ONE WEEK LOAN

Also by Elizabeth Wilde McCormick

The Heart Attack Recovery Book 1984, 1989 (OPTIMA)

Surviving Breakdown 1990, 1997 (Vermillion)

Healing The Heart 1994 (OPTIMA)

Living On The Edge 1997 (SAGE)

Transpersonal Psychotherapy: Theory and Practice (with Nigel Wellings) 2000 (SAGE)

Your Heart and You (with Dr Leisa Freeman) 2002 (Piatkus Books)

Nothing to Lose: Psychotherapy, Buddhism and Living Life (with Nigel Wellings) 2004 (Continuum)

Praise for *Change for the Better*

Elizabeth Wilde McCormick's creativity in *Change for the Better* brings to life the essence of Cognitive Analytic Therapy. The book serves as a guide to self help through practical psychotherapy. It also provides a clear explanation for trainee therapists of how to integrate Cognitive Analytic Theory with practice. I place this book at the top of the reading list for my trainees.
Dr Shakir Shyam Ansari, Consultant Psychiatrist & Senior Lecturer; Founder Member, ACAT

The joy of this book is that it is written in a language readily accessible to all who are interested in the emotional tangles to which human kind is heir.
Dr Sheila Cassidy, UK doctor, known for her work in the hospice movement, human rights activist and author

Elizabeth Wilde McCormick

Change
for the Better

self-help through practical psychotherapy

third edition

SAGE

Los Angeles | London | New Delhi
Singapore | Washington DC

First edition published by Unwin Hyman 1990
Reprinted 1996
Second edition published by Continuum 2002
This third edition published by SAGE Publications 2008
Reprinted 2008, 2009, 2010 (twice)

SAGE Publications Ltd
1 Oliver's Yard
55 City Road
London EC1Y 1SP

SAGE Publications Inc.
2455 Teller Road
Thousand Oaks, California 91320

SAGE Publications India Pvt Ltd
B 1/I 1 Mohan Cooperative Industrial Area
Mathura Road, New Delhi 110 044

SAGE Publications Asia-Pacific Pte Ltd
33 Pekin Street #02-01
Far East Square
Singapore 048763

Library of Congress Control Number: 2007932205

British Library Cataloguing in Publication data

A catalogue record for this book is available
from the British Library

ISBN 978-1-4129-4825-8
ISBN 978-1-4129-4826-5 (pbk)

Typeset by C&M Digitals (P) Ltd., Chennai, India
Printed in Great Britain by the MPG Books Group
Printed on paper from sustainable resources

To Tony and all CATs

Contents

Foreword

We are all born to particular parents at a particular time and in a particular place and our early experiences combine with our inherited temperaments to form us into recognisable individuals – ourselves. The journey through infancy, childhood and adolescence to adulthood is a complicated one and, while most of us acquire a more or less stable and satisfied sense of ourselves and an adequate grasp of the world we live in, we all collect some habits or dispositions or beliefs which serve us badly but which are so much part of our sense of ourselves that we do not question them. Unless and until, that is, we find ourselves suffering from unreasonable anxiety or frequent depression or unexplained physical symptoms or become aware of ways in which our life is not going as we hoped or intended. At this point we may stop and think about how our life has been and we may talk to family and friends and receive helpful support and advice. But for many more troubled people there is a limit to how useful that may be, partly because those we choose to talk to will often be selected (not consciously) because they can be trusted to respond to us in the way we expect and not to challenge our problematic aspects and partly because, if they do challenge them, we may be unable to take on board what they are saying. This is not because we are stupid, it is because, to a far greater extent than we usually realise, we all live suspended in a web of relationships with others, some from the past and some present, and it is this web of connections with others which sustains our sense of being ourselves. Or it may be that, in the face of early experiences that were emotionally unmanageable, we have learned to conceal ourselves and to mistrust others to the extent that there is nobody we can feel safe enough with to show our pains and to expose what we may feel to be our weakness.

It is at such a time that this book can be of particular value. Liz McCormick combines a wealth of experience as a psychotherapist with a gift for writing and an attitude which is fully respecting of the reader. Those seeking simple categorisations of distress or illness linked to prescriptions of how to get better will be disappointed, for there are no oversimplifications of the problems and no dispensing of ready-made solutions. Instead, readers are invited to think clearly about their difficulties and to feel directly the meanings of their past and present experiences. The common tendency to think about psychological symptoms as if they were analogous to physical illnesses and to treat them with medication or simple symptom-oriented therapies is reinforced by some psychiatrists and by the power of the pharmacological industry. It can be difficult for many people to realise that their moods and symptoms are the physical manifestations of difficulties in living and can signal the need for change. That symptoms may be partly physical in origin and may sometimes require medical treatment is of course acknowledged here, but the book aims to emphasise the value of understanding the links between one's distress and how one leads one's life. By indicating the possibility of understanding and changing the thoughts, feelings and behaviours which underlie our depression, anxiety or headaches and our unhappiness or difficult relationships, it allows passive suffering to be replaced by an active engagement in identifying and changing damaging and restricting aspects of our own natures.

To help in this task the book starts by offering clear descriptions of common problematic patterns of thinking and acting. These usually repeat unhappy patterns experienced early in our lives or represent our early attempts to solve problems through means that have themselves become harmful or restricting. We are usually only partly aware of our own patterns and here common ones are usefully illustrated by examples and are linked to exercises that support self-discovery and indicate possible alternative ways of coping. This is unfamiliar territory for most people and exploration needs the help of a guide. A particular strength of the book is the way in which one has the experience of being in dialogue with the author; one is not being given instructions and a guide book so much as one is invited to participate in the construction of one's own map and to conduct one's own exploration. This means that readers, to benefit, must accept their share of the work. This is not a book to read while waiting for the bus; it demands concentration and the ideas need to be thought about actively through the day. Change will not come about in a flash of realisation, it will require sustained attention. The structure of the book supports this and it will be most valuable to those who go through it systematically and at their own pace. As well as helping one to think clearly about negative aspects of oneself Liz McCormick draws on her knowledge of Buddhist ideas to propose mindfulness techniques which can enlarge self-awareness.

The book can help many people through many problems and can contribute to enlarging what can be called emotional literacy but it does not claim too much for itself. Enduring what cannot be changed is not a skill that can be taught but learning to recognise what can be changed and knowing how to begin to change will be greatly clarified by reading this book. Further reading from a wide spectrum of viewpoints is listed and guidance on how to find appropriate psychotherapy is provided. But whether or not further help is needed, I warmly recommend it as an excellent place from which to start the journey.

Anthony Ryle

Acknowledgements

This book is based on the model of time-limited therapy created and initiated by Dr Anthony Ryle at Guy's and St Thomas's Hospitals called Cognitive Analytic Therapy, CAT for short. Since 1984 CAT and CAT therapists have grown in numbers, and this method of focused therapy is now taught and used in different settings within the National Health Service in the UK. I am extremely grateful to Tony Ryle for encouraging me to write a self-help book based on his work, and for his help with the first, second and now the third edition, as well as his supervision and clinical support over many years of my own practice as a psychotherapist. Dr Ryle, now retired to Sussex, and I spent two days together going over the new material for this edition. Most of this third edition is new writing and the changes reflect the most recent developments in CAT theory, particularly the use of reciprocal role relationship understanding, less stated in the second edition. Dr Ryle's contribution has been invaluable. He brings not only his extremely finely focused clinical mind but also his ability to get to the root of something and simplify it, and his great humanity.

Many, many CAT colleagues have contributed to the formation of this self-help book, based upon the collective work in CAT therapy. For this third edition Sage sent out a questionnaire about the use of the book in different settings to thirty colleagues. All of them took the time to reply in detail and nearly all of the comments I received have been addressed in this edition, with enormous gratitude.

Grateful thanks go to Annalee Curran and Shakir Ansari who read the original early drafts, and to my many other CAT colleagues, particularly Deirdre Haslam, Jackie Baker, Dr Julia Clark, Liz Fawkes, Jon Sloper, who runs the ACAT website, the late Angela Wilton and Mark Dunn, all of whom contributed ideas and cases for this book. Thanks also to Susan Needham for editing the chapter on couples and to my partner, Keith Maunder, for his inspiring idea for the cover.

At a wonderful meeting of CAT supervisors and therapists in March my questions and issues about the changes in CAT theory and practice were shared with a group of colleagues to whom I am extremely grateful. This most recent work has, I think, helped me to see that I, as writer, and this book also, have been able to 'Change for the Better'.

I would also like to acknowledge my many teachers of the practice of mindfulness: Ven Thich Nhat Hanh, Vietnamese Zen Buddhist; Tibetan Buddhist nun and author Pema Chodron; Buddhist psychologist Dale Asrael; Becca Crane at the North Wales Centre for Mindfulness, Bangor; my dear friends and colleagues Nigel Wellings and Philippa Vick, with whom I have sat, and mulled over tricky questions around spiritual practice. There are countless others whose texts and practices I have been enriched by and learned from, including my Suffolk coastal sangha. For all spiritual teachings I am profoundly grateful.

A special thank-you goes to all the patients who agreed to have their life stories, charts, letters and diagrams used for publication. All names and some details have been changed to protect their identities. Their examples show us how difficulties can be faced and how lives can be changed.

Change for the Better has had a curious journey since its first publication by Unwin Hyman in 1990. It became an 'orphan book' when its publishers were taken over by HarperCollins two weeks after publication, and for the years following was not readily available in bookshops. Nevertheless it survived, largely thanks to the continued interest in CAT and the growth in training programmes for therapists at ACAT. In 1997 a new edition was prepared for Cassell who were soon to be amalgamated into Continuum Books. And then, in 2002 Continuum sold its health list to SAGE, where the book currently rests. I would like to thank Sage for commissioning this new edition and for their interest in achieving such a thorough production and completely revised content. So for nearly twenty years *Change for the Better* has survived the vagaries of publishing and found its way into many different settings keen to focus on change and self-help: universities, day centres, career counselling services, psychotherapy training and GP practices. As well as being offered to patients on waiting lists or as self-help, it has also been used usefully for students in training, particularly in CAT. It is easy to read and user-friendly. It takes complex ideas born out of research and practice in psychotherapy and simplifies them for general reading.

I am grateful for the interest in the book and to the number of readers who have written to me about how they have been able to make use of it. I am particularly grateful for the support of ACAT.

The author and publishers would like to acknowledge and thank the following for permission to quote material from: *My Father's House*, copyright Sylvia Fraser, 1989, with permission of Virago Press; *Understanding Women* (Penguin Books, 1985), copyright Louise Eichenbaum and Susie Orbach, 1983; *Treating Type A Behavior and Your Heart* (Knopf, 1984) by Meyer Friedman and Diane Ulmer; a report by Anne de Courcy in the *London Evening Standard*; an interview with Jane Fonda by David Levin in *You* magazine (17 September 1989).

Also, Becca Crane at the Centre for Mindfulness, North Wales, Bangor, and Jon Kabat Zinn, author of *Wherever We Go There We Are*, for permission to use the One Minute Breathing Exercise and the Awareness of Difficulty Exercise, and the Mountain Meditation and the Loving Kindness Meditation; Dr J Fisher and Pat Ogden at the Sensorimotor Institute, Boulder, Colorado, for use of the arousal diagram in Figure 1.2; and M. Broadbent, S. Clarke and A. Ryle of the Academic Department of Psychiatry, St Thomas's Hospital, London, for the use of the Personal Sources Questionnaire in Appendix 2.

Introduction

> The present is the only time that any of us have to be alive – to know any-
> thing – to perceive – to learn – to change – to heal …
>
> John Kabat Zinn, *Full Catastrophe Living* (1990)

How many times in a day do we think about change? I wish. I wish I hadn't.
I wish they didn't. I wish I could. How often when things go wrong do we
wish it were different, that perhaps *we* were different? And how often do these
wishes remain as remote dreams that can only come true with the help of a
magic wand?

Perhaps we try hard at something. We strive hard to make it work, employ-
ing everything we know. We work at our jobs, at being nice to people, at making relationships, developing hobbies; we try something new. But still we feel
inside that something is wrong; we feel unhappy, lost, hopeless, doomed.
Things go wrong outside: we don't fit in, our jobs perish, partners leave, or we
can't rid ourselves of habits or thoughts that make us feel bad. So we try to
make changes – a new look, job, partner, house – and for a while we are glad,
and things are different. But then the same bad old things start happening
again and we feel worse – worse because our hope of change fades. We feel
stuck or jinxed and anger and helplessness begin to well up. Perhaps we are
beginning to believe we actually are that miserable, stuck person we see in the
mirror every morning at whom we want to lash out.

This book is about change. It sets out methods of identifying what we *can*
change about ourselves and our behaviour. When we lessen the hold of
assumptions and attitudes based on our early need to survive we allow more
space for developing the natural 'healthy island' within. The 'healthy island'
is comprised of our own basic goodness, and all the positive experiences we
have had where a healthy sense of ourselves has been reflected. The healthy
island is always near, even though often we do not see it or feel it because it
is eclipsed by our problems.

This book suggests practical, manageable ways to make changes:

- We *can* learn to become better observers about what happens to us.
- We *can* identify the patterns, based on our earlier need to survive, that dominate how we conduct ourselves.
- We *can* revise these old survival beliefs which we take for granted, but which
  become redundant when they get in our way.

- We *can* then allow space for the healthy island that is always in us even when we cannot see or feel it.
- We *can* help to nourish the healthy island within by identifying and practising different ways of expressing ourselves.
- We *can* change, by recognising the difference between the old survival self, dominated by faulty thinking, and the energy of the healthy island.

When we change the problematic patterns, we change our lives.

We don't, however, change the fundamental core of our being, the individual seed of our real selves with which we were born, and I will explain that more fully in Chapter 1. But we can change the hold that survival-self-thinking has on our life: the way it limits our choices and leads to things going wrong. We are usually unaware that such processes inform our everyday choices because we learned them very early on, and they are all we know. The wild deer in the forest who wounds her leg might lie low so as not to be seen and preyed upon. Alternatively, she may remain with the other deer, but limp behind at a distance; she may even find someone who will shelter her for life. People are no different in their survival responses. If we survive a harsh early life by developing a brittle coping self, we come through the hard times when otherwise we might have gone under. However, we emerge into adulthood with survival presumptions that make it hard to get close to others or to be touched by life's beauties. And the difference between the deer and a human being is that we are able to contemplate alternatives. And it is when life challenges us through our difficult feelings or habits, or when things have gone very wrong for us, that we confront aspects of ourselves we had previously taken for granted.

This book aims to help people who wish to do something active about their lives, who find themselves saying: 'Does it have to be like this?' It will provide methods for individual self-examination, for checking out patterns, for self-monitoring, for making personal maps to illustrate the kind of thinking webs we weave that ensnare us. And it will offer ways for changing the patterns that are no longer working.

Here is an outline of the steps we shall follow:

1. We identify problems and the thinking, feeling and reciprocal roles that accompany them.
2. We begin to name the sequences or patterns we take for granted, but which actually limit our choices.
3. We write our individual life story, how it has been for us since the beginning, and link what has happened to us with the traps, dilemmas, snags and unstable states that have become our everyday reality.
4. We begin to notice the sequences when they occur in daily life, and write them down.
5. We make maps so we can look at where we are in the sequence throughout everyday life.
6. We make realistic goals for challenging and changing the sequences.
7. We begin to experience more of a healthy island inside, more 'real' bits of ourselves, because for the first time, we have more space and energy.

8. We process and bear the shifts that come with change.
9. We find helpful ways to hold on to change.

The changes we may make from this book are achieved by using conscious will and effort to revise old patterns that are no longer working. Once we do our part, using strengths developed by actively thinking about how we operate, we often stimulate other changes which are less conscious in origin. Many people who actively engage in the process of helping themselves find surprises and treasures. They find they have more inside them than they thought. The numerous threads running through our individual lives which may have felt chaotic start to make sense. We begin to feel there is more in life than the tunnelled-vision way of keeping going that many of us are reduced to when things are not going well.

We all carry a part of us which is wounded in some way. How we carry this wound makes the difference between a passive attitude of 'I am a depressive, no one can help me' and the active 'There is a part of me which is depressed and I will address it and take care of it'. Once we engage with ourselves in this way we are much more open to enjoy and use our inner world of imagination, dream and insight, and to accept ourselves.

Each of us can take up the challenge of looking at ourselves afresh: to see what things we can change and to accept those we cannot, and to know the difference. Setting aside time to ponder on what we can change, and actively working to achieve those changes, means that we free ourselves from the restrictions of the past, and that our changes are changes for the better.

About Cognitive Analytic Therapy

CAT evolved as an integration of cognitive, psychoanalytic and, more recently, Vygotskian ideas, with an emphasis on therapist–patient collaboration in creating and applying descriptive reformulations of presenting problems. The model arose from a continuing commitment to research into effective therapies and from a concern with delivering appropriate, time-limited treatment in the public sector. Originally developed as a model of individual therapy, CAT now offers a general theory of psychotherapy with applicability to a wide range of conditions in many different settings.

> The practice of CAT is based upon a collaborative therapeutic position, which aims to create with patients narrative and diagrammatic reformulations of their difficulties. Theory focuses on descriptions of sequences of linked external, mental and behavioural events. Initially the emphasis was on how these procedural sequences prevented revision of dysfunctional ways of living. This has been extended recently to a consideration of the origins of reciprocal role procedures in early life and their repetition in current relationships and in self management. (Anthony Ryle and Ian Kerr, *Introducing Cognitive Analytic Therapy,* 2002)

Cognitive Analytic Therapy was pioneered by Dr Anthony Ryle at Guy's and St Thomas's Hospitals in London as a time-limited integrated therapy. It has been used with increasing demand in numerous different settings within the British National Health Service since 1983, and CAT is now available in Finland, Australia, Spain, Greece and France.

About mindfulness

A basic definition of mindfulness is 'moment by moment awareness'. This awareness helps us to stay present, with whatever is arising, so that we may experience it fully. Developing the capacity for mindfulness helps us in the journey of exploring our inner worlds. It helps us to see things clearly and also to develop great calm. When we combine a non-judgemental acceptance to our mindfulness we are able to look deeply at the more difficult things, and to find compassion for these difficulties.

On retreat at Arnhem in Holland in June 2006, Zen Buddhist Thich Nhat Hanh said:

> The practice of mindfulness is to remain in the present moment without try-ing to change or avoid it. It has the quality of attention that notices with-out choosing, a sun that shines on everything equally. The energy of mindfulness carries the energy of concentration and establishes us in the here and now. It allows us to touch the island within. Only when mindful-ness is established can we know what is happening in the present moment.

part one

all about change

The new information that science has offered in recent decades makes it clear that something can be done to alleviate many social and mental health problems.

Sue Gerhardt *Why Love Matters* (2004: 217)

1

Change is possible

Why change?

Everyone seeks change for different reasons – to feel less anxious perhaps, to overcome debilitating problems like depression or phobia, to feel more in control of life, to stop making destructive relationships. Or perhaps we seek change because we feel sad or bad, unhappy or empty; because things keep on going wrong, but we aren't quite sure why. We may not necessarily be aware that change is what we want until we begin to look more closely at ourselves and at our familiar patterns of behaviour. Just being prepared to look at ourselves from a different perspective is already embracing change.

We all have our own unique character, gifts and tendencies, as well as our genetic patterning. In early life this potential self is a bit like a seed planted into the garden of the family. Using this image it's easy to see that its growth and development is bound up with the nature of the soil and its environment. We cannot isolate ourselves from our context within culture, language, family, our own biology and history. Inevitably some seeds will be planted in an acid soil when their growth is more suited to alkaline; others may be pruned too early as their shoots are only just beginning to grow; some will land on stony ground. Some seeds, which perhaps have the potential to develop into peaches or pears, experience alienation when those caring for them are trying to raise oranges or apples and their own pear or peach nature goes unrecognised and unfulfilled.

All of us must find ways of dealing with these early experiences in order to survive. It is usually later on, when we have suffered a blow, that we have an opportunity to take stock, and to see our part in things. This gives us an opportunity to revise the patterns of behaviour based upon adaptations to others that have restricted our natural self. There are five reasons we might seek change:

1. Getting fed up with feeling like a victim.
2. Wanting to see and understand our part in chaos or crisis.
3. Becoming aware of our own destructiveness.
4. Realising that there is more in us than our 'coping' selves.

5. Longing to feel well and 'whole'. 'Whole' in this context means accepting and living our own true nature just as it is, pleasures and suffering, likes and dislikes and embracing the hand we have been dealt, however meagre and limiting it may have once felt.

Survival self and seed self

Using the metaphor of nature, we know that Mother Nature brings different seasons, and that her laws decree devastation and death, as well as care and nurture and birth of the new. We have rains and deserts, earthquakes and hurricanes as well as spring and summer. Just as nature constantly shows us its creative adaptations, so most 'human' seeds have to develop a 'survival self' in order to manage the less than ideal conditions of their early life. Few seeds are given the ideal soil. Developing a survival self, together with a package of coping tactics for adapting to a difficult, hostile or just strange environment, is always necessary, and a mark of the human capacity for adaptation. Human beings are extremely creative!

Understanding and contrasting the difference in energy and flexibility between the survival self, with its often restricting ways of living and relating, and the potential of a healthy self that is able to reflect, observe and transcend identification with suffering, is at the heart of the experience of psychotherapy.

The healthy island

Throughout this book we will be looking at some of the ways in which we have become accustomed to think and feel about ourselves and other people. When we train ourselves to use our conscious mind to reflect on the patterns and choices made from our survival self, we can challenge the patterns that are no longer useful or which can actually make things worse. In so doing, we are clearing the ground for our healthy island, with our natural observing self and its creativity.

Reciprocal roles in relationships with ourselves and others

No one grows in isolation. The seed is in reciprocal relationship with the soil in which it is planted. We are intimately bound up from the time of our conception with an 'other' and our brain wiring and nervous systems develop in reciprocal relationship with 'others'. Our model of 'other' may be built from

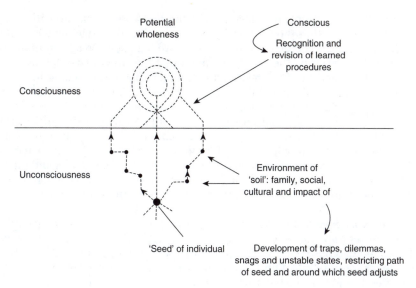

Figure 1.1   Seed and soil diagram of reciprocal role of seed in relation to soil

a mother or series of mothers or fathers, by siblings or caregivers, and later in life by friends, partners, employers or even the government. We also carry this learned 'other' inside us. The way in which we experience the responses from these 'others' in early life starts a process of reciprocal learning and lays down patterns for relating, both to other people, to the outside world and to ourselves.

Let's look at how it all starts. If, as an infant we get fed when hungry, warmed when cold, held when anxious, we learn that our non-verbal signals are effective, that we are understood and the appropriate response is given. *Imitation plus exchange is the basis of communication.* We learn that it is safe to be close to another, and this is how we begin to experience our value, to feel that we are worthwhile and lovable, and to love others. This secure attachment, and our anticipation of it, gives us the space and freedom to express ourselves in a natural way as we grow into a speaking child and expressive adolescent. We learn that it is OK to be ourselves, to be different, to be separate, to go our own way, all within appropriate limits.

Most of us experience 'other' as a mixture of good, bad and indifferent, sometimes there and sometimes not. A lot of us experience 'other' as having conditions based upon their own patterns and expectations, with which we have to comply in order to remain in relationship upon which we are dependent. Because of our adaptability we learn to respond to what our caregiver wants of us. If this is to be good in order to receive care and acceptance then

9

we may develop compliance, always wanting to please others, and thus get stuck into a placation trap. We may develop a rebellious style, refusing any kind of relationship because of its demands. We may develop a form of anxiety over 'other', fearing their disapproval, or that they might abandon us, and become clingy and needy in relationships, which may last into later life.

During infancy and from childhood our brains are tuned to be fantastically responsive and adaptive. Professor of neurology and musicologist C. Trevarthan (1993) speaks about the music of preverbal contact between the infant and other, of how the baby will respond to the communicative sounds of the parent and then wait in anticipation of the continuing response, the baby altering its sounds as the parent alters theirs. The baby's tiny nervous system and brain is finely tuned in responsiveness, like a whole orchestra at concert pitch, waiting for the mutual chords to be struck, the dance of the conjoined music to begin.

If we experience 'other' as unsafe – perhaps as 'not there', as constantly changing, as unpredictable or neglectful, our natural anxiety rises. Our tiny autonomic nervous systems become flooded with adrenalin and cortisol that has no means of release. Our fight or flight mechanism is not yet mature. We may 'freeze' and become flat, avoiding contact for fear of more anxiety; or, we may become hypervigilant, always on the lookout for something unpredictable or difficult. These patterns protect a young nervous system from more unmanageable fear and are to be welcomed and valued. However, the anticipation of responses from 'other' as being in a certain way governs our inner dialogue – the way we think about ourselves inside and what we allow outside, and continues into outside relationships. These patterns will continue in a variety of ways – some more problematic than others – until they are recognised and revised, and alleviated or replaced with other, more helpful ways of relating.

Problems in relationships occur when, in anticipation of 'other' being conditional or abandoning or rejecting, the individual sees even the slightest difference in attunement as extreme and reacts accordingly, as if it were a foregone conclusion. Because we are so helpless in infancy we make all kinds of arrangements not to be abandoned. This might mean being very good outside whilst feeling very bad inside; it might mean compulsively longing for relationships but, once engaged and fearing the old patterns will return, become desperate to get out and cut off or attack.

Understanding the fundamental building blocks of inner and outer reciprocal role relationships and how they dominate emotion and behaviour is the cornerstone of this book, and throughout the different chapters we will be returning to this in many different presentations.

No-go areas

If we have had to adapt to a difficult environment in order to manage our early life, we will have 'no-go' areas. Feelings of being worthless may link with feeling abandoned because of a painful life event such as bereavement or illness which was never explained. We may feel bad most of the time, or find our mood switches from one state to another in a desperate bid for safety. One person described the different and shifting emotional states she adopted with people wanting to get close to her as 'catch me if you can'. If our life feels like a jumble of mistakes or a mess we may discover that cutting off, kicking out, going numb are aspects of our adaptive responses to neglect and abuse, to getting bullied, punished and banished.

The 'no-go' areas are full of unexpressed difficult feelings and fear. We tend not to look too closely until life pushes us into them again. A broken relationship can often trigger earlier feelings of loss that had been left unresolved. And we often carry on judging or punishing ourselves in the way we have experienced earlier because this is what we know.

Until we can begin to describe them, these 'no-go' areas limit the healthy island, our range of response choices and block our natural growth. A clear description of how things have been, together with an understanding of the ways we have learned to cope, help to begin the process of change. Revising our old learned adapted ways of proceeding offers freedom from old patterns that hinder and limit us, so widening our choices and releasing energy.

Core, chronically endured emotional pain

When we start to take our problems seriously and want to change our life, the most important first step is one actually away from the symptom we suffer – whether this is related to depression, relationship failure, dissociation, eating problems or addiction. **We need to get off the symptom hook** and understand what patterns contribute to our symptoms. A good beginning is to reach underneath our symptoms and find words or images that best describe the chronic emotional pain we carry; the pain we try to get away from but end up with when things go wrong.

In this next section we are going to start looking at possible words for our core pain. Core pain and core pain statements tend to become so entrenched in our ways of thinking about ourselves that we take them for granted. We then see life through a lens coloured by these attitudes. In order to inspect the lens we need to identify its nature and then to ask ourselves whether it is still appropriate. Then we can start finding ways to challenge the limitations such a lens may be having upon our life. Read through the following examples of core pain commonly experienced and see if you can find your own words to describe your own assumptions. See if you can identify the pain-suffering and the pain-maintaining reciprocal roles: for example, judging and criticising oneself maintains the feeling of being criticised and worthless.

'Whatever I do, it's never good enough'

Our experience is that however hard we strive – to be good, work hard, give to others – we never get the approval or the love we long for. Our response may be to overwork or become addicted to work or to give up and fall into depression. We may develop a form of perfectionism and achieve a great deal. But whatever the fruits of our striving in the outside world, we are unable to feel good inside, and we are snagged by this core feeling of limitation and judgement. We may end up exhausted and martyred, suffer burn-out, or even suicidal urges.

A learned reciprocal role of *anxiously striving* in relation to *conditional and demanding* maintains the core pain feeling of rejection and worthlessness.

'Everything has to be difficult, whatever I do'

This is a 'yes ... but' snag. It's also a depressed way of thinking and being where no matter what improvements are made we cannot allow them in. The core pain feelings are connected to emptiness. The inner dialogue is between a restricting pessimist in relation to a restricted and defeated small self.

If you recognise this pattern, consider whether you are caught in any of the following patterns of thinking:

I identify myself with my hard work, at least I keep on going. If I don't have a struggle I might be more depressed.

If things weren't difficult and I was happy with my life I would be asking for trouble, pushing my luck.

Mother/Father said, 'Don't count your chickens before they're hatched' – so I never take anything for granted, I prepare for the worst all the time. Whenever I've looked on the bright side I've always been disappointed, so I gave it up.

I need to be admired for my ability to struggle or I'm a wimp.

If you have identified a fear of being pinned down, depressed or being seen as weak, you may view your struggle as being similar to the myth of Sisyphus, doomed endlessly to push a boulder up a hill, only to watch it roll down again. In Part Four we will be gathering information about our early lives and about how we came to the attitudes we have. You may find relief in understanding the nature of your own boulder (which may not be yours in fact!). *Pause here though, and ponder or fantasise on what it would be like if the boulder, or difficulty, were not there. What would it be like if you could change the lens that makes things difficult?* As you begin to recognise the times when this lens colours the way you do things, experiment with leaving this assumption to one side, and moving into things with an open mind.

'No one ever helps me. I have to do everything myself. If I didn't, nothing would happen'

This struggle grows out of an early environment where it was hard or impossible to ask for help and we were expected to do most things for ourselves. The harassed single mother or too busy parent may reward their child for self-sufficiency. In families where parents were ill or absent for long periods, or when children have been moved from one foster home to another, the art of self-sufficiency may be the only means of survival. As a child it is very hard to bear the helplessness or inadequacy of a parent as well as our own. We may develop the fierce independence of a brittle coper, masking unmet emotional need of our own helplessness, fear and loneliness. *This core pain may be maintained by the internal dialogue between our neglecting internal bully in relationship with our needy wimp.*

In some of us this assumption is so well developed we have no concept of being allowed our own needs and feelings. We survive by our independence, 'gutting it' through many of life's crises without apparent difficulty. Problems arise when loneliness or exhaustion become severe. We may develop a cynicism and bitterness in our belief that we are the only people who do anything, and become exacting, demanding company. The fear of letting go enough to allow someone to help us or be close makes us cold companions. Try the following Exercise:

---

exercise: 'no one ever helps me . . .'

Monitor the number of times you find yourself doing things automatically with a resigned sinking heart, feeling put upon and all alone, secretly grumpy and resentful. You might find yourself thinking: 'Why is it always just up to me?' Do this for a week. At the end of the week look and see how much this happens in your everyday life. Start questioning it. Need it be so, every time?

Experiment with putting off tasks for as long as you can bear and note the feelings that come up.

Note how much the presumption that things will not get done unless you do them actually heightens your anxiety.

Talk about what you feel to someone. Explain how difficult it is for you to leave things to others, but how you would like to do this more.

How serious would the consequences be if things were not always done to your standard? Can you live with what feels like others' inadequacy?

Can you identify the inner dialogue that might go something like 'exacting/ demanding to inadequate and worthless'?

I began to recognise this pattern in myself some years ago. It came up when I had to work as part of a team for the first time. I was always going off and doing things either on my own or without consulting the others. The rest of the team saw me variously as arrogant and insensitive. I started monitoring this pattern, and looking underneath I found that I had not learned to ask others for anything, for help, for opinion, for discussion. I presumed I had to do it myself. So I experimented with asking and consulting, taking the risk of rejection for being seen as 'needy'. It turned out it was a relief to work as a team and not have to do everything. I have also found that I can trust others to do what they feel like doing for me on their own terms and not be so exacting or conditional toward myself and others. I get really nice surprises!

'I always pick the bad ones'

We may notice patterns of feeling excited and carried away by meeting exciting others and having exciting experiences of which we have high hopes and often getting lost in the excitement. We project our ideal into the other person and become enthralled, secretly hoping they will offer all the comfort, love, nurture and satisfaction we have never had. In doing so we become passive, vulnerable to being victim. Sooner or later the rosy spectacles come off and the person, ideology or group become just ordinary or worse, and we feel terribly let down, even abused by the loss of the projection of all our hopes. We end up feeling angry, humiliated, beaten, frustrated and let down. We can get cynical and bitter, fearing that all experiences are the same.

The reciprocal role we are caught in is of a *neglected self* in relation to the *fantasy of perfect care*. We may also notice that throughout the day we have a number of different extreme feelings and no idea how we got from one intense feeling to another.

Notice these patterns in yourself. In Part Five, 'Making the Change', we will be looking more specifically at how to nourish the neglected past of ourselves.

'Only if I am allowed to have what I want on my own terms can I feel I exist'

The core pain feeling associated with this is terror of annihilation. As if our only hope for staying alive, or sane, is to make sure we have control over every interaction. As a consequence, people experience us as rigid and over-controlling, and if we do not have things on our own terms we experience depression and its associated sense of annihilation.

The work with change is to find a way of stabilising the emptiness inside so that we can relinquish control in very small steps. At the end of this book there are exercises for befriending fear so that we can take more risks in varying our interactions. In Chapter 12 we see Alistair's diagram of the void and how he took these steps for himself.

'When I have something nice it is bound to be taken away from me'

The core pain here is unbearable loss. We may have experienced the actual loss of someone or something precious early in life. Perhaps we carry an irrational guilt about something for which we were not responsible which makes us unconsciously sabotage anything good. It's as if, because of our loss, we have vowed never to let anything become important to us again. We might feel as if we are living 'on hold', lonely, unable to get close or be happy, and our core pain may present itself as phobia, isolation or chronic anxiety. There are exercises designed to work through this in Part Seven.

You will see from these examples how important it is to get beneath our symptoms or problems to the underlying patterns. We may not be used to looking back and seeing how we made sense of our world. The symptoms or problems that entrap us are maintained by the internalisation both of our experiences as a child and of those who influenced us. We absorb these learned patterns of interaction which then influence both how we relate and anticipate relating with others and also the conversations we have within ourselves. Many of the powerful beliefs about ourselves maintained by the reciprocal roles are mistaken. They prevent us from living fully.

Throughout the book we will see other examples of how core pain is maintained by particular reciprocal roles. As you read, it will be helpful if you try to identify first your own core pain and then possible corresponding reciprocal roles as well as the traps, dilemmas, snags and unstable states that operate in your own life. These are described next and then more fully explained in Part Three. In Chapter 10, 'Writing our life story', we will be looking at ways to describe our chronically endured emotional pain in the context of how our life has been. In Chapters 10 and 11 we will be looking at exits to the learned patterns and at just how we change our learned but mistaken thoughts.

Traps, dilemmas, snags and unstable states of mind

Survival patterns tend to decree that *only* certain ways of behaving are valid, thus presenting us with a very limited range of options and choices about how to express ourselves. In this book, we describe these limited options as traps, dilemmas or snags and as difficult or unstable states of mind.

A **trap** occurs when we carry on with our adaptive behaviour beyond its sell-by date. Rather than protect us when we are vulnerable, it actually leaves us feeling worse. For example, if the habit of pleasing and smiling even when we are hurt seems to save us from others' anger or rejection, it tends to lead us to feel used and worthless. We feel angry and resentful underneath but have not developed the skills to stand up for ourselves and we feel defeated, stuck in the trap of placation.

When we have bargained with ourselves in a black and white way, either 'I'm this', or 'I'm that' – or we think, 'If I do this … then I am this …', we end up living at one end of a **dilemma**. For example: 'If I'm not living on a knife edge of having to strive constantly to be perfect, I will make a terrible mess.' Dilemmas can also form an 'if … then …' quality: 'If I get close to other people *then* I will have to give in to them.' Either I try to look down on other people, or I feel they look down on me.

And a **snag** occurs *internally* when we unconsciously create a pattern of self-sabotage. We are just about to take up a new job or relationship, for example, when something goes wrong and prevents us from being happy or successful. Or, *externally* when we fear the response of others to our success, as if this would hurt or deprive others.

Sometimes the way we experience ourselves keeps shifting and it is difficult for us to keep in focus or to be consistent. It's as if in our early life we have had to keep on the move from contact with 'other' in order to avoid feeling overwhelmed. These **unstable states of mind** may include intense or uncontrollable emotions, being unreasonably angry with others, blanking off or feeling unreal. They may include experiences of dissociation or depersonalisation. **Depersonalisation** means feeling detached from one's body; it's familiar in phobic anxiety and panic attack. **Dissociation** means that we cut off and dissociate from whatever is going on in the moment; it develops as a way of dealing with unbearable pain or terror.

We may have compartmentalised aspects of experience that have, in the past, become unbearable. When something in current time triggers an unbearable feeling we cut off, usually without being aware this is what we are doing.

Where do we start?

Having read so far you will see that this book invites you to look underneath your symptoms, diagnosis or questions about treatment. There is no specific list of symptoms but many symptoms and problems are referred to.

When I see someone for the first time as a therapist I usually hear a phrase that tells me something about the story of survival and begin to sense the feeling of the reciprocal roles that have been learned. This often arises from what occurs in the space between us. For example I might start to feel invited to rescue a 'helpless victim' survival self; I might start to feel as if my open questions are being experienced as critical or powerful and the other person feels put down or judged. Or, I might feel small and inadequate in the face of experiencing the other's powerful need to control or blind me with their own science. This is all good! It's all information, letting me know the nature and feeling of the survival pattern.

Take a few moments now, to experiment with this:

Imagine sitting with someone you know well. See them in the chair in front of you. Without struggling, see if you can find words that describe the invitation from the other – that you are 'nice', or 'clever' or 'in charge' or that you are just happy as yourself. Find words that might describe the dance of relationship between you.

Fear, stress and self-regulation

Skirting around no-go areas and living 'as if' we had only a limited range of options keeps us linked, through fear, to the past. For many of us the body

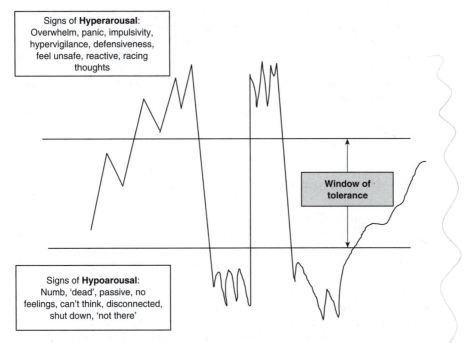

Figure 1.2   The autonomic arousal model. (Reproduced from Ogden and Minton (2000) *Traumatology* 6 (3), 1–20, by kind permission of Dr J Fisher, Centre for Integrative Healing, Boston, USA, and Dr Pat Ogden, Sensorimotor Institute, Boulder, Colorado)

chemistry of fear is dominant and we may find that our sensory experience overwhelms us and stops us being able to reflect or take stock of what is happening. This is called stress. The diagram in Figure 1.2 helps us identify when our responses are dominated by the body reflexes of flight, fight or freeze.

Spend a few moments considering where you might be on this diagram right now. Make a copy for yourself and carry it around with you. Whenever you feel you are out of the 'window of tolerance' stop and try one of the self-regulation exercises described in Appendix 3. Whenever you can, just try to notice the triggers to getting stressed and write them down.

Finding ways to recognise when our stress response inhibits self-reflection, and learning how to stay within the window of tolerance is a first step to taking control of our body stress responses and to change. In regulating stress we are freer to think clearly about ourselves and others.

Our internal core pain will be unique to us. It is based upon what, for us, was both the nature of, and our response to, the people, atmosphere and events of our early life. In searching the past to look at how we have constructed our internal maps, we are not allocating blame. It is not *just* what happens to us, but what we *make* of what happens to us that is important.

Many people carry a strong sense of 'past', of the ancestors and family, contained within the stories and myths of their families, tribes or cultures. This may affect their lives deeply, and may require acknowledgement rather than psychological analysis. The task of the focused psychotherapeutic approach outlined in this book is to offer the tools for revision, adjustment, healing or forgiveness only *where they are needed*.

Different approaches to understanding

There are many different approaches to understanding our selves. This book is based upon the practice of Cognitive Analytic Therapy, as outlined earlier. This is combined with contemplative and mindfulness-based psychology, which offers an understanding that human beings are capable of making a meaningful relationship with suffering. Having understood the patterns that dominate our emotional lives, mindfulness teaches us how to remain present with our difficulties. This book gives us ways to recognise, name and focus upon learned patterns and offers ways, through mindfulness, to assist the development of new, more understanding and kind ways of being with oneself and with others.

This book seeks to spotlight *how* we live with what we feel and *how* we have adjusted, and what changes, if any, are needed. I would also like to add that I have met many people who seem to carry an overwhelming sense of pain and suffering for reasons that are unclear. Not everything has a linear cause. We can only bear witness to the suffering we experience in ourselves or in others, and honour its reality as it lives within the individual, and not seek to concretise or rationalise its source.

The need to tell our own story

Stories have been an invaluable form of communication since time began. Long before psychology the storyteller was often experienced as the one who 'knew things'. He or she could be a wise person, myth-maker, keeper of secrets. The telling of fairy tales was an important form of entertainment in Europe until the turn of the last century, both for adults and children. Stories honour experience, giving it shape as well as containment. The continuum of past, present and future widens the way we collect our ordinary life together. Stories, even about the most horrible and painful of situations, help to bring a dignity to our individual lives when it is *our* story: this is what happened to me; I felt this, I did this, I went there and it was as if ...

In the therapeutic story we find descriptions for the adaptation we want to change and add intention for change and hope for the future. We begin to take charge of our own life and breathe conscious energy into it for ourselves.

As we look at the patterns and myths in our own life story we may find associations with themes from well-established stories: 'Sleeping Beauty'; 'Bluebeard'; 'Hansel and Gretel'. The recognition, as well as wisdom, in these ancient stories can help us to feel not so alone. Others have come this way and their patterns of suffering been woven into story and fairy tale.

And we are not the story! It is merely the context in which we find ourselves, the fabric of everyday event into which our own individual pearl is sown. We cannot escape our context or story but we can make it work for us.

In Cognitive Analytic Therapy, the retelling of the life story, paying particular attention to the learned patterns of coping and survival, is called 'reformulation'. The written reformulation reframes our personal life story and places us as a hero or heroine on a journey of life rather than as a victim of life. This process offers a witnessing process which helps us to feel understood and respected. What follows is an opportunity to understand and respect oneself, to be in charge of one's patterns and one's life.

The stories in this book are from real life. Real-life dramas that are woven with threads from real-life players, scenery, atmosphere and plots, survival patterns and the courage to change. All the stories are moving and graphically illustrate each person's struggle to live a life. I thank again all those people who have given permission for their stories to be shared within these pages, and for allowing their themes to inspire us to look at our own lives afresh.

What is it that changes?

Human beings are not fixed, although patterns of thinking can feel very rigid and dominating. Subtle shifts in our perceptions, feelings and our thinking go on all the time simply because of ordinary living in a web of relationships, and we may change our style or belief because of outside influence. One human life will encompass many phases and changes. The 'global village' liked by the World Wide Web means that there are many more influences than ever before.

We have been looking at the idea that a human being has a combination of an original core self and a 'survival self'. Evidence indicates that the pull of the natural seed gets stronger as we grow older. The desire to be oneself freely, to find our own true way, is strong. This core self does not change but, as understood in Jungian psychology, is always inviting us to individuate, to become who we really are, inhabiting our own healthy island.

What *can* change, however, is the domination of reciprocal roles when they have become fixed and unhelpful. Already, by being prepared to read this book you are growing a new reciprocal role, one of listening, and of being listened to. This might grow into an understanding self that helps being understood and in time you might find that you become more accepting and kindly to yourself and to others in relation to feeling accepted and loved.

Old patterns can move beyond their 'sell-by' date. They can become redundant, to be sloughed off like a snake's skin or chrysalis. We can challenge rigidities and free a space so that our natural self may start to breathe. But we cannot grow if we are living out of mistaken ideas. We cannot take in good things, however much they are offered, if inside we believe we are not entitled to receive them. We cannot relax or let go if we fear being persecuted or abused. And we cannot be assertive if we believe we will lose affection. So in order to change and grow we must challenge the presumptions that limit our freedom to be who we are.

Are there things better left unchanged?

There is an old superstition that it 'doesn't do to meddle with things you don't understand', and the myth of Pandora's box will be used to bear this out, as if all the things we have locked away will wreak havoc once exposed to the light of day. Then there are the old adages 'Let sleeping dogs lie' and 'Better the devil you know than the devil you don't'. These are powerful messages that would stop us searching and ultimately using our power of choice. They encourage avoidance and ensure that we are limited by fear.

My feeling is that if you want to know your devils then make sure that you really do know them. If we fail to know them properly they have a habit of being projected, that is, seen as if they were in other people, who then live them out for us, becoming the very devils we fear; they pop up in relationships, in dreams and they bind us into traps and dilemmas by remaining in the unconscious. The 'shadow' in Jungian psychology contains all that is not in the light, often all that we fear and dislike in ourselves. Accepting this shadow as a valid part of being whole (there is no sun without shadow; no day without night) means we are willing to see it for what it is, rather than projecting it out into the world and making other people or events carry it for us. We have it rather than it having us.

Looking at ourselves isn't easy or pain-free. But what we get out of it is an honest appraisal of ourselves and our choices, and more control and freedom from the burden of unconsciousness.

Is there a burden in knowing ... and in knowing too much?

There are times when we are ready to know certain things about ourselves, and take action. The fact that you are reading this book might indicate that you have started a journey of self-exploration, and are already questioning things you've previously taken for granted. Through honest self-questioning and exploration we find an accurate description of our chronically endured pain. It is through this researching process that we are often rewarded by the gift of insight. Insight – that feeling of 'ah, that is what that meant; that is how it was' – is a leavening process through which we begin to trust that there is inside us something that understands what is going on. Just knowing rationally is not enough; we need to open up our other senses – sensing, intuiting, imagining; then checking it out against what we have learned. When we are open to these other senses we may learn to trust when is the right time to 'know'.

In her moving book *My Father's House*, Sylvia Fraser (1989) describes how for the first forty years of her life she split herself in two – the self that had a secret and the self that lived in the world. The secret self that had been split off leaked out via dreams, impulsive behaviour, irrational revulsions, in rages, incredible sadness and feelings of emptiness. She writes:

> Though my restored memories came wrapped in terror, it is a child's terror that I realise I must feel in order to expel. Thus the adult me comforts the child, holds her hand, pities her suffering, forgives her for her complicity, assuages her guilt. She has carried the burden until I was prepared to remember our joint history without bitterness. I feel only relief, release, compassion, even elation. The mysteries of a lifetime, shadowy deeds dimly suspected, have been clarified. (p. 252)

Is there a right time to change?

The one certainty in life is change! But often we fear it because we fear the unknown. A crisis plunges us directly into new territory inside ourselves, and we are forced to change in order to get through. Sometimes problems become so serious that we have to seek professional help, and that in itself may be the beginning of change. One woman I knew flew back from an expensive holiday, for which she had spent years saving, a week early because she felt unwell and was convinced she had something seriously wrong with her. When it turned out only to be piles she realised the extent of her anxiety and took herself into therapy. She was then in her fifties and she was ready to look. At age fifty-one actress Jane Fonda's husband left her. In an interview given to David Levin in *You* magazine (1989) she describes how she reacted:

> If you are lucky [life] is a continual process of struggle and hard work, growth, learning, setbacks and steps forward. The unfortunate ones are those who stop searching and give up; who don't stay open and are unwilling to grow. That is when the journey ends before it should. My journey is only beginning in fact.

Life has natural phases that involve great change. The greatest change we ever make is from girl to woman, boy to man; we change from little child to questioning adolescent, struggling with emotions and changes in consciousness of all kinds. We change when we become parents, move house or job, learn to drive a car, fall in love. As we grow older we are forced to contemplate a different face and shape in the mirror and the fluctuations of our bodies. Mid-life, growing old, death – all these things involve us in change.

Developing an 'observer self'

Our patterns of relating learned with others are embedded within our inner dialogue and dominate the way we experience ourselves with ourselves. Thus noticing that the extent to which our inner dialogue of *criticising/judging/bullying* in relation to *striving/crushed/victim* governs what we feel, helps us to develop a new, *observing in relation to observed* self. We also need to observe how much our inner dialogic relationship continues in our outer relationships. Developing an observer self helps us to both observe and begin to change the old patterns.

We can prepare for and assist the process of change by moving our concentration into developing new 'awareness muscles':

- Awareness of our breathing and body sensations
- Awareness of our feelings and emotions
- Awareness of thoughts and what follows from thoughts

We can train ourselves to:

- Observe
- Notice
- Reflect
- Revise
- Try something new

Thus, just as a marathon runner develops physical muscles, we start developing strong and flexible mind muscles. We do our daily warm-up exercises, we stretch and limber up.

Psychotherapy nourishes self-observation and self-reflection. Some of the changes brought about by psychotherapy are easy and natural, and are mainly concerned with shifts in thinking, perception and attitude. What is harder to change is the reflexive responses that remain hidden in our bodies. We may know 'about' them in our minds, but we have to learn what they are signalling. This needs our observation and exploration, and many different forms of exercises throughout this book will help with this process.

How to change

In order to change we have first of all to understand the nature of our survival self, its learned patterns of behaviour and our mistaken belief system. We must know something of the roots of our patterns, how they developed and also a good deal about how problematic ways of thinking and proceeding still operate within our life and relationships. Part Three, 'Getting Off the Symptom Hook: Naming the Problem', will assist in this discovery process. Part Four, 'Gathering Information', is aimed at helping us to gather sketches about our early life: what happened and how our attitudes were shaped from our assimilation during this time. Much emphasis is laid upon self-reflection and self-analysis, with the assistance of detailed questionnaires and exercises. By writing down our life story, how things have been for us and how things have come to be as they are in our life, we also begin to look at what it is we need or wish to change. Part Five, 'Making the Change', assists with this process and gives examples from other people who have made important changes for themselves in this way.

For readers wanting to understand their relationships more fully, Part Six, 'Changing Within a Relationship', offers some case examples of how couples used the understanding of reciprocal roles and diagrams to help with their communication. Finally, Part Seven, 'Holding on to Change', offers practical suggestions for holding on to the changes in consciousness this book suggests.

One does not have to be an engineer to drive a car and one certainly does not have to be a professional psychologist to live a life, but if things go wrong in either case it can be helpful to know something of how to go about tracing and remedying the trouble. The chapters are arranged in such a way that the simpler problems are described first; these earlier sections could be seen as a roadside manual, giving only partial explanations of the processes involved but aiming to provide enough to get the car back on the road. Later chapters give a fuller account of how we organise our lives and of the ways in which our sense of ourselves and of our relationships with others can be distorted. The basic assumption is that, in order to overcome our difficulties, we need to alter both how we see ourselves and our world, and how we act.

The limits of self-help

It is important to say at this stage that not all difficulties and symptoms are the reflection of problems in living. Some are the effects of bodily processes and may need medical treatment. Many common symptoms, such as undue fatigue, headaches, indigestion or appetite changes, are most frequently the result of emotional stress, but can, in some instances, be caused by physical illness. If there is any doubt about the nature of such symptoms then medical advice should be sought. It is also the case that being badly depressed may cause, or may be caused by, physical changes in the nervous system which are best treated by medication. Someone whose depression is severe, who suffers from marked physical or mental lethargy, or whose sleep is broken regularly in the small hours with gloomy wakefulness thereafter, should seek medical or psychiatric advice. More generally, if mental distress is severe or prolonged, with experiences of the mind not working normally, it would be appropriate and kind to the self to seek professional help.

Other problems are due to causes that are not primarily emotional, psychological or medical; they are social. The American writer Henry David Thoreau, in *Walden* (1854), observed that 'the mass of men live lives of quiet desperation'. While much of this desperation may be rooted in the personal domain of marriage, family and career and might be eased by the methods discussed in this book, to be poor, unemployed, prematurely retired, discriminated against, badly housed, to have to work at intrinsically boring tasks under the arbitrary control of others are also potent causes of desperation. The impact of these factors is, of course, upon the feelings of individuals, but the appropriate action is political and beyond the scope of this book.

Preparation for reading this book

Having looked at some of the reasons we may wish to seek change, we now need to consider how we might engage in this process through a book! No book can hope to take the place of a flesh and blood therapist. But I will be the therapist speaking to you through the pages of this book as if you were sitting in my consulting room. It might help you to imagine me in a chair opposite you, slightly to the side, as a new witness to all you have experienced and experience now. I could be the compassionate observer who becomes part of your inner dialogue, thus hearing but not joining the voices from the past. I will be encouraging and supporting you. I can become someone who is always there as a silent companion and witness to your discoveries and journey of change. You can yell at me, get cross with me, laugh with me, cry, moan or be silent and contemplative.

The first task is to complete the Psychotherapy File and the Personal Sources Questionnaire which you will find in the Appendices. This helps to distil the issues you are currently struggling with and will help with understanding the patterns of behaviour to which you have become accustomed.

Co-counselling

If you decide to share the process of reading this book with a friend, take turns at being counsellor and client and go through the findings from the psychotherapy file with each other. Each of you can help the other with the process of identifying attitudes, thinking and problem areas, and in answering the questionnaires. In co-counselling the aim is for the counsellor to be an objective observer and questioner. The use of the Psychotherapy File or the Personal Sources Questionnaire is a first step to naming the patterns that are current. Part Four is laid out in such a way that the counsellor may read out to the other from 'Gathering Information' and allow the client time for reflection. Help from another in writing the life story is also important and can act as an encouragement and keep us at the task. If you decide upon co-counselling, set aside a certain time each week to meet in the privacy of one of your homes, and treat the time as you would a counselling session with a professional. Keep to your own individual reflective time in between, for pondering, for painting or sketching the images and impressions that are formed during the process.

Going it alone with the invisible therapist

If you decide to read the book alone to enter into the self-help programme, set aside some uninterrupted time to read the questionnaires and to do the exercises. Part of the programme involves keeping notes, jotting down ideas and associations, keeping a journal of thoughts or ideas. For this you will perhaps need to allocate time for yourself in a way that you may not be used to: marking out time in your diary, or setting aside particular days which you devote to self-reflection and keeping an eye on your aims for change. In each section there are instructions on how to proceed next, and examples from people who have already travelled along this path.

Imagine that I will be sitting there with you. You might like to give me a chair. Whenever you get stuck or feel overwhelmed, look at the chair you have given to me and restore all the qualities you have given me as your unconditional listener who is mindfully listening, and with whom it is safe to be cross or unhappy. When you return to the pondering or writing, write about the presence in the chair who is your very own invisible therapist and give them flesh and blood! Start a dialogue with the invisible therapist.

Notebook, pencil, colours and loose paper

Think of reading this book as going on a journey, and prepare yourself appropriately. A small notebook that will fit into your pocket is useful for jotting down thoughts and reactions as you go through each day. A larger notebook is helpful to keep a fuller journal and is useful for writing down – or making scribblings, drawings, cartoons, doodles – your dreams, ideas, fantasies, open letters to people who come up for you in the course of this programme, your life story, your target problems and aims, and anything else that intrigues you. Choose a notebook that you really like, that you can claim as totally yours. Some people like to have loose-leaf files so that they can add more and more pages. Actor Richard Burton kept his life's diaries in Woolworth's lined notebooks, of which there were hundreds when he died. Keep your notes and thoughts as you would want to, not as others would, or for others.

Creating a safe space through mindfulness

Find a place to sit where you feel warm and comfortable. Close your eyes. See if you can invite into your body memory a time when you felt safe and loved, however fleeting this experience. Stay with the feeling as you identify it in your body. Notice the atmosphere, the colours or shapes, the people or nature of your experience. Just consolidate the feeling in your body and know that you can return to it at any time.

It is useful to keep the image of the safe place close to you. A photograph or magazine picture posted up by your fridge or bathroom mirror can help. Or you could make your own drawing or painting. If at any time you realise you are becoming disorganised in your thinking, overly distracted or ruminative, if you feel disregulated in the way described on page 17, then return yourself to the feeling of the safe place. When you have restored yourself to regular breathing and to the 'window of tolerance' (Figure 1.2), note down what seemed to be the triggers to your disregulation. Knowing your 'triggers' helps you to anticipate or prepare throughout your day.

Once we have made maps that outline the way our survival self has had to operate we might want to use techniques for managing the feelings we are going to allow to emerge for the first time. **Mindfulness** is a practice of resting our attention on the present moment which has emerged from Eastern spiritual philosophies. It is an excellent way of learning concentration and also developing awareness of the minutiae of our responses. Practising mindfulness can help us to be peaceful and to gain insight. It can help us in our relationships to be calmer and more accepting. In Appendix 3 there are instructions on mindfulness and suggestions for practical exercises: the Grounding Exercise; Mindfulness of Breathing; Befriending Fear Exercise; and Unconditional Friendliness or Loving Kindness Meditation.

The early five minutes

It is a very good idea when beginning a programme of self-examination to start each day with a few minutes' silence. It may have to be five minutes when you are alone in the bathroom. For the first few weeks don't try and 'do' anything with this time, just quietly reflect upon yourself, how you feel, how your body feels, and gradually become aware of the first thoughts and stream-of-consciousness impressions you have about yourself. Jot down afterwards anything that strikes you as interesting and unusual, especially feelings. Most of us give very little time, if any, to pondering on how we feel emotionally or physically, and when we have problems we tend either to shut down and go on automatic, or feel flooded with uncontrollable feelings. This early five minutes will be a kind of anchor, a chance to be in silent communion with yourself at the very beginning of the day. And later on, when we have processed the difficulties into your story and your goals for change, you may like to use this time for contemplation or meditation.

Self-monitoring

One of the most useful methods of keeping aware of what is happening inside ourselves is through self-monitoring, and details of how to accomplish this are described in Part Five. However, as you embark upon the reading of this book you might like to make a start by monitoring the number of times you think negatively or unkindly about yourself. Monitoring when we feel depressed, by writing in a small pocket notebook the time of day, what is happening, what we are thinking about, can help us to see if there is any pattern to our episodes of depression. The same goes for any physical symptoms and panic or phobic attacks. As you read through the book you will see how monitoring the occasions when certain traps and dilemmas operate in your life can give you the insight and the clarity of control to get out of the trap or dilemma, and to choose to think and behave differently.

Learning compassion and Maitri

I have said a lot so far about changing the problematic patterns that have had a hold on our lives. Just as important is to value the things we *have* done that we can feel good about and in doing so we nourish our healthy island. Sometimes just the fact of our survival is extraordinary. To have survived a childhood of abuse and yet to be making our way in the world, working at what we can, trying again and again to make a relationship, is brave. Observe your own braveness, and wonder at this capacity you have for endurance!

Survival procedures and irrational guilt often prevent us from choosing joy or happiness. Several people I have met have said that they could envy a dying person, because they no longer had to struggle at life, they could just let go and be themselves. It is a sad thought that we have to wait to live until we are about to die.

Maybe we all need permission to be happy in the present moment. A good example of how this can work comes from meditation practitioners who use the concept of **Maitri** – a Sanscrit word meaning unconditional friendliness or loving kindness to oneself. During conflict, distraction or difficulty, remembering to practise Maitri helps a hardened attitude to be more flexible. It is an extremely helpful concept and one that is rather alien to Westerners who regularly suffer from low self-esteem, self-criticism and self-dislike. These are completely unknown in Eastern countries, where a contemplative way of life is predominant. The Tibetan people, with all the problems of being refugees from their own land, do not suffer low self-esteem.

The formal practice of Maitri, called Karuna or loving kindness compassion (instructions in Appendix 3), begins with practising loving kindness first toward oneself, then to those closest to us, then someone neutral, then someone we have difficulty with and then all people, plants and animals. The concept is that we need to learn to love and accept ourselves in our humanity before we are able to love others.

In my practice as a psychotherapist I often describe Maitri to people and invite them to try it. In Chapter 10 Susannah shares her journey of therapy where she used this concept to help her challenge a reciprocal role that dominated her relationships where she felt merged and lost.

Sometimes just saying 'yes' to life and choosing a joyful attitude makes a difference: to walk in the street and see what is happening rather than what is not; to greet a person and recognise what is in their hearts rather than defending against what might hurt us. And the poets have been there before us. Their words can help:

> To see a World in a Grain of Sand
> And a Heaven in a Wild Flower,
> Hold Infinity in the palm of your hand
> And Eternity in an hour.

'Auguries of Innocence' by William Blake

part two

feelings, emotions and relationships

with ourselves, others and symptoms

We belong in a bundle of life. We say 'a person is a person through other people'. It is not 'I think therefore I am'. It (ubuntu) says rather 'I am human because I belong'.

Desmond Tutu *No Future Without Forgiveness* (1999: 34–5)

2

Reciprocal role relationship procedures

From the beginning of our conscious life we learn to recognise, name and express or contain feelings and emotions through our daily life with caretakers. Like the seed in relation to the soil we are planted in, we grow within the garden of our early environment of family, our social and cultural structure and in response to its demands and prejudices. Feelings and emotions get defined for us from our early reciprocal relationships. What is considered 'emotional' may be responded to in a variety of ways. Many people with eating disorders, for example, have often had their emotional needs responded to with food and not recognised as having individual and separate meaning. Body sensations in response to threat may be identified as the emotion of fear and responded to in a variety of ways. Useful sympathy and support leads us to learn self-care and be able to befriend our fears. Belittling and dismissing leads us to reject expressing fear in words and it remains a body sensation.

Feeling angry, hateful or resentful and responding to anger and rage from others is one of the most charged areas within families. Dr Anthony Ryle, the founder of CAT, says:

> A very large percentage of depressed and somatic symptoms are located in the inability to express anger in a useful way. (in conversation with the author)

So we are seeing that for many of us feeling and emotion get blurred together and develop in the course of relationships that provide definitions. Being seen as 'emotional', or having our emotions interpreted as 'just drama', is often a cultural judgement on any emotion that is seen as excessive. What constitutes reasonable emotional expression in one culture is unacceptable in others. One example is in expressing the emotion of grief after bereavement. In Eastern countries, wailing, rocking, being dressed in black and supported for a year are a widow's rights and offer a rite of passage; in Western countries we are encouraged to 'get over it and move on', as if feeling and emotion had no value or purpose.

When we have been able to identify how our emotions have been interpreted within our growing environment and are starting to understand the learned reciprocal roles around emotion, it is useful to look at a possible difference between feeling and emotion.

Feelings remind us we are alive as human beings and are responding to the outside world! They are in essence quite simple things that communicate through our bodies experiences such as happiness, joy, wellbeing or anger, sadness, fear or jealousy. When not entangled in thoughts, feelings can rise and fall like waves in the ocean throughout our daily life. By practising awareness we can watch this process and allow its natural rhythm without any interpretation from our thinking mind.

Every one of us has a feeling nature. Feeling is an important function in terms of our sensing, valuing and sensitively judging situations. What can be more difficult, though, is experiencing feeling without being 'emotional'.

Emotions are more complex and denser in quality. They are a combination of our feelings, our thoughts and body sensations that have been, in early life, defined for us by our environment. They are the result of feelings getting attached to ideas from our past experiences recorded in inner dialogue about what is possible and allowed and what is not. When feelings are identified as emotions they create distortions in thinking and acting.

Examples of how this might be active in inner dialogue are:

> I'd better not show I'm angry because I will get hit.
> If I show I'm scared they will leave me.
> If I expose my need they will laugh.

Out of our emotions come our actions.

So emotions tend to be dominated by what we tell ourselves inside about what we can tolerate and what not. As we well know, once we have become dominated by our emotional response it is much more difficult to remain centred or express ourselves clearly to others. *Either:* We may just shut down and go silent with everything swirling around inside. *Or:* We may swing from one emotional state to another, feeling out of control.

We may have a particular way of controlling responses that seems to conceal our forbidden feelings but may elicit them in others, such as in passive aggression. We feel angry but anger is forbidden so we sulk, withdraw, eat to excess, and others are furious.

Learning about our internalised dialogue with all the parts of us is an important step to self-awareness and to choosing how to change.

Reciprocal roles and core emotional pain

As we saw in Part One, everything we experience about being a person happens within the context of our relationship with an 'other'. The British child psychologist D.W. Winnicott (1979) said 'there's no such thing as a baby', meaning that the baby does not grow alone, but with 'others' who care for the baby in various ways. We come to know ourselves, and slowly become conscious, through the signs, images and communications toward us and in response to us, from others, and the meaning these communications inspire. The reciprocal nature of relating is learned first via our bodies through touch, holding, sound, smell and atmosphere. Each one of these experiences is accompanied by expressions of feeling and a 'language' of gestures, rhythms and sounds. We have an inbuilt ability to identify with the 'other'. For example, newborn infants stick their tongues out in response to someone sticking out theirs. We have mirror neurons that have been discovered to be the biological basis for empathy, for being with and feeling with another human being. For most of us mirror neurons continue to help us become attuned with ourselves and others throughout our lives.

Our early experience in reciprocation with our all-powerful carers invites a number of what are called in Cognitive Analytic Therapy, **reciprocal role procedures**. The word 'role' is a way of describing our interaction with others, and theirs with us. 'Role' describes how we see, respond and interpret, how we feel and attribute meaning to and how we act with others and in internal dialogue with ourselves.

As we saw earlier, the experience of being held safely creates an internalised capacity to both *hold* and *be held* with the resulting healthy island feelings of secure, happy, loved. An experience of being left or neglected leads to an internalised *abandoning* part of the self in relation to an *abandoned* self with feelings of being 'dropped' or feeling unwanted and bad. And these early experiences are anticipated in relation to both ourselves, and others.

Feeling held when helpless and fed when hungry and crying offers a reciprocal dance between *caring* and being *cared for* and the resulting feeling is contentment and safety. In our growing brains the growth of the frontal lobes that govern thinking and reflecting, is assured, and we are free from the chemicals of fear.

Conversely, feeling hungry and being deprived of food creates a reciprocal experience of *needy and helpless* in relation to *controlling and witholding*, and the feelings, not yet understood, but held in the tissues of the body, are of anxiety and rage. The sense of potential healthy island is restricted.

Most of us experience a mixture of early life care. All of us carry a repertoire of reciprocal patterns learned from early care relating to care and dependency; control and submission; demand and striving. These patterns are internalised automatically and serve to maintain the self in the social world. They become our automatic pilot. Once named and reflected upon they can be made sense of, adjustments may be made to the more problematic roles, and new, healthier, reciprocal roles can be created.

Most psychological problems stem from deficiencies of early care such as excesses of control and demand or a critical, judging and conditional acceptance. Major inconsistencies or unpredictable responses such as violent acting out or traumatic separations and abandonments which are not explained or understood create reciprocal roles that reflect patterns such as *abandoned/ neglected/angry victim* in relation to *violent/aggressive bullying*.

Parent and child reciprocal roles

The analogy of the seed in relation to the soil gives us a context for the evolution of our reciprocal role relationships. As well as environmental influences we must also consider the individual nature that is uniquely ours. **It isn't just what happens to us, it's what we make of what happens to us.** We are not looking to blame an early life seen as fixed and irredeemable. We are looking at that rich mixture of what happened, how we met our experiences, and at what now needs to be revised and changed.

So, in the earth of the early environment we learn a three-way pattern of relating to the world, others and ourselves:

- One pattern is connected to the way we feel towards others and our reaction to them.
- The second pattern anticipates the way we have learned that the other person is going to react towards us.
- The third pattern is the way we relate to ourselves inside.

For example, if my early experience has been with a mother who was perhaps absent for a lot of the time – either because of illness or depression or because of having to go to work, or simply because I didn't feel close to her – my core pain may be around abandonment or rejection and part of me will feel like an abandoned or rejected child. I will also carry an abandoning or rejecting other and act in a rejecting or abandoning way toward others, or toward myself, unable to accept my own or others' efforts as good. My internal dialogue will be reflecting themes of feeling rejected by a rejecting other. I may talk in a rejecting way to myself; telling myself off or not caring for my needs. The inner dialogue may be mild and occasional, and it can become repetitive and ruminative, giving rise to anxiety or feeling obsessed with anticipating rejection.

Sometimes our early reaction to quite small problems with parents, or small instances of absence or neglect, can be quite extreme, and until those reactions are modified and looked at afresh they live on to inform the way we relate to others in quite a profound way.

Sometimes our more problematic reciprocal roles are compensated for or accompanied by reciprocal role procedures derived from good experiences such as kindness or positive examples of care, however small, from others. We may also benefit from a rich imaginative life that supports us through fantasy and dreams that are meaningfully different from the environment we endure, and we are able to make these work for us. There are some people who survive the most neglectful and abusive of backgrounds who have a healthy island beaming openness and grace in spite of it. There is no clear reason for this except for the hypothesis that within their natural being is the means to transform suffering and create meaning and inner strength. Or, this potential for a healthy island, which is in all of us, has been nourished by one good experience of a loving attitude.

Re-enactment of early life parent/child roles

What we learn from early experiences becomes a sort of hidden 'rule book' laying down patterns of relating. We can play *either* role, inviting others to play the reciprocal role. It is important to grasp that we learn *both* roles (the *judged* and the *judging* role, for example). As well as the 'coping child' role, we learn to force others to play the reciprocal role as well as treating ourselves in the same terms. Thus our *core wound* is maintained by both the damaged and the damaging aspects we learned early on.

Look through the table set out in Figure 2.1 and notice how you respond to each section. There may be thoughts, feelings, body sensations. Follow your response, in order to discover your own repertoire of reciprocal roles. Using the words or images that come to you, write down your own connection with patterns of reciprocal roles. Remember that we manage ourselves emotionally as we were managed and cared for. We get used to it, and what we have known becomes part of us. This means that the same sorts of things keep on happening to us in relationships.

These old patterns give us a clue about the structures of relationship patterns that lie underneath. These are the learned patterns we can revise. As you record the relationship patterns you have got used to, you will be finding descriptions of the ways in which you look after yourself, how you expect to be responded to by others and how you relate to others.

First, using your developing new voice, the voice you are internalising in this book, of me as author and therapist also in you, write down the areas in your life that work well and where you can assess the following patterns. For example:

Care we experienced	We felt	Some good experiences
GOOD ENOUGH		
Not 'too good'	lovable	responsive↔held
Not 'too bad'	sense of self	trusting↔trusted
Loving	secure	loving↔loved
Caring	cared for	healthy

Put the words you choose to describe into your 'healthy island'.

There may be many variations in the actual words used to describe your experiences, and it is important for each of us to find our own. We are not looking to find 'literal' answers. For example, it is quite possible for us to recognise feeling punished when we've been criticised as if we have been beaten physically. If the word 'punished' best describes our core pain then it's important to understand the three-way process that lives on in our relating. Our *internalised punished child self* expects others to behave in a *punishing* way towards us. We may unconsciously choose others who behave in a punishing way, thus maintaining the core pain *punishing/punished* and coping devices such as being cowed or pleasing. Our *internalised punishing adult self* may continue to behave in a punishing way, creating demanding timetables or being overcritical, beating up on the *internalised child self* and maintaining a feeling of punishment. Or, we may behave in a punishing way towards others, particularly those who appear 'punishable', and remind us of our own cowed or wounded self. Quite often our coping mode only works partially for us and is accompanied by depression or other symptoms. Sometimes we evoke a punishing response which seems to confirm the original pattern and deepens our depression or other psychological or physical symptoms.

Another example is of the childhood experience of abandonment. This might invite an *internalised abandoned child*, whose experience was either of actual abandonment or of a parent or caregiver who felt remote, depressed or preoccupied. And then there would be the *internalised abandoning adult*, who continually

The way we experienced care	What we felt	Attempted solution (survival pattern)	Reciprocal role (with self and others)
ABSENT			
Rejecting	rejected	placating	rejecting↔rejected
Abandoning	abandoned	parental child	abandoning↔ abandoned
CONDITIONAL			
Judging	judged	striving	judging↔judged
Belittling	humiliated	striving	admiring↔rubbished
split			
Demanding	crushed	hypervigilance	exacting↔crushed
Blaming	blamed	hypervigilance	blaming↔blamed
TOO TIGHT			
Overcontrolling	restricted	rebellion	controlling↔controlled
Fused dependency	merged	flight into fantasy	merging↔merged
Flattening	flattened	giving in	flattening↔flattened
TOO LOOSE			
Anxious	anxious	avoidance	abandoning↔ abandoned
Not there	fragile	anxious striving	
Abandoning	abandoned	'nowhere world'	distancing↔distanced
TOO BUSY			
Overlooking	overlooked	excessive striving	overlooking↔ overlooked
Depriving	deprived	searching	depriving↔deprived
Silencing	silenced	'not there'	silencing↔silenced
ENVIOUS			
Envious	envied	magical guilt	harming↔harmed
Hated	hated	self-sabotage	hating↔hated
Picking	picked on	self-harm	picking↔picked on
NEGLECTING			
Neglecting	neglected	can't take care	neglecting↔neglected
Physical neglect	hurt	mood swings	switching states
Emotional neglect	hurt/angry	feel in bits	unstable states
Mental neglect	fragmented	unstable states	unstable states
Attacking	attacked	develop 'false' self	attacking↔attacked
ABUSIVE			
Abusing	abused	bully/victim	abusing↔abused Fantasy of perfect care
VIOLENT			
Abusing states	hurt/abused	split into fragments	fragmented
		unexpressed rage	hitting out↔hitting self

Figure 2.1 Patterns of care that can dominate our relationships until we revise them

abandons their 'child self' by not attending to needs, or who chooses an *abandoning 'other'* in relationships, which keeps the core wound in search of healing.

As we grasp how these patterns of relating continue, in our present everyday life, we may expect all three 'roles' to be enacted at different times, or within the same relationship. The child 'role' still feels fresh and sore, but it is maintained, within us, by the adult 'role'. Thus the two 'roles' are reciprocal, they go together and need to be understood in this way. It is important when embracing change to look at both ends and not just strive to heal the wounded child. We also need to modify the adult reciprocal role; to recognise when we are picking on, punishing or rejecting toward ourselves or others and find other ways of being.

When we are able to see that the way we feel is maintained by the tension between both roles we can learn to choose healthier ways to relate.

When early experiences offer no relief from painful or unbearable anxiety and fear, and we have no way of processing this, the different feelings may get split off into different parts inside us. Sometimes there is no connection between the parts and we find ourselves in emotional states with no idea how we got there. In Chapter 8, we will be describing the more unstable states of mind and how to create a continuing observer within oneself.

---

exercise

Self to self

Rest your attention on the general flavour of your close relationships, starting with the relationship you have via inner dialogue with yourself. Take your time. Notice how you think about and speak to yourself inside. You may find you have imaginary conversations, with real-life or fictional others, and that there are themes to these. Themes might include trying to be heroic, or happy, or pleasing someone; conversations may be being critical, judging, or encouraging, hopeful or longing toward an imaginary other.

Self to other

Notice how you anticipate how others will behave toward you, especially in close relationships. Notice how this anticipation manifests in the tension in your body, in your thoughts. You may anticipate and hope for special words only to be met with words that do not meet your hopes and expectations and you end up feeling disappointed or dashed. You may anticipate harshness, criticism and hold yourself back or even make yourself vulnerable to what is expected. Notice all your reactions when with others.

As you explore your own reciprocal roles and notice the core pain of the child-derived role such as punished, criticised, bullied, forgotten, think about what you would feel if you saw a child being treated as you were.

3

Emotional states, depression and eating disorders

This chapter outlines three general experiences around feeling and emotion from which you may discover more about your own reciprocal role repertoire. First we look at 'feeling bad', 'not having feelings' and 'unmanageable feeling'. Then we look at two specific problem areas which are predominant in our Western culture: depression and eating disorders.

As you read through, start to write a description of what you feel and what you relate to in the examples.

'Always feeling bad inside'

Reciprocal role procedures incorporate implicit values about oneself and others. When we get into a *critical/rejecting* in relation to *sad/bad* reciprocal role, the way out may be to reverse the roles so that the weight and hurt of it lessens. Often we are not aware of how bad we feel inside until we start reflecting. It might be that we experience others and life as bad, as against us, and things go wrong for us.

Feeling bad inside might influence the relationships we make. We might feel we can only make relationships with people who might be worse than us. We don't like ourselves enough or feel free enough to know what we like, or to have relationships or friendships with people who are attractive or success-ful. The result of all this is that we feel depressed. It might be a general thin veil of depression and worthlessness, or, in more severe cases, deeper depres-sion from which we feel we are never going to be freed. We somehow man-age to carry on, automatically doing things we feel we must do, but never really experiencing pleasure or happiness in any form.

We may try to become 'bad' because, why not? People already think we are so why not live up to it?

You may want to add to this list, naming for yourself what you recognise are your attempts to cope with feeling bad inside.

Sometimes in our early lives we are actually told we are bad and that 'nobody loves a bad girl or a bad boy'. We may pick up messages we interpret to be about our badness. Perhaps we don't come up to the standard required of us. Perhaps our parents' view is that we don't give enough, therefore we're selfish. We might enjoy doing things that the rest of the family doesn't, so we're labelled odd or difficult, and therefore 'bad'. We may find ourselves in the grip of difficult feelings in our early life – fury, a desire to hit out, a sense of entrapment and persecution. We might be the subject of actual cruelty on a mental or a physical level. We are made to feel even worse if we do start to express our feelings of frustration and hit out. When there is nowhere for bad feelings to go, we bury them.

These feelings tend to stay inside festering, like a boil, for years. It isn't until something happens or we start thinking about ourselves that we realise we have believed inside that we are bad. Although logically we may know we are not bad, we may feel that something in our core isn't quite right, there is something wrong with us, something unpleasant and difficult.

But when we don't understand why we feel as we do, those bad feelings are often projected onto other people and situations.

---

exercise: 'always feeling bad inside'

If you recognise that you feel like this, just spend a few moments quietly reflecting. See if you can get some sort of graphic image for the way you feel. Start with the phrase 'It is like …' and let your imagination offer you a picture, colour, shape or image. It doesn't matter what comes to you, just stay with whatever emerges. Examples could be 'heavy black mud'; squirmy tummy'; 'rotten apple'. When you feel you have got a sense of it, make a graphic picture (drawing, note, collage) of what it feels like to be you inside most of the time.

Notice if feeling OK is conditional. See how often you say to yourself 'I will only feel OK if … '.

Can you recognise any of these other ways of feeling bad:

☐ Heavy weight in the body
☐ Feeling sick
☐ Depressed mood

☐ Always think the worst about myself
☐ Sometimes I believe I am evil
☐ I tend to move with a 'bad' crowd
☐ I feel that people always end up hating me
☐ I always return to the feeling I was never wanted in this world
☐ If something good comes my way I can only spoil it
☐ Because I never do anything good, I must be bad

When you recognise any of the above, note it in your own way in your monitoring notebook. Try to notice when and where these attitudes or thoughts come in your everyday life. Monitor this process for a week to give you a pattern of what situations trigger feeling bad.

However many ways of feeling bad you identify in yourself, allow yourself to feel sad at this burden of badness. For it's sad when an innocent child – usually where this mistaken idea began – believes they are bad.

Next, start experimenting with a new idea, that actually, fundamentally *you are not bad*. Challenge the critical nagging voice from the past, whatever bad behaviour you may have indulged in. Always thinking that you are bad might be spoiling your chances of proving to yourself it's not true. *It's a very old message and belongs to the past.* Try to find someone to talk to about it. Sharing the 'I am bad' idea is helpful, because the hurt and pain of the old belief are maintained by the internalised reciprocal role of *critical harsh judge* in relation to *bad and guilty*. Get some help to start a new reciprocal role of *listening* to one of being *listened to* and use it to start listening to yourself differently. Look at the things about yourself that are not 'bad', however small. You have read this page. That indicates that part of you is searching – that's not bad but positive. Believe in that, that you have it in you to embrace something different from the old message 'I am bad'.

Not having feelings

When I ask you 'How does it feel?' what happens? Is it a struggle, or do you find yourself saying: 'I think …'? This may be because you have not been able to develop a language for feeling.

Sometimes we need to ask someone to write a list of 'feeling' words for us to experiment with. Another way is to start noticing what happens in your body when you are asked how you feel. If your answer is 'I feel nothing', see if you can trace what happens in your body when you say those words.

The use of images is also helpful, and descriptive words such as 'tight' or 'tingly' or 'cramped' or 'stuck' can be a good start to exploring more about what you are feeling. Some people presume that they do not have feelings, when in fact their feelings are bottled up and unseen. When feelings have been as firmly shut away as this, we can appear cold. We appear unaffected by the most devastating news as if a reciprocal role of *cut off/controlling* in relation to *controlled/unfeeling* is in operation.

What happens when we shut down feelings? Can you recognise feeling *distancing* in relation to *distanced*?

Feelings may be triggered off when something touches us deeply and gets under our skin and we cannot avoid or freeze them out. Feelings may start to emerge when we are more confident about handling them and are less under pressure from our contemptuous or dismissing reciprocal role to ourselves. I know a man whose bottled-up feelings came pouring out when he was forty-five and fell in love. He surprised everyone who thought he was a cold, unfeeling schemer until that point. Our fear of feelings, defended by denial or avoidance, may wait for a 'safe' environment such as a long-term relationship, or a satisfactory job of work.

If feelings have been so damaged and battered, or if no satisfactory release for them is found, they may get split off into different parts and so our sense of ourselves is fragmented.

- Some people refer to their inner 'rageful bastard' who operates as *angry/abusing* in relation to *terrified/hurt*; or their 'shapeless blob' who always cries, who expresses *belittling* in relation to *put down/worthless*; or a 'rescuing magician/angel' who is always *idealising or being idealised* in relation to being *special*.
- We may have physical symptoms instead of feelings, as if our constrictions, our inflammations, were expressing our unbearable pain.
- We may try to contain our feelings by choosing a profession that will force us to operate only in our heads, using rationale and logic.
- We may act out instead of expressing feeling, by driving fast, drinking too much, taking drugs, taking up dangerous sports and activities, gambling, fighting, stealing.
- When feelings are unbearable and unmanageable we may go numb and our rage, anger, jealousy or happiness is experienced outside of us, in other people, objects or as fantasy. This means that we cannot own them as our own and we cannot integrate them into ourselves as a whole.

If you recognise this splitting off mechanism operating in your life, start by just noticing anything that could be a displacement activity away from expressing feelings you presumed you did not have.

---

exercise

If you recognise that you are suffering from not having feelings, ask yourself when was the last time that you 'felt' something inside? Where did you feel it in your body? What was that feeling? When did it occur? What was happening at that time?

If your answer to the last question was a long time ago (more than two years), what was the result of your recognition of feeling at the time? Did you express it, and if so how? How did others respond? Did something happen to make you decide you would not express feeling again?

If you have been unable to answer the first two questions because you cannot recognise the expression 'felt', cast your mind's eye over the last week. What is the most unpredictable thing that happened? Describe it, and what was happening.

Talk to someone about not having feelings. Begin to explore what feelings are and how other people express them. Become a 'student' of feelings.

Look through the section 'Gathering Information' in Part Four and see if you can identify how your current sense of not having feelings came about.

Feeling WILL arise in its own time. TAKE TIME. Choose music and poetry or descriptive writing to express feelings. Music and poetry bypass the left side of the brain, which is our more rational, thinking

(Continued)

41

brain, and moves to touch directly into the right brain, which is the more feeling, intuitive, imaginative side. So allow yourself to be touched; and to move with, dance to, hold tenderly a tiny bud of feeling; to fire up in a blaze of anger or passion; to hear the sound of your own protesting voice and your own lost poetic soul. In *Finding What You Didn't Lose*, John Fox (1995) writes: 'when your poems become the "container" of your truest feelings, you will begin to experience and integrate those feelings more consciously'.

The void

Sometimes people say they feel that they have a 'black hole' or void inside them. They fear it, because they believe it will swallow them up and they will cease to exist. The reciprocal role is *emptying* in relation to *emptied*. Perhaps we feel as if we are only defined or identified by our work, or our looks. Because we fear the nothingness of the void we may try to fill it with people, food, drugs, work or social activity – anything external. We do not trust ourselves inside, and so we avoid anything reflective, contemplative, or still.

ALISTAIR, once he was brave enough to explore his experience of the 'void', had an image of a 'can of worms' containing everything he feared and loathed about his past and about some of his current feelings. (In Chapter 9 on writing our life story and working on our diagram, we will see how Alistair is currently working to cope with his particular void.) In exploring his 'can of worms' we met snakes who would come up and bite him in the form of an *accusing/judging* in relation to *judged/worthless* reciprocal role and statements such as 'You'll never stay in the fast lane.' The feeling 'I'm unhappy' was strong and was suppressed as quickly as possible. Alistair first realised his particular 'void' when one day he caught himself thinking, as he rushed from one appointment to another, 'I wonder if taking drugs would help?' He believed that if he allowed himself to stop, he would fall victim to the vacuum and emptiness which he associated with the void. All his life he had coped with this feeling by being incredibly busy. We met when his body had begun throwing up symptoms – duodenal ulcer, anal fistula, chest pain – and he had become phobic about illness and death. One of his first tasks was to allow himself half an hour each day for reflection. He found this very hard indeed!

Sometimes the void can be explored through visualisation, through drawing. Often life itself plunges us into the void, and we have to face it the hard way – through a serious illness, accident, breakdown, or being left alone and isolated.

Questionnaire: How do you recognise a void?

☐ I feel as if everything happens to me as if it's behind glass.

☐ I see other people doing things, but I don't belong.

☐ It's like another planet.

☐ I keep very busy with friends, relationships, work, eating, drinking, chaos, 'things', duties, etc., because I know that if I stopped, I would fall in the void.

☐ Inside I feel very lonely. Few people, if any, know this.

A first step in recognition is to accept you feel a void somewhere inside. You could try to monitor when you sense you are either nearing or fearing the void. You could see what happened if you tried to find an image for it, drawing or painting it; using images – 'it is like ...'; telling someone you trust about it. If the void has been created because when you were little you had to spend a lot of time on your own without adult company, it may be that it is very hard for you to get close to anyone, to trust them near to you. You may need help with this realisation and consider psychotherapy. This would give you a relationship with another human being with whom you can take safe steps in getting close and in trusting others. Allow yourself to consider this possibility.

Unmanageable feeling: Too sad, or too angry, or too frightened

If you recognise that cutting off feeling and 'not having feelings' is the way you coped with unmanageable feelings such as too sad, too angry or too frightened, respect that this was the best way you could manage at the time. If your early life included experiences that were traumatic through which you were traumatised – not all experiences of trauma lead to traumatisation – return to the diagram on page 17 and start monitoring your stress levels of hyper- and hypoarousal responses when you are with other people. Find someone with whom you can start naming and exploring safely the feelings you carry in your body.

If you have not already done so, create an image of a safe place (see page 25). This will offer containment for the previously unmanageable buried feelings, which might feel overwhelming at first, to be expressed. As you take steps to make these feelings conscious and you recognise signs of starting to become overwhelmed, or physically disregulated, allow the contained space to hold the feelings for you. **Remember that I am invisibly by your side.**

Sometimes these unmanageable inner feelings can manifest themselves in physical form – nausea, heaviness in the legs, headaches, tension in the neck and shoulders – and in symptoms, both physical and psychological. It's as if feeling is trying to express itself through the language of the body. Unmanageable anxiety, anger, fear and sadness may also be at the root of many eating disorders, in bingeing and starving; in self-harm; and many presenting physical problems that are not organic in cause.

Some provocative risk-taking behaviours, such as driving, drinking, smoking, dope-taking, flying, too fast, too much, too high, may also be a way of trying to manage unmanageable or unbearable feelings. There may be times when we spend too much money, or money we don't have, and buy things we don't need under the illusion that this will make us feel better.

All experiences of depression and suicidality share unbearable and unmanageable feeling: hopelessness, helplessness and trapped and inexpressible rage. As we saw earlier, the creator of Cognitive Analytic Therapy, Dr Anthony Ryle, tells us that a very high percentage of depressed and somatic symptoms are connected to the inability to express anger in a useful way. Understanding this, and finding ways to make conscious, name, express, contain or simply be with, previously unmanageable anger makes a difference. Some shadow of these feelings may always be with us, but we can learn to know and understand the shadows better and be able to use feeling more usefully. In her poem 'Anger's Freeing Power' Stevie Smith (1983) writes that it is the useful and enabling expression of anger rather than love, that frees her raven from beating himself inside the walls of his self-built cage. Also on this theme, the original Brothers Grimm fairy story about the Frog Princess had the princess throwing the frog she despised against the wall in a fit of rage, upon which he was transformed into a prince. It is only later that anger is replaced by the kiss, as if somehow the expression of love needs to exclude anger.

Many years ago I worked with heart patients as a counsellor in the cardiac department at Charing Cross Hospital with cardiologist Dr Peter Nixon, whose work was to understand the link between unmanageable feeling and its somatisation in coronary heart disease. He was challenging to the patients he was trying to help, as in 'Did you not love your wife enough to be angry with her?' Giving permission for anger to be part of love and the expression of it as useful, was part of recovery from chest pain and its associated disease process.

Unresolved and buried anger is very often under depression, it is the underlying cause of most panic attacks, it is now a recognised risk factor in the psychosocial causes of heart disease and can also initiate many physical responses represented in stress-related disorders.

Depression

Depression is an umbrella term for a whole range of difficult and unmanageable feelings which have been turned inwards. In Part One we saw the depressed feeling 'trap' created by depressed thinking and that recognition of the circular nature of the trap and the creation of exits brings about change. When depressed thinking and feeling start to merge into the more blanket term 'depression' it is

44

harder to get to the root of the internal patterns underneath. **But it is vital to do so and not to waste time.** Antidepressant treatment *is* needed for some cases of severe and disabling depression that has biological components, alongside learning about the underlying psychological patterns. It is very sad that depression and drug treatment for depression are so widespread in Western nations.

In *Mindfulness Based Cognitive Therapy for Depression*, authors Zindal Segal, Mark Williams and John Teasdale (2002) write:

> Depression is rarely observed on its own, it includes anxiety, and panic attacks are 19 times greater than someone without depression. Simple phobia and obsessive compulsive disorders have increased odds. Depressed patients spend statistically more time in bed than patients with lung disease. Work loss is five percent greater than non depressed patients. Suicide risk increases with each new episode. Major depression tends to be recurrent and the biological characteristics are: sleep disturbance often with early morning waking, gloomy desperate ruminate thinking in the mornings and a constant overactive neuroendocrine system creating the arousal associated with cortisol. These experiences are not varied with life circumstances such as taking a holiday or getting married. (p. 10)

Let's start by trying to look at what our 'depression' is about. Depression is not just about not coping. It helps to try to unravel the knot of unmanageable feelings, assumptions and old beliefs that depression is made up of and find small manageable exits. Understanding the context for depressed feelings is important for we need to have some idea of what our depressed response is intended to resolve:

1. Depression may be a natural response to a life event – the needed twilight of effort following bereavement, illness or loss. The wasteland experience of rites of passage during adolescence, mid-life, retirement where change in identity is taking place.
2. Depression may be directly connected to a life situation – poor housing, chronic poor health, family disruption, no money, racial discrimination, violence.
3. Depression may be a form of unconscious self-sabotage – a safer internal choice to whatever is feared from success or happiness or from the consequences of expressing anger and rage.
4. Depression may result from a long period of exhaustion – too much, or too little work or contact with others and no way out or to say no.
5. For many people depression is a form of breakdown – the breakdown of the way they have been before and seen as 'normal'.

Maintaining our depressed response may be restricting, and self-limiting reciprocal roles such as *punishing* in relation to *punished*; *critical judging* in relation to *crushed restricted*. There is often the dance of the bully and victim, both within and with others. The core feeling held in the internalised child reciprocal role is often feeling a *punished, flattened, crushed* and *restricted self*, and repressed rage. This is maintained by the tight hold of the *punishing, belittling,* or *judging internalised 'other'.* Other people will also be invited to join this dance until revision and new reciprocal roles are learned.

Questionnaire

Answering 'yes' to more than three of the following may help you to recognise that you are depressed.

I feel and believe that:

☐ I don't have a right to exist
☐ My needs will never be met
☐ Whatever I do I feel bad
☐ There is something wrong with me
☐ Everything is all my own fault
☐ I'm worthless, useless
☐ I can't get over this, ever

Metaphors can help us clarify our experiences. The following metaphors are often used in relation to the experience of depression. Do you experience yourself as:

☐ in a cage?
☐ in a prison?
☐ stranded on a high cliff?
☐ stuck in the desert?
☐ doomed and drowning?

When depressed, our feelings often include confusion, heavy-heartedness, sinking sick feeling, feelings of exclusion, a fear of our own and others' anger and rage, fear of going mad, the feeling of being trapped with something alien, inscrutable and intransigent that does not want to budge. And often deep, deep sadness and loneliness.

The following account is from AMANDA, who has kindly written a piece especially for this book to illustrate her experience of depression. Amanda has had a long history of depression, which has included hospital treatment as an in- and out-patient and also Cognitive Analytic Therapy and learning the practice of mindfulness. Her diagram is included in her account.

'Depression arrived suddenly and without warning. I was assured by the doctors that once the right dose of the right antidepressant was reached I would soon be fine again. Unfortunately it didn't work like that and I was referred for psychotherapy.

'At first I was unable to focus on what the therapist was saying or asking. I had continued to work full-time and I was exhausted. Over many months we looked at the snags, dilemmas and traps that I was falling into. I wasn't quick to grasp the significance of what was developing. The diagrams and cycles of thinking centred largely on my anxiety about most things but in particular about my work and with my inability to deal appropriately with my own and anyone else's anger. It also took me a long time to realise that in fact the diagrams were frighteningly similar in many ways and I needed to understand the processes involved. I could understand it in theory but much harder in practice, finding it difficult to "exit" at an early stage in the process. We also explored visualisation and for me, the concept of a lifebelt, that I could recall to my mind in times of need, was enormously effective.

'Much later, after a third stay in hospital and a long course of ECT, which improved my energy levels but not enough else, I returned to therapy. The lifebelt was still there for me but all too often I still felt desperately low. Suicide was frequently considered and I had started to try to self-harm even though I knew that the exit points of the main diagram were to talk to someone, to be kinder to myself, being "good enough" and not constantly striving to do well and to "get it alright" but at times they felt all too elusive. Now, in addition to this was the introduction to a more "mindful" way of life.

'On the very first session with Liz, she pointed out that I was holding my breath before I spoke. I had been going to yoga classes with different instructors and all would say, as we attempted a posture, to "keep breathing". Breathing appeared to be more difficult than I had thought!

'Practice of mindful breathing became a daily part of my life. It was difficult at first to let go of thoughts that constantly entered my head, something that in yoga I had yet to fathom. To my surprise, just by saying to myself "there's thinking" or acknowledging whatever was happening in the background, letting go of it was much easier. Even if my mind wandered for a while it was okay and returning to the breath was even a matter of congratulations.

'Sobbing uncontrollably has been part of the practice too. Each experience of practice is different but that is all part of it. Sometimes the mind wanders a lot or it is particularly difficult to settle but it really doesn't matter. That is where its beauty lies, especially for me, whose mind tends to be on full alert to what is going on all around. I can use the breathing to give me mental space and to break the negative process from the diagram that I now know so well and recognise my difficulties for what they are.

'Last week I walked into the town centre and started to feel very heavy in my body and mind. I decided to sit in the Abbey gardens and take in the calm of the beautiful park. There were only a few people about so it was easy to find somewhere to sit and breathe. At some point I realised there was a broken beer bottle lying on the ground. William Styron writes in *Darkness Visible* about being accompanied by a "second self" who watches "with dispassionate curiosity" as one "struggles against oncoming disaster, or decides to embrace it".

'Sitting on the park bench I could look at the broken bottle with this observer, taking in with curiosity what I intended to do. Like taking pills, cutting my wrists was a considered idea. But I found myself thinking about what I had learned in therapy, that I had a **choice. It was entirely up to me as to what to do next. That choice in fact gave me strength to resist doing anything except slowly force my legs to move out of the park and back to the hostel.** [emphasis added]

'My depression hasn't gone yet. It comes and goes as it always did. I hope that one day it will go away completely as innocuously as it came, but for now I can manage it much better. I can still feel desperate. I am lucky to have many loving friends and family. Talking to someone can do much to calm me, but then I have the thought that is so welcome; that I can give myself a few minutes of the space and peace that mindful breathing can invoke, however I feel and wherever I am.'

If you have had to bury feeling because it has felt unmanageable, once you begin to touch it again it hurts a lot, and we can feel just as we did when we were two or three years old, just as frightened and helpless. Take it slowly, knowing that now you are older you have help, you have breathing and other exercises to help you accept and process what you feel. You have notebooks in which we are going to find words for what you feel. Accept that the pain you feel is the pain of a little one and feels huge. And during this process we are not so much concerned with the story, as with the pain you feel and the ways you have learned to manage it. See the pain as evidence that your flesh and blood feeling nature is still alive and needs your help at containment and nourishment. Let it thaw out and flow and flourish. Trust it to show you what it most needs.

Unexpressed anger and rage

It can be hard to acknowledge that we have buried angry feelings. Fresh anger is usually a very physical experience, and like all feeling and emotion, involves our bodies. If you recognise after reading this section that you are carrying layers of unresolved anger and rage, just start noticing possible signs of anger, however small. It may be in clenching your jaw or a tightening in the small of the back; your anger may be in forced laughter, in speeded up speech, in cold ruthless prose. You may hold your breath like Amanda or literally swallow your anger with food or alcohol. In Part Three we will be looking at the nature of traps, dilemmas and snags. In each of these you will also find out more about your own anger.

When it first becomes conscious, previously unexpressed anger can feel out of proportion and we will have the same fears we had when we buried it – that others close to us will hate or reject us; that we will be like the angry person in

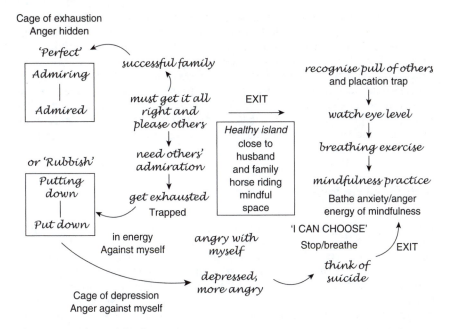

Figure 3.1   Amanda's diagram

our life we feared; that our anger might take us over. This is quite usual. After becoming conscious of anger and how it has been buried under symptoms we need to find a way of containing or expressing what we feel. One way is to write it out in our journal. Another way is to find a safe space to shout and jump up and down. The return from anger is to find ways to express it that are useful, freeing and creative, not destructive or harmful. And, most importantly, what is our anger about? What are the reciprocal roles that lead us to feel angry? What we really need – to feel protected, understood, accepted unconditionally – is often hidden under anger. Learning to find a voice to ask for these things is essential, once we have discovered what our anger is about.

What is the request beneath the anger?

We need to know our own anger and be able to express it and to contain it appropriately. We will probably need to learn to become assertive, to 'sing on the boundary', to speak out, not necessarily our angry feelings, but just what we feel and need, clearly and simply, not in aggression or acting out. We need to acknowledge and learn the language of our own feeling and emotional need and start expressing it in inner dialogue with ourselves, and then with others. Owning anger and learning to walk the talk of anger means that we have tempered the fiery dragons that once threatened to destroy us. Learning the limits of expressing anger and how to contain our anger and its more unreasonable or destructive side is essential.

Lying beneath anger is often hurt. And grief. We may have made an unconscious decision to feel angry or resentful toward those who have hurt us, because acknowledging hurt would have been impossible and also makes us feel so vulnerable. When we are able to reach beneath the smoldering or hardened anger we carry and touch the hurt, we have the chance to befriend and heal our hurt and vulnerability, using compassion and mindfulness. Pema Chodron, an American Buddhist nun, says, 'If someone shoots an arrow into your heart it's no good just railing at them. You need to attend to the fact that you have an arrow in your heart as well' (on retreat at Shambhala Mountain Centre, August 2002). Being able to grieve and mourn what has been lost or damaged, and forgive both others and oneself when appropriate is an essential part of the process of change.

Eating disorders

Eating disorders represent an abnormal preoccupation with food and weight, where food is no longer a simple substance for sustenance and pleasure. Underneath the symptoms of eating disorders are usually preoccupations with issues of control, submission, placation and perfectionism. This preoccupation becomes a means of communicating unmanageable feelings and emotions. It can be seen, as Tony Ryle and Ian Kerr report in *Introducing Cognitive Analytic Therapy* (2002), as a covert way of communicating or coping with feelings of not being heard or being pressurised to 'perform'.

In eating disorders we split food into 'good' and 'bad' food, with which we have a love/hate relationship. 'Bad' food we binge on may accentuate the badness and ugliness we feel inside and we have to get rid of it in order to feel clean; the control of food to the point of starvation gives the anorexic a 'high' and can become addictive.

Too often groups or websites for eating disorders concentrate upon the management of food without attending to the underlying reciprocal roles such as *controlling* (neediness and mess as in unmanageable feeling) in relation to *controlled/withholding*, and *conditionally excessive and rigid controlling* in relation to *empty controlled/worthless and angry*.

FREDA (see life story on p. 171) came into therapy because of her depression. Her eating problem only emerged later, as she had been ashamed of it. Also she had failed to see it as a 'problem', even though she had never eaten with her family or her friends. She was eating only a limited diet and taking laxatives that were seriously affecting her digestion. We made the following chart of the presenting problem, its underlying procedure and the aim for the therapeutic work. You will see that the aim is always directed at the procedure, not the problem. This approach gets us away from only recognising symptoms and being caught on the symptom hook.

Problem 1: Depression.
Procedure: I feel I've never been me or been able to let myself go. I don't think much of myself and get into the 'I'll do this badly' and 'worthless' trap. There doesn't seem much in life for me so far, because others' needs have always been more pressing.

Aim: To monitor everyday negative and depressed thoughts such as those outlined above. To challenge this and to develop more time for the things and occasions that put me in touch with the 'healthy island' – music, certain friends, being in the country.

Problem 2:   Placation trap, 'doing what others want'. Needing to be needed.
Procedure: Recognition of *feeding off* in relation to *fed off*. I have always felt worthless and that others' ways are better, so I give in, and feel cross with myself and anxious. People can easily tyrannise me, and I tyrannise myself by judging myself harshly.
Aim: To be aware of the times when I placate or create tyrants. To bring my awareness into the moment and risk saying 'no' or having a different view when that is what I feel. To trust what it is I feel I want to do much more thoroughly, even if sometimes I am wrong about my decision.

Problem 3:   Eating compulsively, then starving and bingeing.
Procedure: Recognition of *tyrannising* in relation to *tyrannised*. I long to be 'full' but feel bad if I have anything, so I have to get rid of it.
Aim: To monitor feelings prior to, during and after eating compulsions and binges. To recognise 'longing to be full', where I feel it in my body. To risk letting it be just so and letting it speak in words or images.

Problem 4:   Self-sabotage due to irrational guilt about dead brother and mother's depressed life.
Aim: To be aware when I 'sell myself short' or put myself down. To be aware when I let others 'win', or take a back seat when I know inside I could take part equally. To take the risk of expressing myself more assertively, and let go of the family's disappointment and misery. To say, 'I AM ALLOWED' without feeling guilty.

Freda took up her journal-keeping enthusiastically. She said it was like having 'permission to live, even if only inside a notebook'. After a few weeks her depression began to lift. As she challenged her placating, her eating problems got worse. She noticed a craving for food and an intensity of feelings of 'high' followed quickly by heaviness and despair where she sought food for comfort. She found that she could express herself in images. A colourful language emerged, linking early life memories with her current need to starve herself in order to experience control. She found visualisation and drawing particularly helpful. During one particularly moving session she got in touch with the hidden feelings around the time her mother came home after the death of Freda's brother at the age of six days. There was an image of her mother's flat stomach, and a wave of profound despair, the intensity of her weeping (which she showed only to Freda, not to friends). Most of all was Freda's fear and over-responsibility for the insatiability of her mother's need and hunger, for the look in her eyes that Freda believed she had to make better. She saw that she had taken responsibility for trying to fill the space left by the dead baby.

51

Freda described how she felt 'eaten up' by her mother's needs and demands, which returned later when her sister developed anorexia and Freda was once again expected to fill an empty space. One of her drawings showed a huge open mouth into which tiny fish were being shovelled by a thin witch with a child's broken-handled spade. In one of her dreams her right hand was being bitten by a wolf. She drew a picture of the wolf, and came to associate this animal with her own emotional hunger and need, her 'wolfishness' that tyrannised her. The wolf would nip her, reminding her of her own hunger (for something which she needed to name) and of the devouring and tyrannising quality of her mother's neediness, from which she was struggling to free herself. This needing to be needed, or *feeding off* in relation to *fed off* was also recognised in several other relationships – husband, sister, children, family.

Freda was encouraged by her friends' new respect for her holding on to her own ground. Two key phrases – 'selling myself short' and 'I am allowed' – helped her to have the courage to express herself fully with other people, especially difficult people like her mother, to whom she felt duty-bound and very unfree.

[Freda's dream is recounted in Part Six.]

4

Problems and dilemmas within relationships

Relationships challenge all the ways in which we feel about and experience ourselves. It is through flesh and blood human relationships that we experience a mirroring process of the reciprocal roles we have learned. Difficulties in relationships arise when we stumble into the more powerful not yet understood emotions that may be linked to our early life survival patterns, which bring up the more fragile and less-known aspects of ourselves.

All relationships, when our attachment needs are pressed, return us to the world of childhood where we strive to maintain control over what feels like helplessness and powerlessness. We are brought into our vulnerability, our smallness, alongside our need for closeness and intimacy. Often it isn't until we have been in a relationship for some time, or have perhaps had a series of similar relationships, that we realise there are meaningful patterns at work. Because we learn to be a person with an 'other', the patterns of inter-being are the foundation from which we seek attachment to others. So we are naturally drawn towards people with whom we engage in similar learned ways to those significant others in our early life. When this is balanced by mutual sharing and respect these patterns can be mediated, even changed.

But when we realise we are repeating the more negative reciprocal roles, such as being *controlling* and feeling *restricted*, or being *judging* in relation to feeling *crushed* we find ourselves caught up in potentially destructive patterns. Once again we become the child who felt humiliated or rejected, hurt or abandoned, lost, furious, uncared-for and needy.

Our core wound is pressed over and over again by our experience in relationships. We may avoid involvement with others and keep relationships superficial, limiting contact to people at work, or only talking on the telephone, in order to cope with fear of closeness but pay the price in loneliness and isolation. We may rush from one relationship into another hoping to heal the pain inside us. We may long to find 'perfect care' only to feel crushed and disappointed over and over again.

We may suffer from several broken or destructive relationships, including the ones at work or with acquaintances, before becoming aware that there are unconscious patterns at work. Once we start looking, however, our journey toward change has begun. It is possible to shift reciprocal role patterns into being less rigid and dominating, just through our awareness of being invited into them. We can create new reciprocal roles that are helpful and healthy. Reciprocal roles such as: *listening* in relation to *listened to, caring* in relation to *cared for; loving/nurturing* in relation to *loved/nurtured.* By reading this book you are developing an observer self who is witnessing all you have been through, and thus creating *respectfully witnessing* in relation to *respected and witnessed.*

In this chapter we look at the more complicated difficulties which arise from our relationships with other people, which press our core wound against which we defend ourselves in the old learned way. In order to understand this we need to look at the patterns we learned in childhood.

Questionnaire: Relationships

How many of these statements apply to you?

If I get close to someone, I fear:

- ☐ Ridicule: 'I'll be laughed at for what I feel.' And –
- ☐ 'Contempt: 'I will get spat upon.'
- ☐ Humiliation: 'They will look down on me.'
- ☐ Dependency: Being made to feel small and helpless: 'I don't want to have to need anyone.'
- ☐ Being taken advantage of: used and abused.
- ☐ Being teased and taunted: 'They will get just within my reach and disappear.'
- ☐ Invasion: 'They'll get right inside me.'
- ☐ Cruelty: 'I'll be beaten or my words used against me.'
- ☐ Lack of privacy: 'They are watching me all the time.'
- ☐ Overwhelming need: 'No one will ever fill the hole in my heart.'
- ☐ High expectations: 'I'll have to be on my "best" behaviour all the time.'
- ☐ Abandonment: 'I'll be left just when I've let go.' Or, 'I'll be abandoned in the end, no one will stay with me.'
- ☐ Hypervigilant: 'I have to be on my guard all the time. You never know when they will get you.'
- ☐ Suffocation: 'Being close is too much, there is no room to breathe.'
- ☐ Being overwhelmed and overpowered: reduced to nothing, like a slave.
- ☐ Conditional/restricting: 'I'll never come up to scratch, be what they want.'
- ☐ Losing myself completely: disappearing into the void.
- ☐ Losing my independence.

☐ Crying all the time.
☐ Abuse – sexual, physical or verbal.

Do you recognise the following patterns of thinking?

☐ 'No one could ever be as good to me as ...'
☐ 'They will see things about me I hate and want no one to see.'
☐ 'It is only a fantasy, and I'll never get near it.'

Mark which of the above you recognise applies to you and see if you can name your own three-way reciprocal roles.

Learning to recognise the 'shadow'

What was done to us we do to others and to ourselves. Sometimes one way of coping with painful emotional early experiences is to cut off from pain and try to live in a controlled but restricted way. We try to protect the hurt and fragile child in us by looking after it in others, or by hitting out at it in others. It is very hard to acknowledge this in ourselves, because in acknowledging that we have taken on the parental role in our relationships we are admitting that we are behaving like the people who once damaged or hurt us. If we understand that our choices were limited by the unconscious need to be in reciprocation to others we can invite conscious revision and seek help to change. We usually act from both ends of our reciprocal role, but it's harder to acknowledge the more negative role. This may mean facing our critical side, the side that secretly enjoys humiliating others, that likes to be possessive, demanding, cruel, taunting or over-controlling. *[handwritten margin note: Shadow - neg. end of RR]*

When these aspects remain unconscious they cause more trouble than if we face them. If we have experienced humiliation when young we will do anything to avoid it – for example, by living life 'above reproach' or 'beyond criticism'. But the fear will remain, unconsciously. Because we have put it down so firmly in ourselves it's likely we will do the same when we meet it in others. This may present itself in the form of a 'pathetic' old man or woman, someone we see as weak, and from out of the shadows will come our most caustic remark – the very thing we received and fear receiving.

We may get into a relationship with someone we have idealised and admired and wanted to live up to and please. All might be lovely at first, and then we find that they are no longer 'special' and we feel disillusioned and disappointed.

We may find parts of ourselves that do not emerge until we are in a relationship. For example, the successful, ambitious young woman, whose hard work and effort have come from being a striving child, becomes once again the young, frightened child once she's close to a partner. From behind the admired, glossy, confident surface to which the partner was initially attracted steps a small person craving assurance and ready to be pleasing and dependent, whom he does not know or understand.

Dilemmas relating to our relationships with others

If–then and either–or dilemmas restrict other possibilities in relationships. All of us feel vulnerable when we are in a dependent position, which is part of attachment. If we have had an early experience (our very first dependency) which was 'good enough', we do not fear or avoid dependency. When relationships are going well, there is give and take on both sides and a feeling of equality.

See if any of the following dilemmas relate to you.

If I care about someone, I have to give in to them or they have to give in to me

When we care about someone and feel we have to give in to them it tends to be because we want their approval or affection so much that we will do what they want, as in the placation trap (see Part Three). There is no sense of equality in our relating, and relationships feel highly charged. There is no freedom to be ourselves, and others rule the way in which we respond and act. The 'giving in' seems to be based upon self-protection, with the learned assumption that if we do not give in to those we care about something bad will happen. Our sense of self feels under threat.

This learned dilemma could arise from an experience of conditional caring in early life, or from *dominating/powerful* in relation to *powerless/needy*.

The other part of this dilemma is in experiencing our feelings when we care about someone as being quite powerful and demanding. Our sense is that because we feel strongly others must respond and give in to us. We may have internalised the sense of the child who was given free rein or over-protected from an early age, who has become used to their strong feelings being reciprocated in kind and their every demand met.

If I depend on someone, I have to give in to them or they have to give in to me

This is a deeper version of the first dilemma, and can form a very important 'B movie' for what goes on unconsciously within a relationship. Our fear of dependency may stem from the fact that we have never actually been allowed to be dependent and have learned from this to become independent. It feels that, when we do allow ourselves to depend on someone, then they are in control and we have to give in to them. We feel powerless and helpless, which can express itself in passivity and sometimes a feeling of emptiness, coupled with feeling afraid of being at the mercy of another. We may feel that we come near to being just as helpless and needy as we were when small.

56

If we establish a relationship with a strong caring other, it feels as if we can be dependent with nothing to fear. But this may be challenged when we do have to grow up and stand alone. We may accept this and grow within this care, and if the other person is flexible and allowing we can indeed overcome a fear of dependency and allow some interdependence.

However, if we recognise that we feel resentful and cross at having to give in when feeling dependent, and we are expecting others to give in to us, we need to see that we are using our neediness as if it were our only 'strength'. Our fantasy is that were it not for our need keeping someone with us, they would not stay. There might be a fantasy that 'growing up' means others leave us. Sometimes this is related to the actual experience of a mother who found it very difficult to let go of her mothering role and wanted her children to remain as her 'babies'. If we believe that this dependency is our only power or strength we will undermine our ability to grow up and move away independently.

Questionnaire: Caring and depending on someone

If I care for someone, I feel:

☐ Self-conscious and worried.
☐ Eager to be seen in the best light.
☐ I must give in to them in order that they might care for me.
☐ I seem to withdraw and become passive and helpless.
☐ I must control myself, my fear and my anxiety and I must learn all about the other person and please them.
☐ I expect others to notice me, to care equally about me; and to look after me, meet my needs and demands.

If I depend upon someone, I feel:

☐ Afraid and vulnerable.
☐ Frightened of being hurt.
☐ Humiliated and disadvantaged.
☐ I must do what the other wants; give in to the other in dress/manners/ behaviour/religion/work/all standards/looks/sex.
☐ I must give over my whole self to the other.
☐ I expect others to be stronger and therefore able to do as I ask.
☐ I expect others to make decisions for me, to do what I want.
☐ I am in control, as if what I need dominates and makes things happen.
☐ I feel secure that other people know where they stand with me and what I need, and will give in to me.
☐ I feel cosy, knowing what others need and giving it to them and with others knowing my needs. In this way neither of us needs anyone or anything else; safe and 'all wrapped up'.

(Continued)

I never depend upon anyone.

☐ I do not allow myself to be dependent at any time. I notice this in the following ways:

☐ I do not allow myself to get close to anyone in case I feel dependent.

☐ I never allow myself to get in anyone's 'debt'. If I'm given gifts or paid compliments I have to give back as soon as possible.

☐ I never let anyone pay for me; I make sure I always pay my own way. I much prefer to give than receive.

☐ If a woman, I would never let myself get pregnant. If a man, I would never let myself get married.

☐ I like to be in charge. It's hard for me to be a student, to admit I don't know things, to share equally with others.

☐ I'm afraid of being dependent and will do anything to avoid it. Secretly I'm afraid of being ill or getting old, and my images of these are full of humiliation, defeat, suffocation or worse.

If you answered 'yes' to any of the above, ask yourself what you fear from dependency. What gets in the way of your allowing yourself to be in a dependent position? Is it:

pride?
fear (of what)?
fierce independence?
rage?
a yet unresolved memory of being let down, suffocated or other?

Spend some time pondering on what you discover from this questionnaire. Look at the number of times you have shied away from any kind of dependent position. Write about this in your notebook, and let the images or memories stay with you as you read on through Part Four, 'Gathering Information'.

I'm either involved and hurt, or not involved and in charge, but lonely

This dilemma can operate whether we are in a relationship or not. Our vulnerability is towards hurt, and our unconscious antennae are quick to detect it. We have probably been hurt at some time and we therefore associate all relationships with hurt. We expect to be hurt, and we may be highly sensitive to words, nuances, actions and hidden meanings which support us in this belief. To cope with hurt we have learned to withdraw, either literally or inside ourselves, and this remains our position, keeping the dilemma intact. Others may not realise how we feel, because we don't communicate it directly; all they may know is that we are hard to get close to. This may be because we are so brittle and scratchy when we come up against our fear, or because we depart moodily to nurse the fear on our own, or we may fear our own capacity to hurt or destroy if we get close.

Many of us cope with this dilemma by not having relationships or by keeping those we do have very limited and superficial. This gives us control over the hurt, but at the cost of our loneliness. Those daring to enter relationships may find them a torment because of fear and difficulty with trust. It may take a long time before we overcome this dilemma and learn that it is possible to be with someone and not get hurt. Unfortunately when this dilemma operates it's as if we are waiting for our fear of getting hurt to be activated. And, of course, sooner or later something happens which proves we have to stay alone to be in charge. Many people do feel lonely, either within relationships or nursing their hurts alone.

One of PAUL's ways of coping with hurt feelings was to bottle them up. His social isolation was also a coping strategy. He had been very close to his mother, who had died when he was six, and then passed around the family. He promised himself he would not get close, and therefore hurt again. When we met he felt his depression had been caused by personal hurt from the children of his new love. Before this time he had kept in his 'lonely but in charge' position, and it worked up to a point. On falling in love at forty, however, he risked expressing his deep feelings and being hurt. His ensuing depression followed when, inevitably, the initial intensity and closeness of the relationship began to wane. His adjustment and subsequent change involved working through much of the unrecognised mourning for the loss of his mother, and to understand and feel for the lonely boy who had only had encyclopaedias for company.

He monitored all the occasions when he felt slighted or got at by others, the times when he fled to his own room after feeling excluded or misunderstood. He recognised *needing to be special six* in order to feel safe in relation to *perfect but unobtainable*. ['Special six' related to the years he had his mother, which he saw as special.] He saw that his hurt could be triggered by the smallest nuance and was out of proportion. He had to learn that his need to be *special six* meant that what felt like the heartless and thoughtless behaviour of others was just ordinary banter and exchange. It was not people being less than perfect and not caring or coming up to scratch, from which he had to withdraw into his familiar lonely state.

exercise

It is important when pondering on this dilemma to realise that the part of you which feels hurt corresponds to when you were a child. It is he or she who needs your care. When you feel hurt by someone, spend time exsamining

(Continued)

what happened. What was said, referred to, acted out? What was actually said, and what did you hear underneath the words that confirmed your worst fears? Write it down. Try to describe the tone, feeling, image of what happened. Draw it if you can. Notice your eye level when you are pondering this. Are you looking up, or down?

With others I'm either safely wrapped up in bliss or I'm in combat. In combat, I'm either a bully or a victim

This double dilemma refers to our need to return to the safety or hiding of a womb-like environment when we get close to others. We're either enclosed in the relationship in a 'garden of Eden' type bliss, or we react aggressively to others, always ready for a fight and adopting either the victim or bullying role.

In this dilemma there is no comfortable breathing space in between, where we can experience a mutual interdependence. It's as if we have found it hard to learn a model of being with someone which allows for the ebb and flow of energy and difference. We may find that we lurch from one extreme to another: feeling the dependency and flight of being all wrapped up one minute, only to swing into combative mode the next. We may have the 'wrapped-up' relationship with one other person and be in combat in all our other relationships.

The dilemma often arises because of our longing for 'perfect care' and fusion with another. This may be the result of an over-close or 'tight' relationship with mother or sibling, or conversely because we have had empty, deprived early beginnings, where it was left to our imagination to provide an ideal model. The reciprocal roles are of *idealised 'perfect'* in relation to *neglected/forgotten*. So inside ourselves we swing from hope to despair, from clinging to an ideal of how we long for things to be to a position of rage when we are disappointed, at which point we invite a combative situation, bullying others or allowing ourselves to be bullied.

It can be hard to accept that our idealisation is the very thing that stops us having satisfactory relationships. Whilst the fantasy longing for another who can meet our every need can feel good in fantasy, it puts us and others under huge pressure and means we are always doomed to be disappointed. The fact that no one other mortal person can meet the needs of our deprived inner child can make us depressed. But out of this sense of despair we may begin to find the seeds of giving and receiving care from others that eventually becomes 'good enough'.

If we can see that our 'combat' style is an attempt to gain independence from the fantasy of being all wrapped up, we can build on this, finding more robust and realistic ways of relating.

---

exercise

Write a story about 'perfect care' or 'perfect revenge'. Make it as dramatic as you wish. Read it aloud to someone you trust. Allow yourself to experience the feelings or longing behind the words, to identify the 'core pain' of the person in the story, and inside you, who wishes to relate to others.

Write another story about how you might care for the child inside whose feelings you have identified in the first story. Use everyday people and objects that have had some reality for you, or invite characters from your imagination who might serve the needs of the child today.

Either I look down on people or they look down on me

How much do we know of our haughty selves who look down our noses, feel compelled to compete when someone is telling us something, have to cap everything with something of our own? And at the other end, how well do we know the self that is looked down upon, humiliated and laughed at, both by ourselves and, we fear, by others? This dilemma is about the world of despising and being despised, and how we deal with it. Much of the dilemma stems from a particular experience when we felt despised, or were treated contemptuously – by adults when we were small, by admired elders at an impressionable time – and from which we were determined that we are in some part contemptible, laughable, a joke. We may also believe that we deserved our deprivation and are the rotten person we were made to feel.

Believing this is so painful that we have few options. We can go through life with the false belief that we are all the things we despise and that others will look down on us, whatever we do. In this place we may play the contemptible one, or may block out any feelings by going 'on automatic'. We may live only via a 'mask' and suffer the limitations and restrictions of this protective superficiality. Many compulsive workers – men or women – who become addicted to their work in whatever form do so because they are running from this fear and this place. They fear that if they are not sustained by the admiration of others whom they admire, they will be exposed and then will have to feel contemptuous or suffer feeling contemptible. In their studies of post-heart-attack patients, *Treating Type A Behavior and Your Heart*, Meyer Friedman and Diane Ulmer (1984) make the following observation:

As the perilous drive continues (to do more and more in less and less time and against greater odds and with increasing aggressiveness and desperation), the Type A person confines his disdain to those persons he is able to control; eventually he begins to entertain less and less regard for himself. It is when this latter process begins that his own spirit starts to wither, and the urge to self-destruct mounts. Much of this occurs in the unconscious, which makes the tragedy no less profound. (p. 201)

We may only sense that there is something inside us which makes us feel miserable and frightened and from which we are aware of running away, but our external adaptation takes up most of our time. We may not know that what we fear is contempt, and we will not know that at times we appear contemptuous. It is usually when our outer adaptation fails that we feel thwarted and fall into the place of contempt or become contemptuous ourselves.

Questionnaire: Either I look down on people or they look down on me

Can you recognise this statement to be true:

Others I relate to have to be special and see me as special. If they fail, then they are objects of contempt. If I fail, then I become contemptible.

In which of the following ways can you recognise your own contemptuousness:

☐ I have to keep 'one ahead' of others, which makes me competitive. I have to get in my own story, and I am constantly striving to win.

☐ I am judgemental of others whom I see as weak and pathetic. I ignore them, or bait them by teasing and provocation over matters on which I know they cannot cope. Or I sneer, am sarcastic, humiliating.

☐ I enjoy others' discomfort when I have 'found them out' or tricked them into falling into their own mess.

☐ I am envious of others' success but cannot bear this feeling, so I repress it and am only aware of it in my difficulty with being 'less than' at any time.

☐ I find it very hard to be in a learning position where I have to take from another whom I see as being in a superior position to myself and in which I feel inferior.

How do you use your contemptuousness:

☐ I am very uncomfortable with it, but I use it to drive me on in this world.

☐ I am aware I am envious and competitive, and I use it to get me going, to make sure I keep up and ultimately overcome those in whose company I was made to feel small.

☐ I am revengeful to those whom I feel have put me down. I fantasise about situations in which I am the victor over someone whom I feel has treated me with contempt. I practise very hard so that I can get my revenge.

☐ When things go wrong I am aware of feeling more than usually shattered. I swing from being contemptuous, angry and bitter towards others, to feeling contemptible and alone, self-destructive and suicidal.

In which of the following ways do you recognise that you feel others look down on you with contempt:

☐ I always put myself down, usually jokingly, sending myself up.

☐ I sneer at myself frequently and invite others to do the same.

☐ I try to rise above these feelings by being very intellectual and clever. I use complicated words and sentences that few understand to hide my inadequacy.

☐ There is no fight in me. I let others walk all over me, while secretly despising them for it.

☐ I expect others to behave better, but I am not surprised when they don't.

☐ I am bitter. I want others to be better than they are, but I don't give any clues as to how this could be for me. I don't say what I really feel or what I really want from them. I allow others to treat me contemptuously.

☐ Most of my dialogues with others are in fact in my head. I rarely say what I feel or what I would like to say. I presume that others wouldn't be able to cope with it, and so I don't give them the chance.

☐ Although I despise myself, I feel that others should know better and do more for me. I am aware that this makes me incredibly angry, and that I feel angry a lot of the time.

☐ It doesn't take much for people to get through or push me off-centre. I do rely on admiration from others to stop me feeling looked down upon.

☐ I rely a lot on having to be in positions of authority or usefulness to stop me feeling the pain of people looking down on me. But even though I achieve those positions (I look after others well, teach others, am my own boss, have a good job with others working for me) I am still on the look-out for those who would put me down. *There is nowhere I feel really safe.*

What we have to cope with in this dilemma is the feeling that we are contemptible, and the fear that we will be forced to feel this again as we once did. The way in which we lessen the gap between feeling we have to look down on others and their looking down on us is to submit ourselves to the pain of that despised place. In that place we do indeed get in touch with many of the

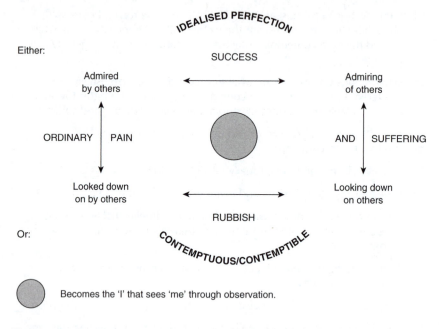

Figure 4.1   Looking down on others or looking down on me. The aim for change is learning to tolerate ordinary everyday pain and suffering

feelings that arose during our experiences of humiliation as a child. But when we experience them during a programme of self-discovery or therapy we bring to the damaged place another awareness of ourselves: that we are more than the child we once were, even though the feelings we suffer may seem overwhelming.

In Figure 4.1 we see how this dilemma operates. If we are not living in the top section (admired and admiring) then we inhabit the bottom (contemptuous or contemptible). When we experience 'the fall' from the idealised heights of success, we so fear being humiliated ('beyond the pale') that we turn our fear into a contemptuousness towards others.

Healing by mourning the loss of idealisation to become 'real' and 'good enough'

As we become conscious of this dilemma we begin to dilute its power and 'splitting' nature by recognition, and by bearing the 'ordinary' pain and suffering of our core pain: This then gives more space to experience a natural 'healthy island'. Here, ordinary pain and suffering, loss and disillusionment will be experienced as we grieve for the loss of 'idealisation'. So healing takes place as we allow ourselves to be ordinary mortals in pain.

Either I'm a brute or I'm a martyr

This dilemma relates to how we cope with our angry and aggressive feelings. If we do get angry and express it we feel like a brute, or we imagine that our anger is brutish. Conversely we get angry but don't say anything. We take on the martyr role, feeling full of self-sacrifice, with all the internal resentment and hostility this evokes. There is no middle place for assertion or appropriately angry responses, and at both ends of the dilemma each position blames the other. For the martyr says, 'I'm not going to get myself involved in anything that's unpleasant or brutish, I am better than that'; while the brute will say, 'It's no good sitting back and letting oneself be slaughtered, it's not worth it. Let's just steamroller over this and get something happening.' Each one serves the other. Each one brings out the opposite, either in another person or within the individual. For everyone who is caught up with the myth of the martyr there will be a brutish side, coming out unexpectedly because of its repression. People who take on the role of martyr are often prone to violent, brutish outbursts, or behave horribly to their animals, children or old people. Many people who appear brutish believe that if they did not act in such a way they would be martyred by others or to some cause in which they do not believe.

We are using the word 'martyr' here in a negative sense and not in the sanctified religious sense of one who gives their life for a believed cause in exchange for a heavenly after-life. If someone consciously chooses to martyr themselves for a cause they believe in, this is conscious acting from a position of idealism. We may say they are brutish to themselves at the same time, and to those whom they deprive of their full company.

However, most of us who take up the position of martyr in our everyday lives feel put upon and deprived of our freedom of choice. Thus, we adopt the role resentfully and harbour a good deal of hidden anger. It is this underlying fury which can be quite devastating to others, precisely because it is so unexpected. We feel guilty if we are not serving others or being slaves to the object of our martyrdom, and we tend to look for ways we should be serving this master. We may expect to receive gratitude from others in reward for our sacrifice. But others may feel enslaved by our martyrdom and unable to go along with it. Martyrdom can be tyrannical and bring out the brute in the best of us! Martyrs can easily become depressed victims, inviting the oppressor in others and thus actualising and extending the period of martyrdom still further.

JOE experienced his mother as a martyr to his macho brutish father. He had a good bond with his mother and was devastated when she died of a heart attack when he was only eleven. He came into therapy because he was very depressed and phobic about death. Unable to go out to look for a job, obsessed with death and the after-life, he was becoming reclusive. In asking him to monitor the feelings he experienced during his panic attacks, we discovered that they came on in situations where he feared he might have to be assertive to someone. A man in the shop, on the end of the phone, when out running with his dog. He was terrified of getting into a situation where he would 'boil over in rage like an exploding volcano'.

When we looked at this we discovered that as well as his father's macho image, which Joe felt he could not go along with, the week before his mother had died his father had thrown a lamp at her in a fit of temper. He had associated his father's anger with a brutishness and murderousness, triggering off his mother's death. He had never put these two together before, but his unconscious had, preventing him from expressing any kind of anger in case it came out in the same way. He had blocked off assertiveness, frightened that it might turn into anger and aggressiveness. When he could see how this dilemma had ruled his life he could begin to learn to be more assertive, to choose his own way of being angry. Then he could begin to go back into the world less afraid, and free himself from the unconscious ties that had deprived him of his own life.

Questionnaire: Either I'm a brute or a martyr

If I am a martyr, is it because:

- ☐ I believe it is the only way I can receive gratitude and thanks from others?
- ☐ I believe it is the only way I can be?
- ☐ I don't believe in my freedom and right to a full independent life?
- ☐ for me it is a form of love?
- ☐ I learned it and am now copying it without revision?
- ☐ I am caught up in a centuries-old-woman-as-martyr-to-men complex?

Name the martyrs in your family, in your experience – from literature, the Bible, films, stories. Do you identify with one of them? Do you fear being identified as a martyr, and so adopt a brutish role?

In what way do I express my hidden 'brutishness':

- ☐ against myself?
- ☐ against my animals?
- ☐ in fantasy?
- ☐ in sudden outbursts of temper directed against others?

If I am a 'brute', is it because:

- ☐ it's the only way I've learned to be from (i) family, (ii) others?
- ☐ if I'm not a brute I'll be a martyr (like someone I know)?
- ☐ it's the only way I can keep on top and avoid victimisation?
- ☐ I enjoy the power and letting others live out the martyr role?
- ☐ It limits my life.

Brutes also have feelings. What are they?

The male/female dilemma: as a woman I have to do what others want; as a man I can't have any feelings

All men and women are influenced not only by the myths about being a man or woman passed on by families, but also by their male and female genes. The most recent research involving MRI brain scans of male and female brains shows differences in speech and language areas. The female brain is highly utilised in speech and language functions. For centuries these myths involved a need to 'placate' the needs of men and play down a woman's own skills for fear of 'emasculating' a man. Are women breaking with these myths today – myths that if we are not subservient we are not feminine and it spoils relationships?

Women are trying to, but it's often surprising how much these myths live on and unconsciously inform what women do and how they behave. Until the last ten years women have felt suppressed by men and masculine ideology, by the force of patriarchy. Although there have always been pioneers, such as Mary Wollstonecraft or Mary Ann Evans (George Eliot) to show that the female spirit was alive, all reflection of women has predominantly come through men. Since gaining more independence economically, sociologically and biologically, women have often still to go through masculine channels to receive recognition, often having to work much harder than men.

In the midst of this transition in women's roles, relationships are changing. One in three marriages ends in divorce. Many women are leaving it until later to get married, and then have difficulty finding a partner who meets their expectations. Many women feel very torn at this point. They want independence to work and express themselves, but they still feel there is a substantial cost involved and that it poses a threat to relationships.

ALICE, a successful architect with two children, is aware of this tension in her own life: 'At work my role is very clearly defined and I am respected for it. I say my piece and it is heard and acted upon. I experience myself as being free and powerful in a creative sense. It is stimulating and exciting and I love the work I'm doing and the feeling of expansiveness and generosity it gives me. But when at home something else seems to take over. I fear being seen as "boss" as I see it as a basic threat to the safety of my relationship. So I give in to my partner's wishes and feel bad after. I don't say what I really think and believe in. I feel that were I to be more assertive he would see me as strident and demanding. He says: "I'm not one of your office minions ... you can't behave like you do in the office here." I don't feel I can answer because I feel he's right, that somehow I've got to be submissive in my private life to make up for "getting away with it" – success – elsewhere. The awful silly guilt. I know I'm resentful. I often get headaches at the weekends and feel unbearably tired when I get home. I associate that with my confusion, not knowing what to do, and a general weariness and lack of clarity about the whole thing.'

Some women actually sacrifice their own views and voice when they marry or enter a relationship, and upon having children. For some it is a relief not to fight or struggle any more, but be content with the age-old passive role of serving home, husband and children. And, indeed, within this role there are many modes of expression. But to give up one's own voice because of a fear of not being feminine causes only conflict and struggle, and leads resentments and angers to build up underneath.

Thanks to feminism these old myths are under revision, but women tend to slip back into them when things get difficult or they try out new ways of expressing themselves that are misunderstood.

Somewhere in this transition of male and female expressions lies the hope for the emergence of a way of being a woman that brings into the light of consciousness the most positive qualities of the feminine principle:

- Receptive, rather than passive.
- Empowering, rather than selflessly giving to others.
- Flexible, adaptable, yielding and creative, rather than submissive with 'no mind of her own'.
- Centred in body and emotions and unafraid of each, rather than overemotional, flighty, frivolous, self-conscious.
- Sexual and sensual, rather than seductive, flirty, posing.
- Nurturing, rather than manipulatively feeding and devouring.
- Containing, rather than possessive.
- Holding close and letting go appropriately, rather than emasculating (men and women) and overcontrolling.

From a central womb of womanhood a woman can then express her masculine side. This would be ancillary to her feminine being, not instead of or to compensate for the negative sides listed above.

As a man, I have to be a 'proper' man, which means not expressing anything to do with feelings

This dilemma will remain unrevised if men can find both work and relationships that avoid the need to get into anything of a feeling nature. If women are still living out the need to define being feminine as not being assertive or having independent views, the men with whom they are involved will be able to dictate the tone of the relationship and look to women to contain the feeling side of things. Many men do manage to avoid having anything to do with feelings, until something happens that hits them personally on that level – their partner leaves them, they get ill and become dependent on others, they fall in love, they lose someone they had never realised was important to them.

With the change in the role of women in society, relationships between men and women are having to adapt radically, and men are finding that they must deal with their feeling side earlier than in previous generations. For many men who have been brought up in a traditionally 'macho' environment, there is little or no developed language for expressing feeling or emotion. The myth seems to be that a man must be in the outside world where his rational, focused side is uppermost, and that the convoluted, diffuse world of the emotions would only impede progress and draw a dangerous veil over the masculine purpose. When men cut off their feeling side because they are afraid of being overpowered by it, they become lopsided. They can get stuck at the extreme end of the masculine principle. They tend to become lonely and are unable to relate to others, their work or the world. They can become depressed because they think they are supposed to act like an automaton, so rejecting a major aspect of themselves and appearing brittle and unfeeling, strident and fixed.

The old myths about men and masculinity persist: tough, macho, in charge and command-driven, strict, controlled, focused, unyielding, unable to compromise. Any show of softness is seen as a weakness. Although a man may have strong feeling instincts and a strong feminine side, he may have been discouraged from using or expressing this aspect of himself because of the powerful taboos that exist against it. There are a hundred little injunctions – 'boys don't cry', mother's boy, cissy, hiding in a woman's skirts, floppy, spineless, weedy, wet, impotent, foppish – all linking the feminine side with negativity.

Questionnaire: The male/female dilemma

What do you feel are the important qualities of being a woman, being a man? How much do you include these in your own life?

My expectations of masculine and feminine

I expect men to:

- ☐ be strong
- ☐ make all the decisions
- ☐ not to be fazed or bothered
- ☐ not to be fazed or bothered by anything
- ☐ be able to take liquor

- ☐ have exclusive male company
- ☐ not be bossed or affected by a woman
- ☐ have the most important role
- ☐ not give in to any weakness

I expect women to:

- ☐ be kind and gentle
- ☐ have warm feelings
- ☐ care about children and relationships
- ☐ keep themselves looking nice

- ☐ be good housewives
- ☐ be the peacemaker
- ☐ have a special 'women's' world
- ☐ never be aggressive or masculine.

(Continued)

Perhaps there is a third position in relating, and sharing:

- ☐ strong ideas
- ☐ strong feelings
- ☐ decision-making
- ☐ assertiveness at all times, and aggression when appropriate
- ☐ an understanding of each other's 'no-go' areas
- ☐ tears and sadness
- ☐ anger
- ☐ other

We may not yet have incorporated the strength of a feeling heart into masculine judgement, but we always know that when these two attributes come together something wise and wonderful happens. A wise leader, judge or company head, for example, will be able both to relate in a heartfelt way and make hard decisions.

part three

getting off the symptom hook

naming the problems

Delusion is the mind's tendency to seek premature closure about something. It is the quality of mind that imposes a definition on things and then mistakes the definition for the actual experience.

Mark Epstein *Going to pieces without Falling Apart* (1998: 126)

In Part Three we begin the process of trying to name as accurately as possible the old patterns that lie behind our thinking, feeling and behaving, which lead to things going wrong. In CAT these patterns are known as learned 'procedures' because they occur in sequential ways in the form of traps, dilemmas, snags or unstable states of mind.

5

Traps

Certain kinds of thinking and acting result in a 'vicious circle' when, however hard we try, things seem to get worse instead of better. Traps are called traps exactly because they feel like behaviours we cannot escape from! In order to remove ourselves from a trap we need to revise what, in terms of our thinking, ideas or presumptions, keeps us there.

The 'doing what others want' trap

When we fear being judged harshly, or feel uncertain of ourselves and our self-worth, we tend not to express ourselves freely but move towards the ideas, beliefs or desires of other people. We do as others dictate. We may please people, doing what they want, thinking their ideas, even feeling their feelings. (One woman said to me once, 'I felt I ought to cry because everyone else was so upset, but I didn't feel anything.') The idea behind our way of proceeding is, 'If I do what they want things are bound to be OK. They will like me, want me, want to be with me.' What tends to happen over a period of time is that our eagerness to please is taken advantage of. Then we feel used and abused, angry, hurt and resentful that we should be treated in this way when we have tried so hard. I often hear people saying, 'I gave him everything he wanted, never argued, never disagreed ... I even changed my hair colour/way of dressing to be as he wanted,' or, 'I stopped seeing the friends he didn't like,' or, 'I gave up my car/hobby for her, and then she went and left me for someone else who doesn't listen to a word she says.' When what one really wants is affection, respect, care, love, it's bitterly disappointing to find it backfiring in this way.

What we need to challenge is the premise that we have to please others in order to be liked. The more we are taken for granted and abused for our attempts to please, the more our uncertainty about ourselves is confirmed. As long as our energy is taken up with pleasing others, moving into their worlds to try to make our own safe, we are not developing our real inner selves as we might; we develop only a coping, or survival self.

When we feel let down or ignored because we are in the 'trying to please' trap our own actual needs *are* being ignored, which makes us feel resentful and needy. Sometimes these needs burst out in a childlike way when we don't want them to. We feel out of control, and because the pressure to please others, and our natural internal fury at this restriction, causes such tension, we may find that we put things off, actually let people down. Or we may hide away, increasing people's anger and displeasure with us, and thus compounding our uncertainty about ourselves.

PAT recognised being caught in the 'doing what others want' trap. She could not bear to say 'no', or to feel she had let anyone down by being different in opinion, view, dress, attitude, ideas or action. To her, failure to comply meant hostility and rejection, which she could not endure. In her self-monitoring diary she wrote:

'Bought new dress. Didn't buy the one I wanted but the one the sales girl insisted looked the best. It was more expensive than I wanted and not the right colour, but somehow I couldn't refuse her. When I got home I just cried, I felt so upset and cross and helpless.'

Pat also wrote about incidents with her children when she had given in to them over bedtimes. She swung from shouting at them and feeling bad to giving in to them, and getting arguments as they tried for more. 'I was giving them what they wanted and they threw it all back in my face.' She recalled similar incidents with her husband and friends, and one friend in particular to whom she had acted as 'agony aunt'. Pat had wanted to confide in her about her own problems, but the friend had cut her off sharply. When Pat seemed tearful and hurt, the friend suggested impatiently they meet the following week. Pat duly turned up on time, but the friend arrived one hour late. Pat was boiling up inside with a rage she could not express and which only made her more fearful of losing her friend. She had convinced herself that it was her fault the friend was late, that she must have written down the wrong time, even though she knew this wasn't true. Pat couldn't speak because she was so upset, and the friend became cross and impatient again. As a result Pat felt guilty, alone and cross, but these feelings were hidden in her headache and sore feet.

When later we looked at the pattern of Pat's need to please and at what compelled her to keep doing this, she selected one of the images she'd written down during her monitoring and got into the feel of it. The trigger point for giving in to, and pleasing others seemed to be linked to a compelling and demanding look from others that hooked her in.

In staying with this she was reminded of two important images. One was related to her English teacher for whom she had written some good essays, and the teacher, who had been very nervous as it was her first job, looked to Pat when things got difficult in class. Pat became her anchor and help. The look said 'don't let me down'. Then Pat told me she'd realised that the look went further back, to her own mother, who had experienced similar feelings of insecurity, and had looked to Pat for help in making her life more comfortable. Pat's adaptation to having to do as others wanted began here. Her most basic

74

fear was that if she did not respond to the eye-call her mother would become cross, upset and withdrawn, and Pat's world would be in chaos. She dreaded her mother's disapproving cold silences, which made her feel isolated and abandoned, and which she interpreted as her own fault. It was precisely to cope with fear and pain that she developed the habit of pleasing. This had served her reasonably well during childhood and adolescence, because her mother responded and things were kept safe. But only on a superficial level, for underneath Pat wasn't developing her own voice or her own ways of being; she was bending and twisting to her mother's.

The habit of pleasing others went on into adult life and wasn't questioned until Pat came into therapy because of her depression. The depression was largely a result of living in the placation trap. She had married a man who benefited from her pleasing skills. He was resentful when she burst out angrily at the children, or when she tried work of her own that was different (she had recently given this up because she felt so guilty). Then everything was thrown into confusion by Pat's depression.

Pat chose to risk getting herself out of the trap. She risked saying no, doing something different from others, risking being disliked. She faced her worst fear. She saw that it was rooted in the world of her childhood and carried with it the force and pain of the child's fear. She recognised that if she wanted to grow and be free she had to take risks she couldn't have taken in childhood.

Although Pat's husband felt threatened at first by her change from placation to being more assertive, he came to recognise that his wife had many more 'real' qualities than he had seen before, and it was a relief when she was not so 'nice' all the time. She stopped being depressed. Pat had some surprises too: people she had previously feared would not like her actually took more notice, and the friend who had let her down said, 'It's good interacting with you now you're no longer a doormat!'

In my experience, people don't want doormats and placators, because they invite the 'bully' in us. To be 'too good' encourages others to behave badly – often in the hope of getting a real response. Also, if people are seen as 'too good', their underlying anger is more fearful because it is hidden.

Pleasing others is a useful and necessary skill in the making of relationships and in human interaction. But when our entire life is lived through it, it becomes a damaging and self-negating trap, perpetuating our worst fears.

Questionnaire: The 'doing what others want' trap

Do you act as if the following were true?

I fear not pleasing:

- ☐ those close to me
- ☐ people I work for
- ☐ anyone and everyone/men/women/authority figures

(Continued)

If I don't please them:

- ☐ they won't like/love me
- ☐ I'll never get anywhere in life
- ☐ I'll be rejected/passed over/ignored/abandoned/criticised/hated/abused

Pleasing people means:

- ☐ doing what they want regardless of how I feel
- ☐ getting to know all about them and what makes them tick so I can feel confident of producing things they would like
- ☐ never getting cross or upsetting anyone, whatever they have done to me
- ☐ squashing what I *really* feel in case it slips out and I am rejected or criticised
- ☐ feeling dependent upon the goodwill of others to feel all right inside

If the feeling you have to please sometimes makes you feel out of control and increases your uncertainty about what to do to ensure the goodwill of others, do you find yourself:

- ☐ putting things off because I'm unsure I've got it right and I can't bear to be wrong
- ☐ being unable to say 'no', and so ending up taking on too many tasks, agreeing to certain things that are inappropriate, and ultimately letting people down

If you find that you have answered 'yes' to more than one question in each section of the questionnaire then you are in the placation trap. You may find that the reciprocal roles are *conditional/disapproving* in relation to *anxious/striving*. Stay with what you have marked and concentrate on the feelings you have identified. See if you can locate any images or memories that help you understand the origin of these feelings. Make a note of them in your notebook and we will return to them more fully in Chapter 10, 'Writing our life story'.

The 'depressed thinking' trap

We may expect that we will do things badly or fail in some way because we feel we have done so in the past. One or two disappointments may make us lose confidence, and this can grow until we believe that we are a failure. Thinking about oneself in a depressed way perpetuates the trap of feeling depressed. Although depression can be complex and have an actual physical basis that needs medication, research has shown that recognising and challenging depressed thinking alters depressed mood.

	Mon	Tues	Wed	Thur	Fri	Sat	Sun
7 a.m.	10						
8 a.m.	10						
9 a.m.	9						
10 a.m.	9						
11 a.m.	9						
12 noon	7						
1 p.m.	7						
2 p.m.	6						
3 p.m.							
4 p.m.	7						
5 p.m.							
6 p.m.	7						
7 p.m.	4						
8 p.m.	5						
9 p.m.							
10 p.m.	5						

10 = very depressed, down, sad, not coping
7 = depressed but coping
5 = mildly depressed
3 = low, but able to take in other things and look around
1 = not depressed but enjoying the moment

Figure 5.1   Chart for self-monitoring depressed mood

Using self-monitoring, over the next week write down how many times you find yourself thinking: 'Oh no, not another day,' or 'I'm not going to be able to do that.' 'I look awful so I won't go out today.' 'I'm too tearful to do anything.' 'Last time I went near that place I couldn't bear it.' Any time, in fact, that you feel 'I'm bound to do this badly.'

To self-monitor depressed mood, make a chart like the one shown in Figure 5.1. Rate each hour, from 1 to 10, to indicate the level of your depressed mood. Low scores start at 1 and 10 would signify a highly depressed state. Mark the chart for each hour for one week and see where your lowest and highest points come. (You might like to use certain colours instead of numbers.) This process asks us to be aware of our mood and what we are feeling; it also gives some loose structure to the shape of our day. So often when people feel depressed they curl up in a ball and do nothing, presuming that whatever they do will not work. These two simple exercises will help you. First, it will show you what times you feel most depressed (often in the mornings), and secondly, that you may not be at number 10 all the time. If you find that you are, then perhaps some professional help should be sought, unless – and this requires honesty and self-observation – it may be that you are angry underneath your depression and don't want this to be relieved until you have been allowed to be angry. We will come back to this in Chapter 7. By monitoring what it is you are thinking about at the times when you feel most low, you will get an indication of where your fears about yourself lie.

There are several ways in which this trap operates, and for everyone who recognises it, it will have different origins.

MALCOLM had become very stuck in the 'depressed thinking' trap. He had got into an increasingly depressed way of looking at himself and life because of his disappointment with other people's failure to recognise the value of his work. On retirement he had hoped for greater acclaim and feared that he would be forgotten. Although on a deeper level his problems were largely to do with an early dilemma of 'having to be special or feeling empty and insignificant', which we will look at in Chapter 6, he was also caught in this particular trap. Every day he contributed to his depressed mood by thoughts such as, 'No one wants me any more.' 'There's no point writing to X because they probably won't reply.'

Malcolm began to see that he was approaching each day with the following attitude: 'I feel doomed before I start, so I jeopardise my own life by not valuing what I do, say or aim for.' One of the ways he got out of this trap was to work at valuing what he had done and did do with his life. As an English teacher, he had many extremely grateful students and many fine examples of his work, which he dismissed. His criterion for acceptance and value was a fixed external idea of fame and public recognition. He could not see how much he was already valued without this. Malcolm's depressed thinking about himself was accompanied by feelings of hopelessness and pointlessness, and by thoughts of death. Fortunately he was angry enough about this feeling of 'stuckness' to use his anger to get out of it and to re-evaluate his approach.

We may also be trapped by our negative and depressed thinking in a passive way, which makes us feel victimised.

CLARE felt very weak after a period in hospital for a knee operation. She had been feeling depressed before this because she was unable to carry on with her work at home or at the consultant engineering company where she'd been a valued member of staff for five years. She was depressed when she was 'out of role', when the ordered world she knew was removed during her hospitalisation, and afterwards when she felt she couldn't cope very well with everyday chores. She became more and more depressed, because she told herself, 'I'm useless,' 'I can't do anything,' 'No one will want to see me like this.' She feared that her husband would not understand her and that she would not be able to make him understand. Eventually, she got to the point where she was almost permanently in tears because of this trap.

She and her husband both attended a therapy session, where we drew up a self-monitoring chart to record her depressed mood (Figure 5.1). When she realised that she was not depressed all round the clock, but that there were some grey areas, she rallied enough to use the better hours to draw or paint what she was feeling and write down what she wanted to say. At first she dismissed all of what she wanted to say as: 'It's silly, he'll never listen to this ... ', but with the help of her husband she was able to make use of the less black periods and free herself from the more depressed times.

When you have monitored your own negative thoughts for a week (the 'I'll only do things badly' ideas), spend some time with your findings and try to see if you can identify where these thoughts and ideas stem from, and how much they are in fact self-perpetuating.

Questionnaire: The 'I'll only do things badly' trap

How much do you exaggerate your fear of doing things badly? Use self-monitoring methods to get a really accurate picture together. Use the chart in Figure 5.1 or monitor the time and place when you expect a negative outcome to:

(a) a thought/idea
(b) what you say
(c) what you do

If you feel you have done something badly, what were the ingredients of your involvement in that work? Were you:

☐ doing something you liked?
☐ doing something you wanted to do?
☐ doing something new?
☐ doing something you had admired others doing and presumed you would be unable to do yourself?

How much understanding did you have about what it entailed?

If you find that indeed your depression is made worse by constant depressed thinking that needs to be challenged and consciously adjusted, it will help to read on and perhaps find some clue to the source of your depressed feelings about yourself in further chapters.

The 'I'm better off on my own' trap

Sometimes we take the view that the trauma resulting from contact with other people just isn't worth it. We feel so anxious that people will find us boring and stupid and we get so hot and bothered when we have to talk to someone that we decide to avoid contact. It isn't that we would rather be on our own; it's that we believe that because things don't go well for us socially we have no choice. When we are forced to make contact with others, and because of our internal beliefs about our abilities, we don't look at others properly, we find it difficult to know what to say and we appear actually unfriendly and standoffish. For these reasons people tend to leave us alone. This is the very opposite to what we really want, and, rather as with the pleasing trap, we are not developing the skills for meeting and talking to people that we need to gain confidence and break the negative cycle of the trap. The other aspect that tends to increase is the fantasy level of our ideas about our own incompetence. We can become phobic about it, building it up to dramatic proportions. Our sensitivity to other people's reactions to us can also be heightened, as we imagine rejections and criticisms in an exaggerated form. Jeff recalled his own experience of this: 'When I began to speak to a group of people at the party, I felt as if my whole being was lit up in stage lights and everyone was watching my performance.'

PAUL decided very early on that being involved with people wasn't worth it. In his early life he had been in hospital for eighteen months. He had no conscious memory of that time, but it is not hard to imagine the powerful effect such a long separation would have on a small infant. As we saw in Part Two, in early life we cut off from feelings when they are unmanageable in order to survive. When Paul was six his mother became ill and died the following year. The rest of his childhood was particularly isolated: his father worked very hard and was absent for much of the time, leaving Paul with a grandmother whom he did not like. Paul withdrew into the world of study and encyclopaedias.

When we met, Paul had a successful career as a scientist, but tended to be very split inside himself. He felt he was either the powerful scientist at his word processor or the very lonely boy. One way in which he had ensured that this split would perpetuate itself was by falling into the 'I'm better off on my own' trap. Then he fell deeply in love and all his deeper feelings of longing, excitement, togetherness, came to the surface. At first things were wonderful, but when the initial wonder and magic was at all threatened he once again became the six-year-old boy who feared abandonment by the woman he loved (originally his mother). We will return to Paul's story in Chapter 6, but having identified the way in which he kept his split going by his isolation he was prepared to look more at his internal world, instead of the external, carefully controlled world of the scientist. He took risks in order deliberately not to isolate himself in situations at home, by going with the pain of his feelings and trying to find ways of expressing them.

In another case, Mary saw her problem in this way too. The chart shown in Figure 5.2 helped her to see how she was trapped into being 'better off on her own' as a way of coping

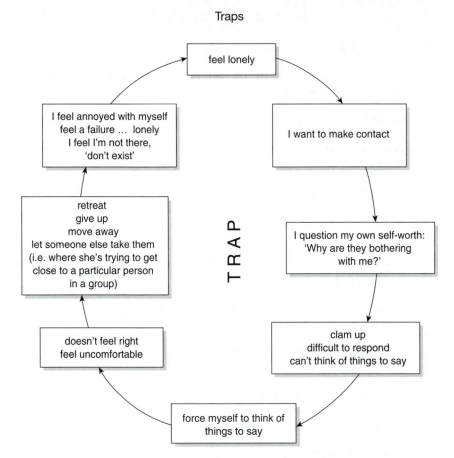

Figure 5.2 Mary saw her problem in this way. The chart helped her to see how she was trapped into being 'better off on her own' as a way of coping

Questionnaire: The 'I'm better off on my own' trap

Make a list of all the things you do on your own. Include activities like making breakfast, going to work, walking, shopping, holidays.

Make a chart showing the number of hours you are alone each day, for a week.

If you do work within an organisation where there might be opportunities to talk to others and form friendships, how often do you avoid contact?

Do you join clubs or associations, go to eat with others, stay on after work?

Do you seek the company of others at weekends or do you feel 'People have got to come to me', or 'It's not worth making an effort as others never appreciate it'?

(Continued)

Do any of the following ring true:

☐ I'm not used to being with people and don't know what to say to them when they start talking to me.

I'm not used to being with people because:

☐ I don't have enough practice
☐ I don't meet people
☐ I don't join in at work
☐ I don't join outings
☐ I don't make sure that I set up meetings where I can practise being with people

I expect people to talk to me because:

☐ I don't feel I'm an outgoing person. (Where does this come from? Who said this? Is it really true? Check it out by asking someone)
☐ if people don't come to me then it's not worth it
☐ I don't feel I should have to make an effort. Nice things should just happen

I lack confidence with others. I presume I will be:

☐ rejected, that people won't like me
☐ criticised because I am not like others
☐ ignored – people will find me boring and stupid because I believe I'm not clever/attractive/rich/don't speak with the right accent

When I do meet people:

☐ I can't look at them, my hands sweat or I can't get my breath
☐ I feel as if my whole body is lit up and that everyone is looking at me waiting for me to make a mistake

I fear if I open my mouth I will:

☐ say the wrong thing, and people will laugh at me
☐ get in a muddle, panic, perhaps become cross or start swearing, that I will say something awful

What is your image of how you would like to be with others? Describe the qualities you would like to have.

Mark down in your notebook which statements in the questionnaire apply to you. Again, we are gathering important information, which we will use when we reconstruct our life story and make our plan for change.

The 'avoidance' trap

If we avoid things we find difficult, we will discover in the long run that our avoidance only increases our difficulties and our sense of ineffectiveness and lack of control in life. Perhaps the most powerful example of this is people who suffer from agoraphobia.

Every agoraphobic will have experienced something frightening outside, or when they were waiting in a bus queue or a shop, or just walking along a street. Sometimes it can happen in a cinema or other public place. Knees turn to jelly, the pulse increases and it feels as if the heart might jump right out of the body; breathing becomes difficult, there is a feeling of faintness or nausea, buildings and surrounding vistas may become distorted and the overwhelming terror can be momentarily incapacitating. People have said, 'I really thought I was going to die.'

The physical manifestations of anxiety have always startled people with their depth and insistency, and can often easily be confused with real organic illness. The symptoms are identical, but the cause is different. What tends to happen in these instances is that the person becomes frightened to go out again in case the same thing happens. The feelings are so fearful that we become involved in the fear of the fear itself and stay indoors, thus avoiding the situation of the fear. This may give temporary relief, although many sufferers from agoraphobia also feel very anxious about being alone inside a house and project their anxiety onto families or friends, so that they only feel safe when everyone is home safely tucked up in bed. Avoidance of anything fearful may relieve us from the anxiety, but it is at considerable cost to our freedom and may restrict our life severely. Many agoraphobic sufferers do not go out of their houses for years.

We may not feel that we go to the extreme lengths experienced in agoraphobia, but we may relate to all the feelings outlined in the next questionnaire in other situations in our lives. Some people avoid contact with others for fear of being rejected; others avoid making decisions in case they are the wrong ones; many people avoid telephoning in case they get a difficult response; others avoid their everyday tasks, leaving them for others to do or until they are forced to do them. All of which results in frustration and feeling bad – which can be worse than the fear the person is trying to avoid.

Most people get into the avoidance trap because they do not believe that they can cope with unforeseen or imagined circumstances. The sense of 'what if … ', followed by the dramatic scenario of rejection, anger, ridicule, or worse, can make us feel incapacitated, and so we avoid the situation.

TERRY lost both his parents before he was three and was brought up by his grandmother. She felt very protective towards him, and he was never encouraged to go out and experience the world for himself. During his early school life he was often absent due to long periods of hospitalisation to rectify a birth defect, and he missed out on a lot of schooling. When he was asked to give answers in class and found he couldn't reply, he felt embarrassed and 'stupid'. Later, when he wanted to ask a question about something he didn't understand, he avoided it lest he be called 'stupid' again.

Unused to having to deal with confrontation and nastiness, and with no preparation for an outside world that was so very different from life with his grandmother, Terry developed avoidance tactics to cope with potential stress, mistakenly believing that he couldn't handle whatever might be asked of him. The 'avoidance' trap meant that he didn't stay in any one job for long in case he was asked to take on more advanced things that he believed he wouldn't be able to handle. He had avoided making any commitment in terms of his work or future, and was plagued with the idea that he shouldn't have to ask but should just know.

When he was able to face his imagined fears he took the risk of not avoiding things, and experienced all the physical symptoms described previously in relation to agoraphobia. But he did overcome his fears and entered into a training programme for a proper professional career.

Questionnaire: The 'avoidance' trap

Do you avoid things because of false beliefs: 'I'm no good at that so I won't try'?

Examine why you may have written something off. When did this attitude start? How far back does it go?

Who told you were no good?

Have you been discouraged by not coming up to certain standards? Were they your own standards or those of others? (Important early figures: for example, father, mother, teacher.)

Has there been a period in your life when you felt left behind, when you didn't understand something and were unable to ask or get someone to go over it with you?

'Fear of failure means that I don't want to start anything.' Have you put off starting a course, applying for jobs, making contact with people you know can help you?

What does failure mean to you?

When did you first come across it?

What are the examples of failure from your own life, or the lives of your family and friends?

If you feel you have failed to live up to your own or others' expectations, do you feel it is what you attempted that hasn't worked out, or do you see it as a reflection of your lack of ability?

When you fail at something do you identify your whole self with this failure or do you recognise it is only one aspect of what you do? (What I try for is not what I am.)

Which of these things do you cope with by avoidance:

- ☐ writing to friends
- ☐ inviting someone round
- ☐ applying for promotion
- ☐ starting a new course
- ☐ getting angry with someone
- ☐ reading something different because we envy others' knowledge about it
- ☐ trying something new
- ☐ sorting out sex problems
- ☐ confronting my partner
- ☐ being angry with someone who has hurt me
- ☐ mending something that's broken
- ☐ tidying up
- ☐ planning things to do with my toddler/children

What are your fantasies about what will happen if you don't avoid things:

- ☐ become ill
- ☐ rejection
- ☐ confrontation with things I don't like about myself
- ☐ fear of getting it wrong, not knowing what to say, how to assert myself
- ☐ get angry
- ☐ make a mess
- ☐ be judged

Can you recognise the personal price you are paying by your avoidance?

You will perhaps have recognised some of your deeper fears from this questionnaire. Give yourself time to allow an acceptance of these fears, because we do not go to the trouble of adopting avoidance behaviour unless our fears are profound. Write about it in your notebook. Knowing and naming what you fear is the first step to overcoming it. Working with your fear will be central to the development of your target problems and aims in Chapter 11.

The low self-esteem trap

Many people suffer from low self-esteem. This means they place little value on themselves or their contribution to life. And in feeling such worthlessness, they become self-effacing, automatically presuming they have nothing to offer. This might manifest itself in an obvious form, such as speaking negatively about themselves, putting themselves down or leaving themselves till last. Or it may take a more subtle form and remain hidden under a brittle, successful exterior or beneath the mask of a 'salt of the earth' coper who always manages. This subtle sense of uselessness may be so well hidden that friends and neighbours are shocked when the person they saw as marvellous and competent takes an overdose, revealing perhaps for the first time just how bad and worthless they feel.

People with low self-esteem find it hard to ask for anything for themselves, because they have very little sense of 'self' and therefore do not know what they might ask for, or they fear that in asking they will be blamed or punished. Feeling worthless tends to derive from having been criticised or judged as bad or wanting at some point in our development. We are left feeling that what we express, indeed often who we actually are and what we want, is in some way wrong or not up to scratch. How often have you heard someone say, 'I feel wrong' or 'I feel bad'? And this can be said even by people who have accomplished much, or who are actually well loved. It's as if the self they wake up with in the mornings feels that it has no right to any self-expression or desire, or sometimes even to existence.

What is frequently most difficult about feeling worthless is that the standards we assume we 'should' be achieving are unclear; we are just sure that whatever we do it will never be good enough. Such a negative sense of self-worth means that we feel we cannot get what we want because (a) we don't know what we want, (b) we fear being punished for even mentioning it and (c) anything good we do receive is bound to be taken back or turn sour because, actually, we don't deserve it anyway.

This becomes a trap when we feel so hopeless that we give up trying to express ourselves, at the same time as punishing ourselves for being weak. Such a circular movement in our thinking merely serves to confirm our sense of worthlessness.

SUSAN came into therapy because she felt unable to make any decisions in her life. As she described it: 'I don't know who to please for the best.' When, after the birth of her second child, a doctor told her that she was suffering from postnatal depression, she thought to herself, 'What does he mean, this is just how I always feel.' She identified feeling worthless, and had often been depressed, sometimes suicidal, claiming the only thing that had stopped her walking out in front of a car was her guilt about how the driver would feel.

She had very few early memories but many images of suffering, and some of these came forward more poignantly after her own children were born. She described her mother as 'hard-faced' and had experienced her as critical, demanding and conditional. Her mother boasted that she had 'never had a dirty nappy' from Susan, but that right from infancy she had been in the habit of 'holding her over a newspaper'. Later on Susan was left out in her pram in all weathers, even snow. Susan learned to survive this early start by expecting nothing from anyone and by fitting in with what other people wanted. She was terrified of feeling cold or hungry, and always wore too much clothing and carried food in her bag.

After the birth of her younger sister, the family's 'golden girl', she became 'mother's little helper' and rather than going to college left school early to contribute to the family.

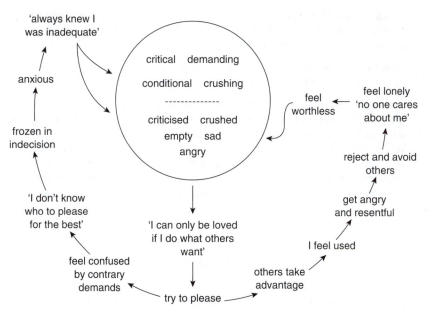

Figure 5.3   Susan's trap diagram showing her reciprocal roles maintained within the trap

Despite these beginnings, Susan had somehow held on to a belief that her life must have meaning. Towards this end she had joined several philosophical, political and religious societies, but still the feelings of worthlessness did not fade, as the groups could provide only outer rather than inner guides.

She expressed her understanding of her particular traps and dilemmas in the following way:

'Feeling unsure of my worth and afraid of rejection, I try to please others by doing what they want. This results either in my being taken for granted and abused, when I feel angry, guilty and start to avoid people, which leads to isolation and confirms my low self-esteem. Or in my feeling confused about whom to please, leading to being frozen in indecision which makes me feel stupid and worthless.'

Susan's dreams variously depicted her as a prisoner in a cage, a dead person underground who hears a voice bidding her to come out, and finally as someone who falls out of a tree but manages to somersault and land on her feet. As she worked with the dream themes and with the diagram of her trap (see Figure 5.3) she began to find a way out. She got in touch with her 'seed' self, and began to let this inform her of its value. This became a part of her which had its own sense of worth, meaning and direction, which was not dependent on the approval of others and which was able to make choices. She wrote:

'I realise now that "yes" to everything is wrong and "no" to everything is wrong, and leads to a difficult existence. What I must brave is the disapproval of some people. It's hard, but no harder than the life I lead now.'

Susan eventually decided to go to college to study for her O and A levels. About two years after her therapy she wrote the following:

'I am going to do things on my own. Not carry food in my bag and eat it on the bus. I'll wait and buy something in a café. I'll sit at a table on my own and not feel I'm doing something wrong because there isn't anyone with me. When I was young I had an imaginary friend who travelled on buses with me and slept with me at night, who went everywhere I went. Here I felt on my own and obvious, so I'll bring that back to myself. I'll feel I've got myself with me and rely on that, not on what someone on the outside has to say.'

exercise

Monitor for one week the occasions when you think in a 'I'm worthless' way, and make a note of them in your diary. Try to isolate a tone of voice, attitude or look that accompanies you at these times. See if you can give a shape or image to this internal judge. Does it remind you of anything from an earlier time in your life? If your internal judge is a parent, teacher, priest, nun, sibling, friend, write down all the things that person has said to you, and all the messages you have received. Read it out loud. Then ask yourself: 'Is this really true? Do I have to go on living my life according to this judgement, as if there were no court of appeal?'

Spend some time discussing these things with a friend you trust, and begin to value yourself in a new way, concentrating on what you find you do and feel, rather than on what you do not. Every one of us is worth something. We each deserve the chance to find something of our own truth, and it is this search which can help to both create and maintain our feelings of goodwill towards ourselves.

exercise: the 'low self-esteem' trap

How do you rate your own value? What words do you use to describe yourself?

If you are struggling in the worthless trap you probably have little sense of yourself at all and are afraid of thinking about yourself. Sometimes it helps to give yourself permission to take time, and as an experiment just to look at your face in the mirror. Notice what happens when you read this idea.

Notice how you think about it. Do you think, 'I'm awful', 'I'm ugly', 'I'm nothing', 'I'm bad', 'I'm useless', 'I'll never amount to anything'? Or, 'I'm not going to do any of this, it's useless'? Just notice how much this thinking affects your mood and your sense of yourself.

If you notice that you think in this way, what part of yourself are you referring to? Is it your body, or mind, or feelings? Or does the voice that says 'I'm bad' mean the whole of you? Go back to the mirror again, and be an observer to that face. If it were the face of a friend, you would probably be objective and find something positive to say about it. Try this approach now, still as an experiment. You might come up with nice eyes, hair or smile (try smiling into the mirror). Try this exercise each day for a few minutes and see what comes out of it.

Do you compare yourself with others? If so, which others? Think how you judge yourself. Is it by comparison with those you presume are superior or better? Are your comparisons fair? For example, Sibyl was always comparing herself with someone heroic she thought might represent the boy that would have made her parents happy and saved their marriage. It was a point she could never win, and her efforts merely reinforced the feelings she had about her own worthlessness. The question we must ask is how helpful is it to compare ourselves with what we were never intended to be? However you judge yourself, do you always find yourself wanting?

Do you presume that you and what you want are always 'wrong'? If so, try to isolate what this part of you wants to do or say, and let it have an airing. Then be your own judge as to whether it is 'wrong'.

Can you get help to express the bad feelings you have inside, and recognise where and when they originated? Can you see how much guilt you have assumed for not being what you thought others wanted, or guilt for some failure for which you could not possibly be responsible? Read Chapter 7, 'Snags and self-sabotage', and see if this might throw any light on your experience of the worthless trap.

Have you got so used to feeling worthless that it has become a habit? Sometimes people are afraid to get out of the worthless trap because they feel that more will be demanded of them if they try. I've heard people say, 'If I did it well, people would expect it all the time. This way at least I can just be unhappy.'

exercise

Are you in touch with what you do well? It might be something straightforward like keeping a nice home, being kind to others, writing letters. Make a list of what you feel you do well. If this feels too difficult, ask someone to help you with the list. When you have done something well, how did you respond to this inside yourself?

The 'fear of hurting others' trap

In this trap we believe that if we say what we think or feel, or just express ourselves to others, we will hurt them in some way. So we either avoid self-expression altogether, allowing others to ignore or abuse us, or we find our real feelings bursting out in a display of childish anger that surprises, even alarms, others, thus confirming our original feeling that what we think or express is harmful. And because we believe we will be hurtful, we avoid standing up for ourselves in case we are seen as aggressive.

So where does this idea that we might hurt others come from? Sometimes our early feedback emphasised that 'children should be seen and not heard'. Sometimes we have the impression that the way we express ourselves is just too demanding, and we get judged harshly, as if there were some better way to be. Anger is often a problematic emotion in families. It can be forbidden or punished, or evoke even more furious responses. We learn that to be angry is bad and dangerous, so we bottle it up fearing the 'devil' inside. Sometimes people have felt so oppressed in their early life, either by strict parenting or schooling, that they find it impossible to trust what they feel or need. It's as if their way of being has never been respected.

Sometimes we are frightened by the kind of thoughts and feelings we have inside. We fear that if we let these feelings out they will hurt others as we have been hurt. It's as if we have no way of judging the nature of our responses that we have bottled up. This sometimes applies to people who have been abused, either physically or sexually, early in life. They come to mistrust their own instincts and impulses, believing wrongly that it was something in them that made the bad things happen and that they, and what they feel inside, are not to be trusted.

The consequence of being bound in the 'fear of hurting others' trap is that we fail to assert ourselves with others or to stand up for our rights. We carry around a poor sense of what is reasonable, and are so afraid of expressing what we think that we do not develop our own ideas. Sometimes we feel stuck in a kind of childish sulk, weighed down by the unfairness of it all. We cope with this in a number of ways. We may turn what we believe to be our hurtful ways upon ourselves, inflicting harm by cutting or bruising, drinking or drug-taking. In so doing, we avoid contact or blot out the reality of what we feel, making ourselves so isolated that we become depressed and despairing.

exercise: the 'fear of hurting others' trap

Monitor for one week the number of times you are aware that you fear hurting others when you are with them. Notice the way in which you think about yourself, or anticipate hurting others, and the words or images you use.

When you find yourself alone in a sulk or feeling badly because this fear you have has forced you to withdraw, notice the feelings you have and their nature. Keep a diary of them.

How angry do you feel? What are your ways of coping with anger or expressing it? Have you buried old anger?

How long have you felt like this? Was there a time when you felt that you had hurt someone? Who was this person? What did you either do or say that you feel was harmful to them? How old were you then? What were you feeling at this time? See if you can put words to the feeling. Did you feel angry, shamed, upset, abandoned? What has happened to those feelings now?

Ponder on how you carry your own hurt. What is its nature? How do you express it?

Take a piece of paper and crayons or paints, and draw or paint what you fear coming out of you. Don't censor it as you do with people. Just let the images form. Share them with someone you trust if you can, and see what they might be telling you about the fear involved in hurt.

Aggression and assertion

Many of us are helped out of the 'fear of hurting others' trap by a reappraisal of aggression and assertion. We may have been taught that to speak our own mind or stand up for ourselves is aggressive, and are put down for appearing this way. But aggression is part of our survival and we need to acknowledge its force and power. We can then claim our right to a relationship with it, as well as the right to choose how to express it. Mindless aggression leads to violence and the loss of power that often triggers it. Natural aggression becomes *assertion* when we use it to name or speak out about something important to us, and to stand up for our rights. It becomes our way of 'singing on the boundary', as the birds do in claiming their territory.

6

Dilemmas

Part of adaptation to environment involves developing a 'persona' – the safe-enough mask we present to the world. Sometimes our choices about how to 'be' become polarised. Our ways of being and thinking are reduced to 'either/or' or 'if ... then'. When we become lopsided and live at one end of the pole of the dilemma, it is usually because what we see as the alternative is much worse. If we have recognised being in the 'doing as others want' trap, we might also recognise the dilemma about feelings – either I keep them bottled up, or I risk making a mess. In dilemmas there is no middle way, no grown-up greys!

We choose the pole of the dilemma which is most comfortable for our 'survival' self, thus creating part of our persona, or 'mask'.

The following are widely held dilemmas in being. Read through and see if any of these apply to you.

The 'perfect or guilty' dilemma

This dilemma is dominated by the need for perfection. In striving to be perfect we are trying to live up to an image of what we feel is expected of us, originating in our early environment. Being perfect might mean getting everything right all the time and each one of us will have a different model of what is 'perfect' for us. It might involve standards of excellence in work, behaviour, morals, lifestyle, accomplishments. Perfection might mean having to climb one mountain after another; it can mean trying never to have a cross thought about anyone.

In this dilemma, if we are not striving to follow the learned pattern of perfection we feel guilty, and the gap left by not striving makes us angry and dissatisfied. Because the dilemma is based on a false choice about how to be, it carries with it the weight of feeling we have to be a slave to a system that is not fully our own, and we become angry at the imposed restriction. Even the external 'success' that our perfect standards bring about does not relieve us.

Many people live with this dilemma for years, striving for often impossible standards and unaware that this is based on a false presumption. However high the external achievement, it brings neither joy nor satisfaction; in fact there is often a sense of irritation and feeling trapped, and a nagging sense of meaninglessness, and something missing. When you are caught up in this dilemma you have to go right on trying to be perfect, regardless of any success, until the dilemma is revised.

Perfectionists caught up in this dilemma tend to live on their nerves. If they try to be perfect they feel depressed and angry; if they don't try to be perfect they feel guilty, depressed and angry. Sometimes it is an admired and strict authoritarian role model in early life that stimulates the creation of this dilemma. The old saying: 'If a job's worth doing, it's worth doing properly' can be useful, but if it becomes too rigid and carries an unconscious message, 'You're nothing if you're not trying to be perfect', then we can become lop-sided. (See Part Five, 'Making the Change'.)

Another way in which this dilemma can develop is in an environment where the person only feels safe if self-enforced models of perfection are brought about.

MARY was the youngest daughter of a factory worker. She was beaten and abused by her brother (eight years older) and teased at school for being clever and different. There were no books in her house, but she craved the life she escaped to in the safety of their pages. So she allowed her brother, who found ways to get books, to barter with her for them. She survived this deprived background by holding her feelings inside and never showing them or asking for anything, and by learning to despise the environment which she called 'in the grime'. Her way out of the grime was to work obsessively hard in order to get above those who persecuted her.

Her coping mechanism worked and she is now a successful doctor, but for years she has had to struggle with the depression caused by this dilemma. Her fear was that if she did not try to be perfect she would slide back into the grime, and she had been unable to develop a place that did not involve this slavery to perfection. Slowly she is separating herself from the rigidity of this dilemma – which also cuts her off from other people – and is starting to express not only what she really feels but also how to be content with 'good enough'. She has surprised herself with how philosophical she can be.

Questionnaire: The 'perfect or guilty' dilemma

In which of the following ways do you try to be perfect:

In my home:

☐   I have to be always cleaning and decorating
☐   everything has to be in its place

(Continued)

With other people I have to be:

- ☐ kind
- ☐ polite
- ☐ interesting
- ☐ helpful
- ☐ clever
- ☐ unselfish

In the way I dress I have to be:

- ☐ colour co-ordinated
- ☐ very neat
- ☐ fashionable
- ☐ young-looking
- ☐ smart

I must get everything right by:

- ☐ knowing what to do in all situations
- ☐ aiming for the best
- ☐ striving for the highest goal possible
- ☐ being always in control

If you don't try to be perfect, how do you feel:

- ☐ depressed and empty
- ☐ in terror of being criticised
- ☐ vulnerable to being called names like 'lazy', 'sloppy', 'has-been', 'no good'
- ☐ envious of others who I perceive as getting it right
- ☐ frightened of being left behind
- ☐ angry that I should be caught up in this need: who's it for anyway?
- ☐ lonely and lost without a goal
- ☐ frightened of chaos
- ☐ dissatisfied with myself, with life

List in your notebook the number of times you recognise this dilemma. Record your frustration, depression, anger, petulance, or other difficult and unwanted feelings which may result from you or others failing to meet 'perfect' standards. Note any anxiety, guilt, fear or sadness which may be connected to your feeling prevented from reaching the state of perfection you seek. The search itself can become like a drug-induced 'fix', which, when withheld, causes withdrawal symptoms.

Experiment with allowing yourself to be in a less than perfect place from time to time. Allow the anxious or guilty feelings. Begin to accept and care for them. In Part Four, 'Gathering Information' you will be able to look at the source of this dilemma for you, and what fears or judgements you have learned to internalise which keep this dilemma going.

The 'perfect control or perfect mess' dilemma

This dilemma is dominated by the need for control of anything seen as 'messy'. This may be to do with the way we express ourselves at work, at home, or in our dress. It may extend to our speech and thoughts and may be severe enough to involve all kinds of rituals of checking, touching, repetition of words or thoughts, or placing things and ourselves in certain positions at particular times. The need for perfection is linked to our need for control of, and freedom from, feeling guilty or messy. We may not be specifically aware of our fear of mess and its consequences, only dominated by the need to control it in particular ways. We may need to exert this control inwardly or outwardly, organising things in such a way to make sure we keep safe and in order.

What may have begun as a ritual of protection in early years grows into something more rigid and detached from what it was originally meant to protect. We know from the work of Dr Donald Winnicott (1979) that children grow attached to objects early on – teddy bears, blankets, thumbs, fluff, cotton – and that these objects are important talismen for the dangerous threshold of separation. They represent the safety of the mother, or whoever is the main carer, when that person isn't there. These objects help reduce separation anxiety, until healthy separation has been achieved. When psychological separation from early carers is never truly achieved it's as if crossing into adulthood or the newness of the outside world is still full of early fears, however grown up we may appear to be on the outside.

When as a child we are confronted by difficult feelings we use objects around us to try to help us: teddy is poorly today; the witch in the story is very, very wicked; the dragon in the dream breathes fire and is very cross. The reciprocal role of *distancing/controlling* to *fearful/overwhelming* helps to mediate the *controlling/judging* in relation to *controlled/fearful* reciprocal role from overzealous parenting where anything messy has to be quickly rushed away.

If we learn that 'mess' is bad and in making this mess our security is threatened, the fear of mess may extend to our natural excretory functions over which we do not have control at first, or to our sexual feelings. In order to keep feelings of rejection and abandonment away, we may develop rituals of control, initially with toys or champions in stories. If the fear of mess remains, the rituals may extend in later life to objects such as floors, surfaces or door handles, as if they carried our dirt or mess and have to be repetitively controlled and cleaned. What we are struggling to make safe are primitive instinctual feelings and also our fear of unmanageable separation from what has been held as 'safe'. When we can actively engage in doing something about our fears such as counting, checking, wiping or cleaning, we have our fear under control. And often, the rest of our life feels hostage to our rituals.

Our need for control may also involve limiting ourselves to certain experiences, and insisting on organisation and order. We may seek to control our anxiety by limiting our lives only to 'comfort zones'. We might manage our anxiety about being attacked or invaded by arming ourselves with weapons, locks and alarms. Today this is becoming epidemic in our world. Whilst it may be an appropriate response to urban and rural violence, the reciprocal role is *persecuting control* in relation to *persecuted/terror* dominated by the terrorist in both political and street life.

The outward expression of control may also tell us something about the nature of our struggle with internal invasions of feared violence. Any early influence which restricted our natural growth, which was against us rather than for us, will be internalised and as such will carry on restricting us from inside in later life. We will continue to believe there is something frightening that must be controlled at all costs. We may have experienced these restrictions as frightening episodes of anger or temper, as an overemphatic concentration upon morals, or in the dogmatic insistence on 'right' and 'wrong' behaviour that is characteristic of religious fervour. We may also experience it via the obsessional or repetitive behaviour of those around us.

THEA was adopted by a couple who had already adopted a boy two years older. She spent her first few months with her biological mother, then time with her adoptive parents, and then her first Christmas with her biological mother. She was officially adopted when she was nearly two. Her adoptive family emphasised being in control, especially of anger and 'tantrums'. When she was three she remembers her grandmother saying, 'Put your anger in the wardrobe'. Her life was very contained, both by her tight family unit and by a strict school where little self-expression was encouraged and any kind of risk-taking severely restricted. At sixteen, on moving to a different school, Thea discovered an aspect of the world that felt 'wicked, naughty, dirty, sexy and very out of control' and which she was ill-equipped to handle.

Since this time, when she broke down under the strain, she has been bravely learning to cope with this different and difficult aspect of outside life triggering inside feelings, which threatens her safety. One of the ways she copes with strong feelings, especially negative feelings, and with her fear of sex and physical closeness, is to make sure that everything in her house is kept very clean. She may wipe over her doorknobs three or four times when she comes in from work, even though she knows that no one has been there during her absence. She explains:

'If everything is in its place and tidy then I feel I can let myself off the hook and relinquish my obligations. I get cross if people mess up my order. If my bag isn't tidy and I haven't tidied up before I leave the house, then I'm all at sea and things will go wrong.'

Thea sees her 'perfect control or perfect mess' dilemma as rooted in her early life's anxieties about being sent away or orphaned if she were not very good, which meant in her family being neat and controlled, especially with her feelings. This also kept her in a dependent position: 'If people feel I need them they'll stay around more than if they had a free choice.' She feels that if she gave up being dependent people might make decisions over which she would have no control.

Thea is an attractive, very intelligent woman who has done a great deal to separate herself from the early survival modes that helped her get through very difficult beginnings then, but which can sometimes get in the way of her current relationships now. She bravely monitors how she feels when the need to clean is at its most pressing, and these occasions are usually connected with a time of transition or change which threatens her security. She has recently taken the huge step of committing herself to a relationship, where her fears of closeness, of sex and of being out of control of what she most needs are challenged, and she is managing well. She has been able to express many of her hidden feelings about being adopted, and her sense that 'anyone could have picked me up', and the helplessness this puts her in touch with. She is working towards the possibility of freeing herself from the tyranny of 'perfect control' in the future by feeling more loved and 'allowed' as a person.

If you recognise yourself in this dilemma, make a list of all the ways in which you keep in 'perfect control'. You may not be aware of some of the ways immediately, but let your awareness of this problem stay with you and inform you as you go about your everyday activities.

Two of the most frequent ways of keeping in perfect control involve continuous cleaning and checking external situations. A young man came to see me because he had to get up three or four times in the night in order to re-clean his bathroom. When I asked him to describe exactly how he did the cleaning, he began to recite his ritual in great detail. Suddenly, as he was describing how he pulled on 'his pink rubber gloves', he exclaimed, 'I know ... it's all the dirt inside myself I want to clean out, isn't it?' This sudden piece of insight allowed him to work back to the core issue of what he considered the 'dirt inside himself' to be. In unravelling how this idea had originated, he was able to release himself from the powerful internal terror of dirt which was manifest by his external, ritualistic cleanings, and which was threatening his everyday life and work.

Use the questionnaire to identify any issues that apply to you in any way. Write them down in your notebook.

Questionnaire: The 'perfect control' or 'perfect mess' dilemma

Cleaning obsessively (more than is appropriate):

☐ going over the same area more than twice after it is already clean
☐ cleaning something before you sit down, eat, go to bed or relax in any way
☐ cleaning at inappropriate times

Checking obsessively (more than is appropriate):

☐ gas
☐ taps
☐ electricity

(Continued)

- ☐ windows
- ☐ valuables (jewellery, money, books, etc.)
- ☐ things needed for work outside the home or journeys
- ☐ children
- ☐ telephone

Record in your notebook how many times you have to check your 'perfect control' rituals. The next time you feel compelled to move into a 'perfect control' mode, spend a few moments allowing your feelings to surface. Do not worry how vague they may seem to be. Do this on as many occasions as you can. When you have a sense of the feelings underneath the 'perfect control' mode, feel into what it is you are trying to achieve through the method of control. Are you:

- ☐ keeping things safe (later on ask yourself, what things or feelings)?
- ☐ keeping something out?
- ☐ saving something?
- ☐ bestowing a blessing?
- ☐ other?

What do you most fear will happen if you do not check, clean or control in any other way?

- ☐ flooding
- ☐ invasion
- ☐ dirt
- ☐ contamination
- ☐ ruin
- ☐ disaster
- ☐ chaos
- ☐ annihilation
- ☐ death
- ☐ unbearable stress

What is it in you that tells you whether you would or wouldn't be able to cope, or eventually ask for help in some way, if any of the above were to happen?

exercise

Try to imagine how you would cope. What would you do? What could you do? Have you got an image of how others cope with such situations? If you have difficulty in imagining any coping strategies, it may be that it is difficult for you to imagine anything other than the 'distaste' itself. Is there a voice in you which tells you that you would be unable to cope? Or a voice which informs you that you would be helpless or unable to enlist help? One of the most useful positive thoughts to develop is the idea that, whatever happens, you will either find a way of coping, or you will ask for help. This is all you can expect to ask of yourself.

The 'greedy or self-punishing' dilemma

This dilemma is related to our basic needs and desires, which have, in some way, been thwarted from an early age. Left with a sense that we are not fully entitled to anything freely for ourselves, when we approach something we need or desire we inevitably feel as if we are being greedy. To cope with this we deny our needs because the pressure of the guilt about feeling greedy is unbearable, and we end up being miserable and punishing ourselves. This dilemma is very painful, and at its core lies our struggle to cope with early deprivation. Whichever end of the dilemma we inhabit, the experience is equally painful, and so often ritualistic to-ings and fro-ings from one end to the other seem a way to cope.

One of the most symbolic ways in which this dilemma finds expression is in people who have problems with eating, sex, gambling, spending money, or any other ritual attached to something important which symbolises having our needs met. The person suffering from bulimia, for example, will allow themselves a certain amount of food. If he or she goes beyond this limit, the solution is to vomit up the residue or take laxatives. Sometimes the self-imposed limit is very small, and the sufferer will feel in danger of becoming fat and being seen as out of control and greedy. Such is the terror that she or he enacts the self-punishing end of the dilemma by getting rid of the food. Equally, someone with a gambling compulsion will be able to have money for only a short time before he or she risks losing it. Some people will allow themselves to spend money on buying things, feel immediately greedy and have to store them away, never to be worn or used. Others may have decided that their needs are simply never going to be met, so they will deny all need or desire or pleasure and 'give themselves away' to anyone, being sexually profligate or exchanging body and sex for money and power.

Sometimes we may feel that the sense of deprivation inside is becoming unbearable and we desperately have to grab what we can in an attempt to fill the place that feels so empty and hurt. We may go on a binge of some sort – for example, eating or spending – or we may assume a compulsive pattern, grabbing at something or someone whom we hope will fill the emptiness. We may get into debt, try to resist paying for things. (When you feel deprived inside it's hard to give out without resenting it somewhere in your being. This frequently expresses itself unconsciously, perhaps as hoarding, appearing 'mean', or by attaching an exaggerated anticipation to what other people may or may not give, which always disappoints.) But being torn in this way makes us feel miserable, and the misery may be turned against oneself. When someone in the grip of anorexia nervosa feels longing and hunger of an emotional as well as a physical kind, they feel such terror that punishment through strenuous exercise, or starving for days, soon follows. Other people are compelled to harm themselves by cutting, stabbing or damaging their bodies in some way.

This dilemma carries with it both a social stigma and a religious one, and thus the internal dilemma becomes more absolute as it is judged harshly by the moral tone of society or the Church. Greed is seen as a sin that deserves punishment. Perfectionism and high achievement are admired and encouraged. It may be that the truer source of greed comes, in fact, from the compulsive perfectionist's desire for bigger and better without reflection on need or appropriateness, rather than from the obviously equally compulsive strivings of someone labelled greedy by the exposure of their needs inside. Once basic needs are met – by each of us recognising them for what they are, by having another recognise and name them, by a relationship with another, or by putting energy into something where our needs are satisfied and we are nourished – then the heat is taken out. Greed becomes recognised as need.

ROSE started to look at her life closely when she realised that her spending of money had got out of hand. She would see something very beautiful, usually an antique, and couldn't resist buying it. She was very afraid of her husband's anger when he found out, because he said things she didn't want to hear: about her being out of control, greedy, irresponsible, wanting things 'above her status and income'. She knew there was some truth in all of this, but she felt 'carried away by my tastes'.

Rose had been sexually abused, first by her father between the ages of ten and fifteen and then by her uncle from fifteen to eighteen, when she managed to get away to university. She came to see that, largely because of her secret and forbidden relationship with her father (which her mother refused to believe, and indeed made Rose feel dirty and guilty for revealing), she had linked all of her self-expression, her appetites and her desires and excitement, with guilt, shame and a sense that they were forbidden. She had married a man who helped her 'control' her appetites because he was 'strong, determined, disciplined' and very good at controlling money, which was his specialist field.

For a while she felt safe, that her appetites and tastes were under lock and key. But because she needed her instinctual nature and her appetites to allow her to express herself fully, they had to emerge somehow. (Seeds want to grow.) They tended to emerge guiltily, as in some of her compulsive eating bouts, and in her need to keep lovely 'delicacies' waiting in the fridge. And they started emerging through her compulsion to spend money on lovely things. The way in which her feelings and instincts surfaced frightened her, and at first served to refuel her old learned and mistaken belief that her appetites and tastes were dangerous and out of control and would lead to disaster.

Rose was a wise professional woman who soon talked things over with her husband, got her own separate bank account, and began working on how her life had been controlled by the 'greedy or self-punishing' dilemma. One of her problems listed on the chart we made was: 'Pleasure, excitement, appetite, forbidden'. The aim was 'To free myself from the effect of past abuses and their grip. To allow a fuller range of feeling.' In the letter she wrote at the end of her therapy she says: 'The short therapy has been a wonderful vehicle for my release, and it showed me some of the ways I can manage the chaos that results from that release.' In allowing herself to get in touch with her instinctual nature she was able to revalue her creative self, which had originally expressed itself through music until it had been put away, like all other instincts, when she became the scientific professional. She was also able to have a much fuller relationship with her husband, no longer assigning him the 'controller' role, and she has recently experienced the 'healing' joy of a second child.

Concentrate on the next questionnaire and become more aware of your needs during your daily experience. As we build a picture of what you would most like to change we will also be building a picture of what you most need and desire in your life – something you may not have thought about. As well as actively changing old attitudes that are now redundant, we are also rebuilding a sense of who we are and the ingredients of what our 'seed' self most needs for its growth and development.

Questionnaire: The 'greedy or self-punishing' dilemma

In what ways do you experience yourself as greedy:

☐   with food?
☐   with money?
☐   with possessions?
☐   with wanting more contact with others?
☐   with sex?
☐   do I take on more than I need or can finish?
☐   do I 'hoover up' experiences, books, others, time, events?

What kinds of feelings are behind your experience of greediness?

☐   hunger
☐   exasperation
☐   need
☐   desperation
☐   hope
☐   hate
☐   love
☐   longing
☐   waiting

(Continued)

☐   anticipation
☐   fretfulness
☐   shame
☐   anxiety
☐   emptiness

How do you cope with your experience of greed?

☐   Swinging from one end of the dilemma to the other?
☐   Living permanently at one end?

Have you ever talked about it to anyone?

What do you most hope will be resolved by this dilemma?

How much is your body involved in this dilemma?

What is your image of your body? Draw, look in the mirror, show a friend.

Get in touch with the body that contains these feelings, carrying them out for you in a literal way. (See Chapter 13, 'Techniques for working through the process of change'.)

Draw a picture of the hunger. What is it like, what does it need?

What do you consider are the basic needs of a human body?

Make a list of your basic needs as they come along. Include warmth, care, holding, rest, sleep, safety.

The 'busy carer or empty loner' dilemma

Most of us are familiar with the person who faithfully and selflessly devotes all of his or her life to others, either to a parent or family, or in serving a household or company way beyond the accepted call of duty. They may end up, either in retirement or after the death of the parent or relative they have devoted their lives to, feeling lonely, anxious, unsure what to do with the rest of their lives and fearful of feeling out of control. Many people do serve others and find deep fulfilment without being caught in this dilemma, but here we are looking at those who, unless they are involved in looking after others and keeping up with their expected role of carer and server, suffer anxiety. It's as if our identity is built upon the premise that we are lost without our job of serving the expectations of others.

This dilemma often originates from an early environment where we are encouraged to look after others, be involved in decisions of the adult world and receive a lot of self-worth and praise for doing so. Many people are relieved to find they fit in, and can play a role that is useful. And if there is uncertainty about going out into the world alone, making a career or leaving a comfortable job to do something more risky or courageous, they will be glad to settle for a role where they become indispensable and their worth is reflected in everyday terms.

Out of this comes the need to be needed. It is gratifying to be needed, especially if the need is something we can supply. In being needed we often don't have to attend to our own needs, which may feel terrifying. We may assume a 'holier than thou' pose, adopting a self-righteous and superior demeanour to save our inferior sense of self. If we are doing something worthwhile and selfless, many ways of life encourage this 'service not self' attitude. In communities where this is practised by everyone and there is more of a chance of everyone getting some of their needs met, this may work. But it is when our identities are caught up in believing we are nothing if not in the service of others that this dilemma becomes a tyranny.

When we are engaged in looking after another and their needs, and have devoted much of our energy to this (the person may not be ill or needy) we feel OK, and the reason for the dilemma is borne out. It is only when something happens (we are bereaved or told we are not needed any more), that we come face to face with our fears of coping with our *own* lives, and in particular with our own emotional and inner lives.

SALLY was the sort of person who could be guaranteed to look after everyone and their problems. She was a jolly, large, cheerful person, for whom nothing was ever too much trouble. She had four children, an unemployed husband, and worked as a nurse. In addition, she reported that she ran the Girl Guides and Sunday School, and took in animals and babies when people went away. She filled every moment of her life with other people's needs.

During her forties Sally began to get irritated with people, to snap at them and then feel remorseful and guilty. She began to get depressed, and put everything down to the 'change', until one Saturday, when her husband and all the children were away and she wandered around a shopping centre wondering what to do with herself.

'I sat down on one of the benches and looked at all the people milling around me. They all seemed to have somewhere to go, be doing something important. I saw my life as being one mad rush to get things done, and what for? I felt suddenly very frightened, horribly lonely, and I just started to cry, I couldn't stop'.

This crisis brought Sally into counselling, where she needed to address her dilemma, be able to express some of her needs and understand that her irritation and bursts of anger towards others was not a 'madness' but the result of denying her own individual life and reality for so long.

Many people live with this dilemma in their relationships. Many women, particularly, have learned to be the carer, the one who thinks all around another, anticipates, who knows what the other – husband, partner, family, group – needs and wants, and who knows how to provide it. Many such women receive an early training from their mothers in the role of serving and giving, and in how to respond to another's needs without ever thinking of their own. From this way of being we absorb a lot of good feeling and security, and find a useful place in the community. But if our responding to another's needs is not based on a solid sense of ourselves – who we are, what our needs are – our own desires will surface in some uncontrollable way, making us feel guilty and angry. In *Understanding Women*, Louise Eichenbaum and Susie Orbach (1985) write:

> A woman must learn to anticipate others' needs. Part of her social role as caregiver and nurturer of others involves putting her own needs second. Yet her needs do not remain merely secondary but often become hidden ... for if she herself does not have an emotional caregiver to turn to there is an imbalance in the giving. A woman then carries deep feelings of neediness.

Over the years I have met several men who became carers in a different way from their women counterparts. The men expressed their caring through being good providers and by making sure their partners never needed for anything materially. They tended to choose partners who they secretly viewed as 'weak' and in need of looking after. Although this initially had the benefit of caring for the man's lonely 'inner female' self through its projection onto the partner, ultimately these relationships would become very stuck. The female partner would become infantalised into being the weak needy one who couldn't grow; the men remained in their loneliness, no nearer to claiming their neglected, lonely female selves or child selves.

Many people who have been busy carers for a long time have admitted that secretly they hoped that if they gave out enough to others, those others would turn round and recognise their own needs and desires and return in full the affection, attention and caring they had received. Many busy carers are well defended. If giving out is based on a denial of need and the underlying message is 'I don't need anything', or, 'I don't matter', it is very hard to receive. Others are often rebuffed because carers cannot bear to think of themselves as having needs. It's hard to reach them, because they feel invaded and vulnerable if their own needs are discussed. Perhaps the ultimate fear for carers is that if they really show how they feel inside the outpouring would be unstoppable because the depth of feeling and need is so great.

Questionnaire: The 'busy carer or empty loner' dilemma

How much does the 'busy carer or empty loner' dilemma operate in your life?

How much of your daily energy is tied up with caring for others?
  100%, 75%, 50%, 25%, 10%?

How much of your caring for others is caught up in the 'having to please' trap?
  100%, 75%, 50%, 25%, 10%?

When people question your role as someone who gives out to others all the time, do you answer:

☐ 'I've no choice.'
☐ 'No one else would do it.'
☐ 'I can't let anyone down.'
☐ 'People need me. I can't help that.'
☐ 'I like to feel I'm doing something useful.'

How much of your living is postponed until tomorrow? Do you put off things by saying 'I'll do this when …'?

List any things that you really want to do but daren't while you are in the role of main carer?

How often do you feel you can call upon the help of others to share your burdens, or do you feel you have to do it all yourself all of the time?

How do you spend any time off? Doing things for others or doing something you really like?

How much can you recognise feeling anxious and lonely if people aren't expecting you to do things?

Do you feel guilty when you think about not being a busy carer?

Do you label wanting to do things for yourself as selfish? Do you want to be a selfless person?

What are your dreams of the kind of lifestyle you would like to have?

---

exercise

Feel into your loneliness or emptiness the next time you are about to fill it by caring for others. How does it feel? Can you paint or draw what you feel? Does it remind you of anything? How might you develop this image?

If you recognise that you are caught in this dilemma and fear feeling out of control if your life and identity are not shaped by caring for others, spend some time thinking about how it came about in your life. What is really at stake now in terms of claiming the right to your own life? You still have gifts for caring and giving. These will not go away. If you can develop a firmer sense of yourself, so that you can use your free time creatively, your skills at caring will be all the more nourished. You will be freer to give, and your giving will be enriched. You will not feel so out of control, but will have a greater sense of appropriate boundaries. Others will respect you more and demand less, because you are in firmer control of who you are and just how much you have to give out.

Many people realise that although they have given out all their lives they have actually received very little thanks or regard for it. This may cause bitterness and anger. Depression and a sense that it really wasn't worth it soon follow. Some people may feel their lives have been wasted when they look back on years spent in the service of others at the expense of their own development.

I do not encourage individual development at all costs, but I do discourage lopsidedness. People who are centred, comfortable with themselves, who know how to say 'no' without the accompanying guilt, and have a quiet sense of themselves, are free to give with a joy that is beyond price. If we tie ourselves to the dilemma that if we are not expected to do things for others then we become lonely, guilty and out of control, we are tying ourselves to a life of slavery. There will be a build up of underlying anger and resentment at the frittering away of our own precious life. Many murders are committed by wonderful carers who have suffered and been abused by their tyrannical charges, until the one time when they are pushed too far and boil over.

If as you are reading this you are getting in touch with your own anger, use it. Don't be afraid of it or consider it bad. Write down all the angry things you can think of; hit something (not someone), throw sticks, logs or cushions, go into a tunnel and scream. Get it out. Find out what your anger is like before it turns in on you and swamps you with depression and self-destruction. (See Chapter 13, 'Techniques for working through the process of change'.)

The 'bottled-up or burst-open' dilemma

This dilemma is related to how we cope with our feelings and emotions. We either keep our feelings bottled up inside, or fear hurting others and being rejected ourselves if we express what we feel. For us the world of feelings is dangerous and unknown, full of frightening unstable volcanoes about to erupt. For many people feelings carry a quality which they do not understand. Unlike the cool, clear rational world of thinking and reasoning, the world of feelings can resemble a raging fire, a stormy sea, a sweltering underground pool, a heavy earthen cave, damp and dark. Often we don't like this about ourselves and are afraid. We get used to bottling up feelings, because we don't know what else to do with them. It may be that feelings were not welcome currency early on in our lives and we were told to 'pull ourselves together' when we expressed something emotionally. We may have witnessed occasions where feelings got out of hand and the extremes of feeling were expressed, making us decide secretly never to get that way ourselves.

If we have known the extremes of the emotional and rational in our early lives we may feel we have to make a choice between them, and many of us choose the rational because it feels safer, calmer and logical. We live in a society where words are the main currency. As we saw in Part Two, feelings and emotions tend to come without words and are thus often misunderstood.

Sometimes we are humiliated for expressing our feelings; or laughed at, or made to feel weak, at the mercy of anyone with a command of words.

We usually bottle up our feelings because we don't know what to do with them, and because we have learned and still presume that if they are let out they will be the cause of misery, mess, hurt and rejection. Most of us are unaware that we do this because it's what we know. Again from Part Two, sometimes we presume we don't have feelings, but find ourselves weeping at something on the news or in a film, or find ourselves depressed and lonely for no 'good' reason. We may be aware of odd things happening in our bodies: feelings of apprehension or tension, constant stiff necks, backache, migraine headaches, skin trouble, pain in the chest, difficulty breathing. Although all these symptoms may well have other causes needing medical attention many people who bottle up their feelings do store them in their bodies. Bodies express themselves via symptoms. This may be the only clue we have to the fact that we bottle up feelings.

PAUL, who was referred to in the 'I'm better off on my own' trap (Part Three), would be overwhelmed by a surge of tears and sadness whenever he felt that someone was excluding him. He had a lump in his throat and wanted to cry. His frustration came out in anger against others for excluding him, which he was unable to express except by withdrawing into aloneness, and which others saw as a sulk. He experienced himself in a place where no one could reach him and all he had for comfort were the logic and facts of his encyclopaedias. He had learned no way to express his emotions, for in his early life there was no one to pick up the signals of what he was feeling or to interpret them. Thus, he had kept most of his feelings bottled up reasonably successfully for many years, through one marriage and its subsequent ending, and through the birth of his only child. It was when he really fell in love for the first time at forty that his bottled-up feelings welled up, which he found extremely difficult. His anxiety over making a 'mess' and suffering rejection of his new-found love overwhelmed him.

So most of us bottle-up feelings, because to express them is worse, and feelings become our 'no-go area', the area we are least familiar with and fear most. If you feel you recognise yourself in this dilemma, spend some time pondering over the next questionnaire.

Feelings that get bottled up or displaced tend to be behind many emotions. Understanding the world of feelings plays a very important part in our growth process. Beginning to unravel the different feelings that affect you at different times and finding ways of using your feeling life creatively will be tremendously helpful. As you read on you will see how others have made this journey, and in Chapter 12 there are ideas to help you to anchor what you are feeling and learn how to cope with the feelings of others.

Questionnaire: The 'bottled-up or burst-open' dilemma

In what ways are you aware that you bottle up your feelings?

- ☐ I keep everything inside me, no one ever sees what I truly feel.
- ☐ When something emotional is going on I feel:

  - ☐ tense
  - ☐ upset
  - ☐ afraid
  - ☐ apprehensive
  - ☐ lost
  - ☐ unsure
  - ☐ eager to leave
  - ☐ hopeless

- ☐ Most of the time I am unaware of what I feel.
- ☐ I presume I don't feel anything.
- ☐ I experience physical symptoms:

  - ☐ stomach cramps
  - ☐ tightness in the chest
  - ☐ difficulty with breathing
  - ☐ 'lump in the throat'
  - ☐ difficulty swallowing
  - ☐ neck aches and headaches
  - ☐ clenched jaw
  - ☐ grinding teeth
  - ☐ back pain
  - ☐ wobbly legs
  - ☐ racing heart
  - ☐ thumping heartbeats
  - ☐ dizzines
  - ☐ pins and needles in hands and feet
  - ☐ problems with eating, digestion, stomach

- ☐ I do express some feelings but not others. I find the following feelings very difficult:

  - ☐ anger
  - ☐ frustration
  - ☐ disappointment
  - ☐ sadness
  - ☐ happiness
  - ☐ success
  - ☐ winning
  - ☐ envy
  - ☐ when hurt by others
  - ☐ praise
  - ☐ when shown affection

- ☐ love
- ☐ admiration
- ☐ joy
- ☐ jealousy
- ☐ mistrust
- ☐ hate
- ☐ loathing
- ☐ disapproval
- ☐ embarrassment

☐ I think feelings are messy and you should never wash your dirty linen in public.

If you don't bottle up your feelings what do you think will happen?

- ☐ I will get hurt by others who will take advantage of my weakness.
- ☐ It will come out all wrong and I will be embarrassed and want to disappear into a hole.
- ☐ I will be rejected. No one really wants to know what I feel.
- ☐ Everyone will see what a mess I am inside.
- ☐ My whole world will be totally out of control.

☐ Someone would get hurt. What I feel inside is violent, furious, out of control, intense, huge. If I really let out what I feel the rage and tears would be unstoppable. I would be:

- ☐ like a little baby almost choking myself on my screams
- ☐ screaming into a void
- ☐ swamped
- ☐ drowned
- ☐ People would laugh at me and try to put me down. They would call me names: cissy, mother's boy, wet, wimp, softie, cry-baby.
- ☐ whatever I feel it always comes out as tears, and I can't stand it.
- ☐ whatever I feel it always comes out as anger, and people don't understand.

On what sort of occasions are you aware of your feelings most strongly?

- ☐ when alone
- ☐ when with others
- ☐ when with older people or those in authority
- ☐ after a row
- ☐ when watching a film or news item or reading a book
- ☐ days after something important has happened
- ☐ when others are expressing strong feelings

Think about how feelings were handled in your family early on. Go to Part Four ('Gathering Information') and consider the different kinds of feelings. Ponder on how they were or weren't expressed in your early life, and with whom each feeling was associated. How were feelings discussed, and if not experienced within the family, how were feelings discussed in association with others outside? What kind of family sayings or myths did you grow up with?

The 'if I must ... then I won't' dilemma

Initially, this dilemma appears quite difficult to understand, but take a moment to examine the number of times when you have felt totally overcome by instructions or orders or 'having to'. They may come from inside you or from other people. Sometimes we feel so restricted by these requests and demands that the only freedom is not to do them. The thought pattern is: 'I've got no option.' The feeling is one of tremendous restriction, which can be claustrophobic. The reaction then is to get out by not complying as if this is our only freedom. This can operate in quite subtle ways: we may receive a letter from somebody which we ought to answer but don't, perhaps there is a telephone call we need to make and we keep putting it off. A more extreme and damaging example might be that we fail to turn up for an important job interview.

The seeds of this dilemma go back to restrictive former years, in family or school, where rules, regulations and obligations felt binding. We can feel so rule-bound that there is no room for self-expression. Our only self-expression is in saying 'no'. A graphic illustration of this dilemma comes in the story of Oblomov, who lay in bed all the time because he couldn't bear any kind of obligations to get up and get dressed or go out. His dilemma consolidated itself to the point where he slowly dwindled away and died (a rather extreme form of this dilemma!).

Aspects of this dilemma operate in most of us because most of us have experienced restrictions of one kind or another during our early life. But when the dilemma is severe it affects everything we do, and we are keeping up our sense of control in life mainly by default. It's not what we do but what we don't do that gives us a sense of control or power. But in time this backfires. Our inability to get anything done means that we are never able to develop a decent sense of self-worth or skill.

In the 'avoidance trap' we looked at TERRY's story (Part Three) and how the restrictions placed upon him in early life led him to duck out of challenges to do with work. On a deeper level he experienced his early restrictions as coming from the demand of others that he be both grateful for being cared for by people who were not his parents, and for his (later) inheritance. Because he felt he owed it to his grandmother, and the family who later on adopted him, to 'be good' and do well, and because an overprotective environment meant that he hadn't developed the skills to deal with the challenges of outside life, he believed that the only way for him to cope was not to do anything at all. This was not a conscious decision, but an unconscious drive based upon the mistaken belief that his only option was to say 'no' to a demanding environment.

When Terry came into money at twenty-one, for which he was also unprepared, he took flight into heroin addiction. He could not cope with the demands the money made upon him, and he could not ask for help from those

110

whom he presumed he had to please and be grateful to. He did not believe he was entitled to his powerful and mixed feelings of grief over losing both of his parents, and he felt disloyal for talking about them.

Since this time, several years ago, he has been courageous and brave enough to get himself off heroin and to look at his life more fully. He has begun the painful process of grieving and mourning for his lost parents for the first time, and is releasing himself from his restrictions in thinking about his life and what he was entitled to. As he began to have more choices about how to respond, and as he allowed himself more freedom to take up choices about what to do, he has been able to release energy to put into tasks and training, has become professionally qualified and married. The energy that was tied up in the silent protest of 'if I must ... then I won't' has been well used.

If this dilemma is severely restricting your energy and your life, look carefully at where it originated and what your fears are about embracing something instigated by other people. If this dilemma is allowed to dominate it can take over and immobilise us, to the point illustrated by Terry's heroin addiction. If you find yourself saying 'I won't' when you feel obliged by someone or something, feel into what your own inner restrictions are. See how many ways you can find to respond to the perceived restrictions, other than saying 'no' or 'I won't'. You may find you need to be angry, to hit out, to be sad and grieve, to find a way of thinking about things that stimulate you and which you allow. You will need to go through the 'pain barrier' felt by restriction and to find yourself on the other side – your own freedom.

Questionnaire: The 'if I must ... then I won't' dilemma

How much does the 'if I must ... then I won't' dilemma operate in your life? I respond to an obligation with 'I won't':

- ☐ all of the time
- ☐ some of the time
- ☐ in certain situations:

    - ☐ at work, college, school
    - ☐ with friends
    - ☐ with family
    - ☐ in relationships with men/women
    - ☐ other

If I feel obliged, I feel:

- ☐ restricted
- ☐ caged
- ☐ controlled by others

(Continued)

This then makes me feel:

- ☐ furious
- ☐ frightened
- ☐ belittled
- ☐ threatened
- ☐ defiant

When I feel this way I want to:

- ☐ hit out
- ☐ run away
- ☐ curl up
- ☐ get the world to make me disappear

I see saying 'I will' as conforming to others' ways and ideas:

- ☐ all of the time
- ☐ most of the time
- ☐ in certain situations (name them)

Saying 'I won't' gives me freedom from restrictions imposed by others. I have put this to use by:

- ☐ creating my own life
- ☐ using my defiance to start something new

I am frustrated and feel I can only act 'against':

- ☐ I have been unable to create anything of my own
- ☐ I feel the restrictions I feared from others have now turned against myself

The 'if I must not ... then I will' dilemma

Take a moment to explore this dilemma, even if you don't relate to it immediately. Again, as in the 'if I must ... then I won't' dilemma, this dilemma is concerned with our response to pressures, whether they come from inside ourselves or are imposed by others, especially those in some form of authority. In this case, it's as if the only proof of our existence is our resistance. In our fight against, in our protest, we are struggling to be seen for our real selves. But all too often this dilemma results in harm to ourselves, and in punishment rather than acceptance. We begin to break rules – even our own rules begin to feel too restricting – and so our frustration and fury with life escalate. Sometimes our attitude becomes so entrenched that we feel we will lose face even more if we give in or change our pattern, so we carry on piling up negative responses to command, thus tempting fate.

Many of us will perhaps relate to this dilemma during adolescence, when we need to lock horns or try out our strength against those in authority. The 'cult' of protest is active, and usually appropriate, during this growing time. And many of us forge our sense of ourselves against such testing of authority, especially parents or leaders, for our views on religion, politics, social welfare, dress and addictive substances. We emerge stronger and wiser and go on to occupy those positions of authority we once had to kick against, developing rules or structures we once found so frustrating.

But this dilemma can become a way of life, piling up our anger and resentment without a space to breathe or take stock. If it becomes entrenched, it may move us into circles of friends whose lives, behaviour and choices are all limited by this dilemma, creating a much greater force of 'must not'. Then the life itself can become like a brick wall which feels impossible to break down. Until properly revised and refreshingly challenged, this dilemma only serves to block our path and prevent us from having a life.

Sometimes we learn to resist as our *only* way of survival in a restricting environment, where our resistance ensures our actual body and soul survival. We learn to become guerrilla fighters in our own families or environment, living on our nerves, hiding, being always on the attack against the enemy. And while all communities need this fighting *for* aspect, to challenge authority when it becomes limiting and oppressive, when we fight *against* simply because it has become a habit we court destruction rather than creation.

Many people do experience their lives as being oppressive in this way, as if they were the hunted minority. But if we persist with this behaviour after the war is over, we are not claiming our true freedom. The skills and determination we have learned during our resistance are actually needed much more for the creation of our own rules and standards, where we are forging a life for ourselves rather than having to defend against an imposed position.

Questionnaire: The 'if I must not ... then I will' dilemma

If you can see this dilemma operating in your life now, ask yourself:

In what areas of my life am I fighting the rule 'I must not ... '?

- ☐ at home
- ☐ at work, college, school
- ☐ in religious belief
- ☐ in my social life and sexual or moral conduct
- ☐ over money

Which rule exactly do you experience as 'I must not ...'. Spend time examining this. Write the rule down in your notebook. Try different responses to it in your imagination.

How many times in a week do you say 'I will' in response to another's 'You will not'. Note the time, place, feeling, people or aspects involved. See how these tie in with the first question.

How much of your life is taken up living in a 'must not' cult? List the areas (friends, interests etc.).

Does this serve your needs now?

Ask yourself what would happen if you examined your resistance more thoroughly? Try to communicate with your resistance now, and find out more about it. What are its qualities?

The 'satisfied, selfish and guilty or unsatisfied, angry and depressed' dilemma

This dilemma is to do with getting what we want. If we get what we want and therefore attain some measure of satisfaction, we find that it is inevitably accompanied by feelings of selfishness and guilt. We feel like a spoiled child. At the other extreme, if we don't get what we want, we feel angry and depressed. This dilemma is related to our ability to receive something and possess it freely. At some point we have decided unconsciously that we are not allowed to have what we want. We may even have been told, 'Don't think you can get what you want,' or, 'You can't always have your own way.' These kinds of statements, which are common currency during childhood and at school, can be interpreted internally as 'if we get what we want it's actually at some cost'. So, like a spoiled child we feel rather guilty, because we are not really entitled to it.

At the opposite pole, if we don't get what we want we feel angry and depressed and obviously deprived. This can lead to a kind of spoiling mechanism. Because we feel so guilty and childish when we get what we want, we actually don't allow ourselves anything – we don't even allow ourselves to receive things from other people. But at the same time, we feel permanently angry and depressed precisely *because* we are refusing to receive anything, either from ourselves or from others.

Sometimes it's as if we get permission to get what we want only through being impaired in some way. This might be through chronic illness – for example, migraine, stomach upset, back pain, colds and flu, or in minor repeated accidents where we need attention. This isn't to say that we make a conscious decision to become ill. It may be the only way we can receive something without feeling childish and guilty. But even when we have 'paid' the price, the dilemma dictates that deep down we feel we are not really allowed anything and guilt is just below the surface.

Questionnaire: The 'satisfied, selfish and guilty or unsatisfied, angry and depressed' dilemma

Do you feel that you get what you want?

- ☐ at home
- ☐ at work
- ☐ in relationships
- ☐ with children
- ☐ in sports
- ☐ sexually

If you feel you have never addressed this issue, take a few minutes to consider what you want in your life. Write it down, and then ponder on which areas in your life are satisfactory and which are not.

How do you know when you do get what you want? I feel:

- ☐ bad afterwards
- ☐ selfish
- ☐ guilty
- ☐ greedy
- ☐ too big
- ☐ secretive
- ☐ joyous
- ☐ triumphant
- ☐ satisfied and happy

If you get what you want, do you feel:

- ☐ I will have to pay something back
- ☐ life or someone will get even with me sooner or later

What myths, sayings or 'old wives' tales' about being satisfied and getting what you want can you remember from your early life?

Where do they come from? Whose voice do you hear when you remember them?

If you don't get what you want, perhaps because of any of the above injunctions against it, do you feel:

- ☐ angry
- ☐ sad
- ☐ depressed
- ☐ punished
- ☐ despised
- ☐ vindicated (i.e. the old messages that say 'you can't' are right)
- ☐ spiteful
- ☐ envious of others who seem to get what they want
- ☐ childish and want to cry
- ☐ murderous
- ☐ ill

Do you recognise a pattern of illness after disappointment? Look to see if any of the above feelings could be hidden within the illness.

Identify as clearly as you can the areas in which you believe you should deny yourself satisfaction. Notice the feelings you experience when you go along with something that you actually don't want, but have not yet developed a way of saying 'no' to. Note in your diary or notebook the times when this occurs and the feelings involved. Experiment with asking exactly for what you want in a direct, clear way and see what happens. When you have isolated the mistaken belief behind this dilemma, challenge it as best you can in your everyday approach to life.

7

Snags and self-sabotage

'Yes, but ...' and 'if only'

Snags seem to operate when part of us is saying 'I'd really like things to be better, but ...' Or when we say, 'Oh well, I could never have a life like that,' or gaze very enviously at others and say, 'It's all very well for them.' We may also start to reminisce, 'If only I'd been allowed to do, be, have ...' Part of us has the desire to lead a fuller life, to have better relationships, to feel freer about ourselves, be more successful, to be more imaginative, but it's as if we have been found guilty and sentenced to a life of snag.

Part of us is saying 'if only ...' while the other part of us counters with 'but I couldn't ...' or 'I'm not allowed' or 'something bad would happen if I were to be happy'. It's as if we carry an eternal rebuke for being alive and well, as if we were responsible for bad things that happened early in our childhood. This is called 'magical guilt', for it is guilt for something we wouldn't possibly have taken responsibility for or feel guilty about, hence the word 'magical'. The 'magical guilt' we carry may be for things that happened in the past. It becomes fixed as if 'true' and seamlessly woven into our everyday repertoire without our questioning it. The things for which we have taken on magical guilt may be external, such as having a handicapped sister, or a depressed mother to whom we may, or may not, be able to express our frustration or be cross with. If not able, we turn our more aggressive feelings into ourselves, as if it is we who are responsible for the difficult painful or lost lives of those in our early family.

As you read through this section, remember that I am sitting opposite you in the therapist chair as a third person in your inner exploration and dialogue. I am the mitigating 'judge' you didn't have when you were small, standing in for the new reciprocal role relationship you are trying to develop in yourself that does not blame or envy but understands the forces that formed you and forgives the past where it has become embedded.

Family myths

Sometimes this sense of 'yes, but' comes from powerful people in our early lives: 'She was always such a good child,' 'He was such a clever boy,' 'She was the one that kept the family together.' These can be very powerful myths and often prove difficult for us to challenge. We may be helpful and good and kind, but it may not be the sum total of who we are. We may also want to be fun, frivolous, exciting, naughty, cross and so on.

Another powerful injunction may come from the family myths themselves: 'People in our family never ... smoke cigarettes ... wear loud clothes ... shout a lot ... go into that kind of business ... marry outside their kind.' This means that hanging over us, imperceptibly (because we may not have realised it), is this idea that 'I'm not entitled to be anything other than what my family has made me'. Under this injunction we repress ways of expressing ourselves which don't fit in with what is expected. One woman said to me years ago that although she went through a very difficult patch in her marriage she never considered divorce, because no one in her family had ever been divorced. It was a completely alien concept.

Our attitude to work, friends, religion, health, ways of proceeding are governed by our early family and what the family accepts. Obviously all have an impact upon us. They may suit us well, but when we find that we are snagging ourselves as we've described above, we may need to look at our family's myths about us and what is 'expected'.

Families may also make judgements:

- people who think too much about themselves are self-indulgent
- people who don't have a proper religion and don't go to church don't have moral fibre
- our race never goes with white/black/oriental people
- don't let anyone see you when you're down, they'll only take advantage.

Start making a list of the myths in your own family, from the smaller concerns like dress and appearance to the more major questions of politics, religion and relationships.

It may also be that the snags in our life develop because important people close to us actually do not want us to change. This may not be obvious, but remain hidden within a relationship. Ask yourself if the 'yes, but' in your life is related to what you anticipate from others. Sometimes we think that if we were to improve ourselves, become more successful, happier or healthier the people around us might not know how to deal with it. They may oppose it, because they feel unable to cope with what our changing means to them.

An example of this might be when one person in a relationship begins to enjoy success, while the other – parent, husband or wife, for example – becomes ill or depressed. It's as if they can only thrive when the other person isn't feeling so good. Thus, we may have become unconsciously caught up in the life patterns of another. Our reciprocal roles may be *merging/special* in relation to *merged/safe*, and to separate them feels threatening and betraying. What maintains the relationship is interdependency, where one partner thrives because, and at the expense, of the other. It is as if there would not be enough 'wellness' or 'goodness' to go around for both people.

You may not be consciously aware of snags because they operate unconsciously. Having read this section and completed the questionnaire, allow the concept of being snagged to be part of your thoughts, so that if you are actually snagged you can become aware of it. Be aware of how often you think or say 'yes, but'.

Questionnaire: Snags

I recognise that I snag myself by saying 'Yes, but' or 'if only':

☐ every day
☐ in certain situations (name them)
☐ in certain relationships (name them)

I always feel that others are:

☐ luckier
☐ more successful
☐ happier
☐ more attractive
☐ better than I am

Name any past obstacles you feel have caused a snag and prevented you from being successful or happy:

☐ if it weren't for ... I would be ... now
☐ my parents never let me ...
☐ I never had the chance to ...
☐ if only I'd been allowed to ... I would be ... now
☐ other

Look at these snags honestly and ask yourself: have I contributed to making these events worse:

☐ by resentment, bitterness, anger, laziness?
☐ by using them as excuses for not taking up opportunities?
☐ by letting anger and resentment get in the way of trying for what I would really like?

How much do family myths about how to be and what is allowed live on and influence your choices, forming a snag? (For example: 'There's never been a divorce in our family'; 'We never wash our dirty linen in public' (i.e. talk about our feelings to others); 'No one from this family has ever gone on the stage.')

Do snags operate because you believe that if you make your own free choice of how to be, someone important to you won't like it, or an important family value will be challenged? (For example: 'If I am assertive my marriage won't survive'; 'If I leave the job I hate and train to be a teacher my wife won't cope'.)

Self-sabotage

Other evidence of a snag operating is when we seem to arrange to avoid pleasure or success. Or, if we are successful and happy, we have to pay, either by depression or illness or our ability to spoil things. When success is within our grasp, we find we are not able to claim it. We may have achieved high marks in an exam, we may have got that important interview, we may have lost the weight we wanted, but we don't allow ourselves to fully have it – we miss the appointment, we immediately put the weight back on, we mess up the next paper of the exam – thus actually wiping out the good.

'Magical guilt'

Magical guilt can have a very powerful underlying effect on our lives. As we saw earlier it arises because in our families we felt more privileged than one of our siblings, or even one of our parents. We might be cleverer than them, or healthier. Magical guilt can also occur when a member of the family is ill or depressed or if someone dies when we are young. We may feel that this has something to do with us and it's our fault.

This is not a conscious thought, but a powerful undermining and unconscious process that can catch us like the undertow in an apparently smooth river. We then develop the unconscious, mistaken belief that 'I am strong at the expense of my brother or sister or my aunt, my grandmother, my mother or my father's weakness. I am healthy at the expense of their illness. I am well and fit and happy at the expense of their bad feelings and depression. I am not entitled to my good fortune or my good luck. My talent is at the expense of their misery.' 'If I am successful something bad will happen.'

Because we want to be attached to those early figures who are important to us, it's actually very difficult to manage all this when we are young. We unconsciously take on the burden of guilt, and live feeling (magically) guilty for our successes or happiness. Our only way to cope is to deny ourselves in some way, to deprive ourselves of our success – we may reach the point of claiming a lovely friendship, a good career, or a marvellous travelling experience, and we suddenly spoil it at the last minute. We either miss the boat, or we get ill or depressed or we do something quite extraordinary which prevents us taking it up.

Envy

It's hard to acknowledge feelings of envy or that others may envy us. Envious attacks feel threatening and disorientating. But envy is a natural part of life and there is room for awareness of feelings of both healthy envy as well as malignant envy that wants to destroy.

A snag may operate in our consciousness because we've experienced envy from one of our siblings or a parent for our perceived good fortune, good looks, strength, sense of fun, freedom, abilities and skills. This may not be obvious and few of us are comfortable about actually acknowledging this. If you cast your mind back you may recall comments like 'I don't expect you to be able to do things like that', or 'A great girl like you! I would have thought you'd do a better job', or 'Trust you to do the most difficult thing there is', or 'I suppose with your skills you can have anything you want'. Such remarks are said in a slightly hurt, slightly belligerent way by people whose favours we want to keep. We then begin a process of learning to hide the skills and gifts we have, of jeopardising them rather than risking the wrath and envy of those people whose love we crave.

It can be quite upsetting when we eventually realise how much we are snagging ourselves in our lives and acting as if we aren't allowed to take up our gifts and skills. It can be quite painful to think that this comes from being actively envied in our early lives. We can only free ourselves from this pattern by making all the instances and all the realisations conscious, and seeing them clearly. We can then actually stop the pattern of self-negation and snagging.

Sometimes this is a hard task, because if we have taken on the idea that we were not entitled to what is in fact ours, it's quite difficult to start to claim to have something. When we do begin to claim our lives for ourselves we wake the previously unconscious fear we will be rejected or punished. We will **feel** the heaviness of guilt and the conviction that something really bad will happen. And some of those old voices that made us feel bad about our gifts will come back from the past: 'You're completely selfish', or 'You're a ruthless man', or 'No one wants somebody like that', or 'You give no time to other people' – all the kinds of accusations that originated from envy and jealousy that was not named.

Questionnaire: Self-sabotage

Make a list now of the times and ways in which you feel you sabotage yourself.

I fear the response of others if I:

- ☐ do well
- ☐ look good
- ☐ win anything

I fear most the response from ... (name the person or persons).

Because of my fear of others' envy through their (a) disapproval, (b) withdrawal, (c) sharp words, (d) criticism, (e) saying, 'It's all very well for you ...', I play down what I know and what I can do

- ☐ all the time
- ☐ in certain situations (name them).

I feel I'm not entitled to:

- ☐ success
- ☐ nice things

- ☐ happiness
- ☐ love
- ☐ freedom
- ☐ a good job

I feel that if I get things others will be worse off and suffer. Who will? Where does this feeling come from?

If something good happens for me I feel:

- ☐ it's just luck
- ☐ I don't deserve it
- ☐ it won't last
- ☐ I could never create it for myself
- ☐ I could never keep it going

Once the way you are snagging or sabotaging yourself is clearer to you, you can see how important it is to free yourself from these old patterns. They are magical injunctions: *It's not true* that we are responsible for the depressed, miserable, negative, unhappy lives of those who have gone before us; and *it's not true* that we don't care. *We can care and feel compassion and also live our own life!*

It is possible to claim one's gifts without feeling guilty for them. As we embark on this journey we can only become wiser, more fulfilled and more comfortable in what we are doing, and able to summon up the energy needed. We also become able to inhabit a space where we can look back on what's happened, and particularly on how we've been caught up in these magical guilt processes of the past. We can free ourselves and other people from being involved in them. And of course we are facing these magical guilts from a different place, because we are that much older and the defences with which we had to protect ourselves from the harsh words or the harsh judgements of those around us are much less.

Realising how much we have snagged our lives or stopped ourselves being happy may be rather a depressing task at first. It's important to remember, however, that the way we coped was not stupid or bad, but the only way we were able to manage difficult feelings. But having recognised how this way of coping lives on and gets in the way, it's vital to understand that we don't have to keep on doing it.

By no longer 'snagging' we learn control and this also changes the way other people behave towards us. We learn to stand up to those who, because of their own difficulties, do not want us to change. Sometimes others do resist the changes that we want for ourselves, particularly those who are closest to us. They might say things like 'You're not as you were', or 'All this psychotherapy is making you too inward', or 'I don't like what it's doing to you', or 'I think it's dangerous'. It's important not to underestimate them. Something quite important happens when we stand up consistently for who we are, and this can transform our relationships with others. If we're firm about our right to change, those who care for us will usually accept it. If they cannot accept, however, then we often do have to make a painful choice. Once we have faced the ghost, the ghost is never so frightening again.

Having completed this section, name those people in your life who wish you well. Begin to allow yourself an equal freedom and to allow yourself to claim your own life freely.

8

Difficult and unstable states of mind

The emotional roller-coaster

We all recognise quite different states of mind at different times but sometimes the way we feel about ourselves can be very unstable. We may switch from one state of mind to a completely different one often without knowing why. Until this is pointed out to us we may not know it is happening, because when we are in some of the states the feelings are intense and all-consuming and we have no memory of the others. We will also not know how we got into such an intense state.

We saw in the earlier chapters that if we have internalised harsh reciprocal roles such as the neglectful abuser in relation to deprived victim our inner and outer world of relating will reflect this defensive pattern. It is in response to emotionally unmanageable experiences that we may develop patterns of cutting off, or dissociation. There are two forms of dissociation. One is cutting off from feeling and is often experienced as going blank/detached and unreal. The other is called structural dissociation, or fragmentation; this is the way we protect ourselves from unbearable and unmanageable feeling. The result is often a rather fragmented sense of ourselves, as if we were built out of lots of different but separate pieces. These pieces are described in CAT as **dissociated states**. The shifts between the states are often abrupt and confusing to oneself and to others. They may appear unprovoked but usually follow perceived repetitions of threats of abuse or abandonment or the failure to get the desired response from the other person. Stressful situations and also just remembering past abuses can also provoke state switches.

Some people describe switching from one state into another as being on an emotional roller-coaster. If you imagine the tramlines of a series of separate roller-coasters in a park, it's as if we swing up or down one tramline and then find ourselves right on the other side of the park on a different tramline, with no idea how we got there. All we know is that we end up feeling either confused or overwhelmed or intensely upset with things going wrong around us.

All of us can experience intense and split-off emotional states when we are under extreme stress or have been traumatised by an event. But some of us can identify always living as if on a series of mini roller-coasters. This may be illustrated in our outside life by lots of unconnected movements – many different jobs and relationships, never staying in one place for long or completing anything. Inside we may have volatile mood swings – extremes of idealised longing or reckless abandon and utter despair and self-harm. Each of the different states of mind is governed by a, usually harsh, reciprocal role internalised from early life. If our early care was experienced as neglectful, abusive or violent, our experience of ourselves will be fragmented and unstable. We may have internalised ways of relating that could be described as being powerfully neglecting, absent and unpredictable in relation to feeling powerless, fragmented and neglected. In adulthood it may have been too frightening for us to make relationships with other people and so our main search for safe attachments may be with objects or substances such as food, sex, drugs, overwork or alcohol. Or with groups or causes which give us a sense of containment and meaning without risk. Because we have not been able to internalise a sense of continual self – the 'me' that sees all the 'me's' – our sense of ourselves remains fragmented, and our longing for real care is idealised. Whenever we try to seek connection and therefore risk intimacy, or of being safely close or loved by another, we tend to raise hope and expectation to impossible levels – as if this person, object or substance will save or transcend all our suffering.

Of course, no one person or substance can do this and so we are continually plunged once again into feeling neglected, abandoned, abused, and the violence we have internalised will be directed both at 'other' and toward ourselves. Impossible idealised hope is raised only to be dashed over and over again.

When we are on an emotional roller-coaster our different states of mind are accompanied by intense, extreme and uncontrollable emotions such as feeling intensely guilty or angry with oneself or being unreasonably angry or hurtful to others. In some states we may feel intensely angry towards ourselves, wanting to hurt ourselves, and sometimes this intensity can be projected out toward others, wanting to harm them. We may sometimes find that we feel blank or unreal, feeling muddled and confused. Sometimes the only way to cope with confusing feelings or 'forbidden' anger is to blank off and feel emotionally distant. Quite often there are headaches or other physical symptoms.

If you find yourself identifying with the description of different state switches, our first shared task is to notice them. That is all at first. Then we will find creative ways to describe them. Then we will make a map of them. In this simple process we are already creating a witnessing 'other' inside us. This is the beginning of a new and helpful reciprocal role that could be described as *helpfully witnessing and caring* to *being seen and cared for*. This new self state we will be building over the next few pages has our general co-ordination at heart and wants to help find a way for all the parts of us to live together consciously.

To help this process, on page 125 is a list of descriptions of states, some of which might apply to you. The list is only a beginning. It's good if you can add your own from your experience of just noticing what happens to your mood through one day and finding words to describe it.

DIFFERENT STATES. Everybody experiences changes in how they feel about themselves and the world. Sometimes these are extreme, sudden and confusing. Learning to recognise them, and the shifts between them can be very helpful. Identify any of the above by putting a ring around the item and deleting or adding words. If any state you have circled leads on to another, join them with a line.

zombie – cut off from feelings or from others, disconnected	provoking, teasing, seducing, winding-up others	contemptuously dismissive of myself, worthless	secure in myself, able to be close to others	seeking revenge, stalking, harassing, murderous
feeling bad but soldiering on, coping	clinging, frantic, fearing abandonment	vulnerable, needy, passively helpless, waiting for rescue	intensely critical of myself, and of others	knight in shining armour rescuing others, righting wrongs
raging and out of control	frenetically active, too busy to think or feel	envious, wanting to harm others, put them down, knock them down	cheating others, cheating the system, lying, hiding the truth	as if poisoned or contaminated
extra special – looking down on others, unrecognised genius	agitated, confused, anxious, panicking, desperate	protective, respecting myself, respecting others	feeling hopeless, no one can help, life is pointless, suicidal	like an unexploded bomb
control freak – in control of self, of life, of other people	feeling perfectly cared for, blissfully close to another	hurting myself, hurting others, causing harm or damage	spaced out – distanced from others, as if acting a part, double-glazed	watchful, suspicious, jealous, paranoid
cheated by life, by others, untrusting	misunderstood, rejected, abandoned, desolate	resentfully submitting to demands, a slave, under the thumb	flying away, running away, escaping	
hiding secret shame	hurt, humiliated, defeated, always in the wrong	frightened of angry others		overwhelmed by grief and loss

Over time see if you can add other words that describe this state of mind. Perhaps: furious, confused, upset, lost, afraid. There may also be colours, pictures or images. Sometimes when we do this actual memories arise of earlier times when you felt this way. Don't be alarmed. Just record them in your notebook and return to them when you are ready.

Any time you find yourself becoming overwhelmed, turn to the exercises in the Appendices which are designed to help you maintain stability whilst you do this work. The Grounding Exercise and Mindfulness of Breathing are two good ones to practise in a short time. When you have got your breath back and your heart rate is steady, return to your task. Be the best observer of all the different states and their content that you can. You are doing important work of becoming a co-ordinator.

The next step is to see if you can recognise the reciprocal role within the state itself. For example: if you are wanting to hurt yourself whilst feeling hurt and humiliated you may recognise the reciprocal role of *violently rejecting/ dismissing* in relation to *abused/rejected/crushed*. If you recognise craving, wanting to be lost in bliss, you might describe a *perfectly admiring* in relation to *specially held* reciprocal role.

In the rage and hate of 'monster' you might find *belittling/punishing* toward others or yourself in relation to *punished/humiliated/shamed*. The reciprocal role of *judging/blaming* in relation to *blamed/put down* may have kept your natural anger repressed and feared as 'monstrous', leaving you unable ever to express natural anger and only either turn it on yourself as self-harm or threaten others in distorted ways.

The diagram from GRAHAM, who had a long history of drug abuse and self-harm, illustrates the internalised reciprocal roles at the beginning of therapy and, in bold lettering (which represents red used by Graham in his diagram), the new roles he learned to develop through self-observation and reflection. As his self-observation grew, he started to feel more in charge of the different states and their sudden switches. The pull of the dissociated

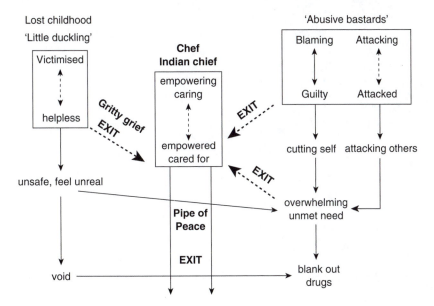

Figure 8.1 Graham's diagram

states felt less extreme. There were fewer episodes of blanking off and feeling unreal and fewer episodes of cutting himself. In their place there came lots of very painful and difficult feeling. He called this 'gritty grief' – a mixture of longing, despair, rage, loss of innocence and hope for good things. He wanted to kick out at the helpless little ducklings in the park in spring, squeaking and following their mother. He longed to cry 'a normal bucketful' for his own helpless little duckling but was too scared at being overwhelmed. He wrote about his lost childhood spent in numerous foster homes.

In the centre of his diagram in bold type is an Indian 'Chief'. This figure, an image representing a new self-state, is made up of one of the few good figures in his life, an institutional chef who once befriended him and taught him snooker, and an Indian Chief in full head dress who appeared to him in a dream. In the dream, toward the end of therapy, the 'Chief' showed him how to ride through a herd of buffalo. He understood this as an indication that he could learn to ride amongst his roller-coaster states with greater consciousness and also be in charge. This was the beginning of the creation of his 'healthy island'.

The energy of this dream figure also allowed us to talk of different 'pipes of peace' from the crack cocaine that had long been his habit. At follow-up he was finding some benefits from meditation and had joined a group that met weekly.

part four

gathering information

A person's consciousness awakens wrapped in another's consciousness.

M.M. Bakhtin *'Speech Genres' and Other Late Essays* (1986: 138)

9

Examining the impact of our beginnings

By now you should have a notebook of ideas about difficulties you are having, some of which may go back a long way. Perhaps you are ready to ask, 'Why do I get myself into traps and dilemmas?' 'Where do these conflicts come from?'

Remember the concept of the individual carrying the seed of their own nature with its potential for individual life. If our own core nature is a bit like an apple pip it will want to grow into an apple tree. Whilst we are naming and studying our 'no-go areas' it's important to understand that they are the result of our own 'appleness' meeting the early outside world. As you look back over your early life in this section, remember to look for signs of your own 'seed' nature, which may have been eclipsed by your environmental history. Try to keep hold of it, feeling your way in to what it was trying to accomplish. Remember also the concept of Maitri – unconditional friendliness to oneself.

Use this section of the book in the way that you would flick through a photograph album. Focus on what feels right for you. **Push where it moves**!

Before you start, sit quietly somewhere by yourself and ask: What has brought me through the dark times?

Opening boxes

In this section we are going to be opening a few boxes. We are going to use everything that you discover about yourself to write your own life story. In order to create an accurate description of what goes wrong we need to know exactly where difficulties are rooted so that we can build a picture of the reciprocal roles that influence your inner and outer relationships. Then we need to create appropriate aims for change that you will be monitoring each week.

Some memories will feel painful. It's the pain you have tried to manage all your life. Whether you are reading this section in co-counselling, or you are on your own and are concerned about dragging up old ghosts, imagine that I am sitting right alongside you. Imagine that my voice and face is smiling and encouraging you to be both courageous and also mindful of what you can manage. Use the diagram on page 17 (Figure 1.2) to keep yourself in the 'window of tolerance' by monitoring your body responses to all the material you are exploring. Our task is to find ways to accept the emotional pain you feel and to respond to it differently.

Psychotherapy is not easy, but it does bring relief if you stick with it. It can help to make us stronger.

Self states

You probably realise already that your experience of yourself varies throughout each day as if you were composed of many different parts. Some you may know well, others not at all. Some you may like, others not like so much!

The different self states that comprise our personality and fund our behaviour have been developed at different times of our lives. Many of them are rooted in early life. Some parts of us may feel very small, like a child who has a specific need – to be looked after, or helped to grow up. All of us tend to have a dominant 'coper' to control chaos inside; or an 'insister' to cope with feeling needy.

Understanding where our conflicts are rooted helps us to see how very powerful fears, often unconscious, act to keep us behaving 'as if' the circumstances that produced the original problem are still in full force. Although over the years we have grown to be competent adults, there is a part of us who has not yet learned that new outside circumstances are prevailing. We still behave as if, unless we please, avoid, cut off or act in a particular way, our emotional life is threatened.

Recognising how our everyday feelings and images may be rooted in our childhood, and thus can be reframed, is an important part of the change process. So we are now going actively to shine a light on the bits of ourselves that have been hidden, because they were too scared, too rejected, too damaged. The purpose is to bring a listening ear and a caring heart to the places that hurt. To relieve the small part of us from isolation and rejection, fear and limitation. This work is done in psychotherapy all the time. No book can hope to step into the place of a living person met each week in the privacy of the same room and time. But these pages may offer a beginning for the safe exploration of our misunderstood self, challenging old assumptions and messages, and facilitating the discovery of previously hidden parts of us that we will come to value.

Am I odd?

Another reason for looking into the past is that we often take what we feel for granted. Many people say to me 'Doesn't everyone feel like this?', as if they were trying to find what was 'normal'. I think that this is a very basic concern when someone embarks on a path of self-discovery. Am I odd? Am I making a fuss? Freud tells a story of a young man who visited him early in his career. When Freud asked the man to describe what he did each day he said, 'Same as everyone else … get up, throw up into the toilet, dress, go to work …'.

Claiming our uniqueness is part of allowing ourselves to be real and to put our experience into context. When I suggested to Freda that it sounded as if she had had to grow up quickly and become a 'little mother' when her brother was born and her mother became depressed, she responded with a good deal of feeling. Suddenly she had an explanation for why she felt responsible for everything. In making sense of her experience she felt relief. She could then chose of her own free will how to take up responsibility or not.

The rest of Part Four really forms one long questionnaire about your early life. As you reminisce, make notes or you can draw or paint any of the feelings or memories that come to you. Try not to underestimate the powers of your own imagination to create symbolic language, our very first language, which often has much information.

If you notice that you have blanked off, become stressed in your body, or desperately want to eat, just note this feeling. Write about it in detail as much as you can.

Early life review

Prebirth

There is an increasing awareness that interuterine conditions affect the growing infant. Just over a hundred years ago, Geog Groddeck was writing, in *The Meaning of Illness*, about the womb as our first container, our first contact with sound, space, warmth, movement.

> In the mother's womb the child is made for nine months; it lives, grows, and develops in the womb. Never again in his life does the human being have relations as intimate as those he entertains with his mother during pregnancy. The extent to which we harbour the wish to be loved and to love is conditioned by this period of intimate togetherness. (1977: 65)

And one hundred years later neuroscience is corroborating Groddeck's findings through brain studies that show the effect of the mother's endocrine system on the growing infant in the womb, and on attachment behaviour after birth. If a mother is stressed by depression, anxiety or trauma her cortisol levels are raised and so also are her baby's. These high levels of cortisol may disperse with the post-birth mothering, or, if not regulated, can remain thus giving the growing person an anxious start which is difficult to regulate until this has been taught.

Birth stories and reciprocal roles

The late psychotherapist Angela Wilton made a study of birth stories – the actual birth as well as the earliest postnatal experience – and their link with the reciprocal role procedures. She asked people to tell the story of their birth and its impact on the family, using any anecdote, story or image from any source – parents, siblings, doctors, midwives – that added to the picture. She included jokes, myths or catch-phrases, as well as any actual memory of the birth itself.

As she worked with different birth stories she began to notice how the atmosphere around the birth story was often mirrored in the person's ways of relating to others. For example, a mother exhausted and angered by a long, arduous labour might be less able to bond with her baby than a mother who found giving birth exhilarating. This birth story would carry an atmosphere of pain and struggle, inducing possible hidden and 'magical guilt' in the child. These feelings might well be carried over into other relationships. Parents who hope for a child of a certain gender may have difficulty covering up their disappointment when their baby turns out to be the opposite. This disappointment may give rise to the person feeling worthless, especially when they get close to others, and to the belief that they have to strive to justify their presence.

Sometimes when a baby is born after a bereavement or loss, he or she becomes associated with this rather than being greeted in their own right. As a result, the person grows up believing that they were 'born under a shadow' or have become a 'replacement child'.

Over half of the people in Wilton's study felt they had damaged and hurt their mother during the birth, so burdening them with the reciprocal roles of either *hurt* one or *damaging* one (as if to be alive is to damage others), evoking guilt and a need to make compensation. Another theme was 'just we two', where an easy birth was followed by close and uninterrupted bonding between mother and child, with the father absent. The stories tended to emphasise an idealised central and perfect position in relationships, from which there could be, in reality, a long fall! Relationships in adult life with the 'just we two' emphasis could be over-close and dependent, mutually admiring, with a tendency to over-idealisation; or, if this was not met, a crash into feeling rubbished or, conversely, rubbishing anything too 'ordinary' (see Figure 4.1, p. 64).

The 'unwanted' theme was also prominent, leaving the person with a sense of ambivalence about commitment and an anticipation of rejection: the rejected/rejecting reciprocal role.

> HELEN came into therapy because of difficulties in close relationships. She had a pattern of desperately trying to get close, getting close for a minute and then fleeing. The myth in her family was that she always had her 'knickers in a twist'. It turned out that she had been a breech birth, in spite of being turned before birth to come out head first. She had turned again to find her way out. Her mother always felt that she 'couldn't win' with Helen and thus was born the reciprocal role of stubborn/defeating to defeated/depressed with the resulting feelings of anger and resentment that made intimacy and acceptance hard.

Facts of our birth used to be shrouded in mystery. But today, as conditions for being born in the West have improved, I hear an increasing number of stories where a sense of *joy and celebration* is evident. Perhaps with the number of fathers now taking an active part in the birth process, increasing, as well as a greater sense of control over the nature of the birth, these stories will be on the increase. My grandson Harry told me, aged three, with a serious look in his eye, that his mummy had to be cut open in order for him to be born, but that there were lots of people there and when they pulled him out they all shouted 'It's Harry!' and a huge smile came over his face.

The reason for examining your own birth story as part of gathering information about your life is to bring what has been hidden into the light. I have found that when people begin to ask friends and relatives about their birth or their early life, a few things start to make sense. It also offers an opportunity for corresponding or meeting relatives who may have been scattered over the world, as well as the family 'black sheep'.

These times of gathering can offer an opportunity to express rage and fury at what appears to be the unfairness of our lot. They also can lead to expressing forgiveness: of a mother or father who one learns was immature or ill, suffering from hardships we can only imagine, given little or no help, dominated by others, and living in poor and inadequate housing. While it's important to experience those feelings that have become blocked or split off by our need to survive earlier life events, part of moving on into maturity is to let go of our feelings about the past.

Sometimes the atmosphere of our birth seems to accompany us on other transitions and we can feel the flavour of a 'long difficult birth' in starting a new job or relationship, or in moving house. Or, feeling impatient always, as if we've always had to exit early, as in premature birth. Some people describe their lives as being like 'waiting in a passage'; others report a life-long sense of restriction around the throat which intensifies during change and subsequently discover they were born with the cord around their neck.

The atmosphere of our birth will not necessarily dominate our lives, for many people overcome difficult or protracted births naturally. But if you feel there is a link between the flavour of your birth and the kind of physical experiences you have while undergoing change or transition, it is worth reflecting on the nature of your birth, especially if there is still someone you can ask. Even if there isn't, your symptoms and intuition will be enough to let you know what to concentrate upon. Perhaps those of us who had slow and difficult births need to recognise that this may be the way we go into new things, and accept it for what it is. In knowing it consciously we can choose whether to get help to push ourselves on a bit, or whether to let the slow, difficult way take its own time.

The following questionnaire is designed to help you ponder on the nature of your own birth and the atmosphere into which you were born.

Questionnaire: Birth and prebirth

Our time in the womb is our first experience of unconditional being. How much time do you allow for *being* rather than *doing*? Weekends only, evenings, two hours per day, only holidays, never?

(Continued)

How does your need for containment – a house, room, building – reflect itself in your life? Does the place you live in suit you? What is it like? Describe it, and see how much of it is an extension of your original container, offering retreat, safety, protection. If you find it does not offer these properties, where can you go to get in touch with them? For all-round good health all of us need safe and appropriate containment, whether this is a caravan, tent or hut that is our very own.

How much sleep do you allow yourself – enough, too little, too much? Are there restrictions against sleep in your life (internal voices telling you to get up and not sleep)? Look back over your life and see how you have used sleep, whether it has been allowed or not in your life. Babies and teenagers require a lot of sleep, as if they needed to balance the enormous growth in consciousness and physical change with darkness and rest more than at other times.

How much care do you take of yourself – warmth, safety, protection?

Do you allow rhythm into your life – music, dance, sound? When was the last time you felt in touch with the rhythms of life and felt you were part of it – today, yesterday, last week/month/year? Where did you feel in touch most? By the sea? In the country watching the seasonal changes? How much do you allow this to affect you positively – all the time, partially, not enough, never?

How much do you know of your actual birth? Was it a natural birth, forceps delivery or Caesarean? Was it easy or difficult? Were you breast-fed or bottle-fed?

Multiple births

This means that several lives share the same space right from conception. Sometimes this creates rivalry and a keen competition for space and attention. Sometimes there is a complex mixture of strong feelings: those of intense love and bonding to the person with whom you have shared your whole life; and intense hatred and jealousy for when the other or others would seem to be favoured, and you feel your already slender share of the goodies is threatened. Multiple-birth children are actually deprived maternally, however hard the mother works: those moments of being alone and special to Mum are rare. But even short regular moments of being recognised as unique help to consolidate our sense of 'self'.

Many multiple births also include deaths, especially today with the new *in vitro* fertilisation techniques where several embryos may be implanted. When one child or more is born, and one or more has died, there can be a tendency for medical staff to be so pleased that there are any survivors at all that they can overlook the impact of the deaths of those who have perished. There is anecdotal evidence that if you have had a twin who has not survived you are subtly aware of it in some not yet understood way. If that person has died but not been accorded his or her due recognition, there may be uneasy feelings such as survivor guilt. Fearing we were greedy will not be conscious, but may be around unconsciously, subtly undermining our freedom to live.

136

Adoption

In adoption we are carried by one woman and then nurtured by another, or many others, during our first years. We come to each one as a stranger with whom bonding has to be achieved and new signals learned. All of us are now much more aware of the importance of the early years to our psychological development. People who have had many fosterings, many different 'mothers' and many moves seem to suffer the most in terms of insecure or disorganised attachment and lack of self-esteem. But sometimes, if there has been one central kind of influence, even the most deprived early backgrounds can be compensated. During the process of self-exploration, people who have been mainly in touch with the negative side of their backgrounds do often unearth the memory of someone who was kind and helpful, someone who showed care and introduced the person to something of value in themselves.

JAMES, who had had several difficult fosterings before living in a reasonable children's home for several years, kept his life very ordered and unadventurous, not making many friends and not risking relationships. He had a fine sense of colour. He would wear coloured socks and have an attractive tie and handkerchief. When I commented on this he looked startled and embarrassed. Teased for his 'foppishness', he had tended to repress this side of himself, but on exploring it further he did acknowledge his love of colour and design, and his attraction to beautiful things. He had a knack for picking out small objects like glass and silver, at markets, but he felt it to be 'wrong' in some way. What we discovered was the influence of an old lady he used to visit as a community service 'punishment' during his early fostering days. He hated being associated with the 'cast-offs' of society – babies and old people who weren't wanted. But this old lady had a room that resembled an Aladdin's Cave, and when he showed an interest (which he had in him naturally) she encouraged it. It was the only concentrated attention and appreciation he received during his early years. The memory of it was buried underneath years of basic survival in a difficult competitive world that revolved around who was going to get the best parents or foster parents. It was a moving moment when he realised how much kindness he had received for himself and who he was, and it raised his self-esteem. He started to value his appreciation of colour and shape and took it seriously enough to begin an evening course in design.

Many people who are adopted carry the sense of rejection all through their lives. In an interview with Anne de Courcy in the *London Evening Standard*, the writer John Trenhaile explained that many adopted children are overachievers, struggling to compensate for some sin they are not even aware of having committed:

> ... the feeling that you have failed a test you didn't even know you'd been set ... In my case I felt I had done something so unspeakably wrong that my own mother gave me away. But it took a long, long time to realise this.

Sometimes people who have been adopted carry an *abandoning/rejecting* in relation to *abandoned/rejected and worthless* reciprocal role. This may express itself as an obsessional interest in security, being attached to objects or rituals of checking, or fear of emotional commitment. Or, the *conditional* in relation to *striving* reciprocal role may include rebellion, testing out all attachments to see if they will last, to prove oneself 'lovable'.

Some people split their biological and adoptive parents into good/bad or ideal/second best. Biological parents may be idealised, and the split between the two sets of mothers or parents may be reflected in later relationships, or form a 'snag'. For example, a pattern of allowing a 'second-best' relationship while yearning for the unattainable idealised 'real'. Now that adopted children can search for their biological parents this split has a chance to be healed, both by the reality of finding actual parents less than ideal, as well as healing through self-exploration or therapy.

Do you recognise that any of the following underlie your feelings about yourself: I unconsciously behave as if I'm about to be: (a) given away; (b) abandoned; (c) teased by being given life but nothing else; (d) rejected?

Many people who have been successfully adopted, and who are tremendously grateful to their adoptive parents, also carry some of the intense feelings that less successful adoptees carry, but feel guilty about expressing them. They feel they should be grateful and give all their loyalty and self-expression to these parents, and that it would hurt or harm them if they were to search for the biological other. The cost of gratitude may feel as if it damages the 'real' parent or image, thus developing a pattern of spoiling hope or longing. It is often only in later life that people feel able to look at their past and their attitudes in a fresh way. It is possible to find ways to release this hold and to allow a full, accepted life that our biological mother felt unable to offer.

Questionnaire: Our first reception

Were you expected; wanted?

Did it matter if you were a boy or a girl?

How long had your parents been married when you were born?

Where did you come in the family: eldest, only, middle, youngest, etc.? (See Figure 9.1, p. 141.)

Were there any miscarriages, stillbirths, other children who died but were perhaps rarely referred to?

Were you welcomed with open arms and smiling faces?

Was much expected of your presence, for example as the first boy, girl, grandchild, mixed race child, child for generations; or as the heir to title, fortune, family business etc.?

Was your birth an attempt to redeem lost other lives or disappointment?

Was there an unwritten hope that you would carry on a tradition or break with tradition; that you would pioneer something new, such as being the child of a gay couple, or redeem parental restrictions?

Development of a sense of oneself in the world

Infancy

Reciprocal roles describe the internalisation of patterns of relating, to ourselves and to others. These roles begin during pregnancy, through birth and infancy into childhood, when we are at our most impressionable, before we have started to form thoughts about anything. Our infant world is experienced mainly through our bodies – hot, cold, wet, soiled and uncomfortable, hungry, empty, full; held gently, firmly, roughly, not held at all; stroked gently, soothingly, lovingly, roughly, angrily, harshly, or not at all. Because we are so dependent and vulnerable when we are infants we experience a great deal of anxiety if what we have known as keeping us safe is threatened in any way. Dr D.W. Winnicott (1979) uses the term 'primitive agonies' to describe the unbearable anxieties of the infant in fear of falling forever, in fear of being abandoned.

When our early infant life is adequately provided for, our fears are allayed and our anxieties do not get out of proportion. We learn to trust that what or whoever goes away will come back; that it is safe to know love and be loved, and to know and love oneself; and that there are parts of us we can trust to be safe and to where we can retreat. We form appropriate boundaries between ourselves and others as we grow from infancy into childhood, a process that takes from the time of birth to between two and three years.

When the early environment is experienced as non-nurturing, but neglectful, hostile or inadequate, our development is thwarted by anxiety. We learn to adapt in order to accommodate, and, before thought process, and before we have separated what belongs to ourselves and what belongs to others, our only defence against what is experienced as a hostile outside is to compartmentalise our experiences. This might involve states where we withdraw, become zombie-like; states of helplessness and states where we are overwhelmed by unmanageable feeling and can only writhe and scream. We may also split off the things that are unpleasant and experienced as 'bad' from the good experiences, setting a pattern for later on of things appearing as either totally good or totally bad, with nothing in between.

Projection

For example, it could become difficult, if not impossible, to be angry and love someone at the same time, or to receive someone's anger without feeling hated. When we are split off in this way we may project any negative aspects onto others, thus experiencing the other as bad or against us, as chaotic or hateful. These feelings can be projected onto our employers, friends or relatives, who we then invite to live out for us the unresolved difficulties or rejected parts from our early life.

From birth to about the age of seven the ego is developed against the background we have just described. In order for the ego to grow healthily and be of use to us as a lens through which we see and operate in the world, we need a 'good enough' background. We need to feel that we are loved and therefore lovable; liked and therefore likeable; accepted and therefore acceptable. We need to know that however 'bad' we are, we will not be rejected.

If our early years are accompanied by a 'too tight' environment, where a parent or guardian is too attentive and protective, we get little experience of the outside world and therefore lack the tools to cope with adult life. We tend to grow up to be afraid of life and our instincts, unwilling to take any risks, avoiding challenge and thus isolating ourselves. Our reciprocal roles tend to involve *restricting/controlling* in relation to *restricted/crushed* and we may recognise the dilemma 'if I must, then I won't'. We may be drawn to want to merge with another.

If there has been too little interest, too loose a soil, we feel ungrounded and 'dropped', which can emerge later in depression and a lack of ego strength or self-esteem, a sense that we inhabit a 'nowhere world'.

Recollecting early life and influences

The following section offers exercises and questions for gathering together and reflecting upon your early life.

---

exercise

Figure 9.1 is an example of how to lay out your own family map. Make your own family map or tree in your own way. Use different colours for different people and different shapes. Alongside each person put their date of birth, occupation, style, personality traits and any other description you feel is significant. See if you can find words to describe the reciprocal roles of the family members in your map.

Spend a few moments with your eyes closed, and feel into the type of early childhood you had and the type of early environment. Did it feel (a) too tight and enclosed, or (b) too loose? See if you can get an image of your mother, or whoever was mother for you, the feel of that person. Where are they in relation to you? What does the image tell you about your early life and the child you once were?

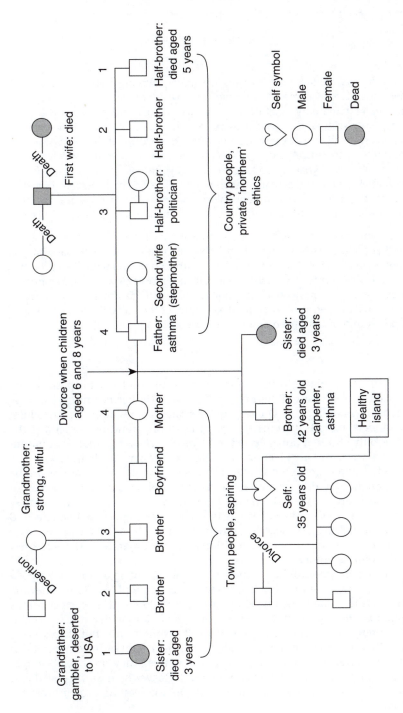

Figure 9.1 A family map

Many people have few or no early memories, although sometimes early memories start to come back during therapy or self-questioning. What is your earliest memory? Picture it, in all its colours and shades. What is happening, with whom, who is there? Set the scene for yourself down to the tiniest detail – what everyone is wearing, the texture of the cloth, smells around you, sounds. Again, closing your eyes, feel into your own place in the recollection. What are you wearing? Feel your feet on the ground, feel how small you were, actually become yourself as a small person in that picture. Write down what is happening, and what the feelings are. When you look at it now, what do you sense are the reciprocal roles being invited?

When you have got this memory, anchor it by writing or drawing. Make another picture inside yourself, of the early life you would like to have had, painting in all the feelings, objects, ideas, atmosphere you would have liked as a small person to have had. See if you can, from this exercise, begin to understand the world you inhabited as a child, and the kind of choices you had to make in terms of survival. Make a note of the parts of you that went underground or unnoticed and undeveloped.

Ponder on where you fit in the family network and on how this position has influenced you. Eldest children are said to have similar beginnings as only children: they are 'King or Queen' until a sibling comes along. As the eldest you had 'new' parents, inexperienced at the art of parenting. Sometimes the eldest or only children are expected to be more 'grown up' than is appropriate for their age, and are given responsibilities way beyond their years.

Second children are often treated more leniently, because parents are by now experienced and more relaxed. If the elder sibling is making a success of things and fitting in with the family network, a second child may feel they have to keep up. Or, if the eldest has in some way disappointed parents and family expectations, the second (and this can apply to any children who come afterwards) can take on the position of the eldest, making the eldest feel redundant and a failure.

If you are a middle child then there is a sense of having to 'jockey for position' in a family, often feeling in between or in a 'no place'. Sometimes the youngest child is the 'sunshine child' who has it easy, with few expectations or demands. Siblings often divide into pairs, as families with two parents and two children can become two pairs. Pairs are comfortable, but threes make complicated triangles. Youngest children may have a lot of freedom, but can also be neglected or taken for granted. Sometimes they are babied longer than is appropriate because they are the last to leave the nest. If spoiled and cosseted, they may find it difficult to grow up and lead their own independent lives.

researching signs of our 'healthy island'

in early life

1. Play

Were you allowed to play as a child? What kind of play was it? See if you can remember games, toys or stories. Notice the quality of this remembered play and how it made you feel. See if you can find a word to describe what you were naturally drawn to. There may be both negative and positive aspects that emerge from exploring the games we had as children. Play can often be creative and nourish our imagination, our sense of colour, shape and image-making capacity. It may also have been a way in which we safely expressed difficult feeling. Telling dolls or teddies off or mending them with bandages sometimes tells us something of our internal world at a particular time. Burying things in the garden, learning to punch, throw darts may help us see our natural defences emerging.

How do you play now?

2. Longing

How have you experienced longing? For what have you longed? See if you can follow where you own natural longing, or your own heart, has been trying to lead you.

3. Happiness

Write down the times in your life when you:

felt happy
experienced joy
were respected
realised you were being taken seriously
felt you mattered

Note how you experienced these feelings:

in your body
in feeling words

How might you write about these good feelings now and about what you received?

(Continued)

4. Connection

Write down the number of times in your life when you have felt connected to someone – person, animal, situation or group, part of nature, belief. Note the feelings around this sense of connection.

5. Spiritual awareness

Write down what for you gives a sense of spirituality. How important is this capacity to you? Do you give space for this in your everyday life? What are your spiritual practices and how do you nourish them?

Whatever you discover about your healthy island, make a space for it in all your writings, diagrams and in your own self-monitoring. When, later on in the book, you make a diagram of the problematic reciprocal roles, remember to put your healthy island on to your diagram.

---

exercise: using objects to create our family map

Have some fun by gathering a number of objects – for example, shells, stones, plates, glass – that might depict your family members. Choose a favourite object for yourself and place this on the floor first. Then gather objects that represent other family members, including steps, fosters, halfs, aunts, grandparents and any animals and neighbours if they were part of family life. Move the objects around to indicate times of change. For example, if one parent left, became ill or died, when you went to school, when siblings were born or other people joined the family. We can often remember something happening in a certain house, but not how old we may have been.

Allow the objects to show you something of your early family atmostphere.

Qualities of early caregivers

Describe the one or two main people in your early life and list underneath in columns the main qualities of each: their likes and dislikes; their sayings and ambitions.

Mealtimes

Mealtimes can be highly charged family gatherings that can tell us a lot about what is going on in a family.

What were mealtimes like? Did you eat: together as a family, or separately?

What kind of atmosphere was there:

- ☐ silent
- ☐ formal
- ☐ informal
- ☐ tense
- ☐ happy
- ☐ chatty

Were there rituals about food, such as preparation, washing up, washing hands, saying grace, 'I always sit here'?

Were mealtimes in front of the TV?

Recall your favourite and least favourite foods. What was the difference?

What habits, fears, difficulties, pleasures, have come out of your experience of family meals?

Celebrations

Name and remember one good and one not so good celebration, a birthday perhaps, or Christmas.

Recall your memories of any of the following:

- ☐ being dressed up
- ☐ poverty
- ☐ worry
- ☐ rows
- ☐ feeling spoilt
- ☐ feeling neglected

Which visitors were allowed?

Relatives

Who were they? (Go back to your family tree)

Who spoke to whom?

Family feuds: what was their nature? What was the history, story, mythology? How did it live on? Who perpetuated it?

Were those who were a bit slow treated equally and well, or secretly laughed at, ridiculed and ignored?

In cases of great social or financial change, how were relatives who had not 'made it' treated:

- ☐ slighted
- ☐ with shame
- ☐ ostracised

(Continued)

☐ looked down upon
☐ kindly
☐ generously
☐ willingly

Religion

What was the family religion or belief system?

How did it manifest itself? Did you go to church every Sunday? Was there fierce rejection of anything 'funny' or irrational? Any other memories?

Was religion talked about in a free way?

Were you allowed to have your own view as you were growing up?

Was religion important to you – the idea of God, Jesus, Allah, Siva? Was it:

☐ frightening
☐ reassuring
☐ wonderful

What lives on today from your early experience with religion and religious ideas? The concept of:

☐ sin
☐ guilt
☐ love
☐ discipline
☐ wonder
☐ awe
☐ belief

School

Take either primary or secondary school or both.

What was your first day at school like?

Were you prepared or not prepared?

Who took you?

How did you react to:

☐ teachers
☐ other children
☐ the classroom
☐ tasks

What lives on in you today that comes from early schooldays?

How did you cope with:

- ☐ lessons
- ☐ the playground
- ☐ other children
- ☐ teachers

Did you ever run away or want to come home?

How did your parents cope with talking to teachers about anything to do with school and school meetings?

Did you have school dinners or take your own lunch?

Did you feel different from other children? If so, why? Was it:

- ☐ clothes
- ☐ hair
- ☐ hygiene
- ☐ parents
- ☐ where you lived
- ☐ colour of skin
- ☐ religion
- ☐ being clever
- ☐ being not so clever
- ☐ speaking in a different language
- ☐ not understanding others

Were you bigger or smaller than others? Did this matter?

Did you follow in a brother or sister's footsteps?

Did Mum help with school or was it Dad?

Did you get rewarded for achievements, or did no one notice or seem to care what you did? What were the rewards?

Did you travel on your own or with others?

Did you have to care for a younger sibling? Did you mind?

If things went wrong at school – bullying, fights, teasing, taunting, unfair treatment by staff – who did you talk to?

If things went wrong at home, was there someone at school to whom you could turn?

How did it feel to come home after school?

Friendships

Were you allowed to bring friends home?

How were they treated?

(Continued)

Did your parents' morals and ethics become judgements on your friends? What was this like for you? Did you:

☐ remain divided in loyalty
☐ continue the friendship anyway, but secretly
☐ give in to your parents and drop the friends

Were you allowed out in gangs or groups? How early?

Money

Did you know how much money your parents earned?

Were you given pocket money?

Were you encouraged to, or did you have to earn your own money?

Was money important for:

☐ saving
☐ buying things
☐ having power

What were the myths about money in your family? Was money never talked about, worshipped, or was everything priced or referred to in relation to its cost?

Were you hard up or poor? Was this:

☐ like everyone else
☐ sad
☐ a disgrace
☐ humiliating
☐ painful

exercise

Write something in your notebook about what you learned about value systems from the family's attitude to and handling of money.

Spend some time looking at your own attitude to money and how you may have used money over the years:

☐ Do you feel you have to hold on to it if you have it?
☐ Are you afraid of it?

☐ Does it burn a hole in your pocket?
☐ Do you never have enough, however much you earn or are given?
☐ Do you hate and despise it?
☐ Are you embarrassed about talking about it and cannot discuss money matters?
☐ Are you comfortable with money matters?

Talents and gifts

Many people grow up not knowing that they are really good at something because this is never appreciated and mirrored back. In Chapter 7, 'Snags and self-sabotage' we looked at the effect of envy upon someone whose skills or gifts were more developed or extended than those of a parent or other family member. We can be made to feel guilty for our talent and hide it or leave it undeveloped. Only later, when perhaps we are able to succeed, can we begin fully to claim this part of ourselves. But sadly some people do feel very crippled by their guilt about having gifts that they never develop, and remain thwarted in some way, envious of others' successes, frustrated and living out only half of their capacity.

What gifts do you feel you have? Make a list. If appropriate include things like communication, good listening, good with people, patience, kindness, ability to analyse or put things together, intuition, as well as being good at sport, writing, science, selling, making things, reading, storytelling. Add this to your healthy island.

How did the family remark on your gifts:

☐ kindly
☐ proudly
☐ encouragingly
☐ took no notice at all
☐ denied them
☐ called you names when you did something well – 'Don't let it go to your head', 'Show off'
☐ compared you with others, themselves or their ancestors

The things we are good at may also not be properly understood by our parents. They may appear to discourage our talent or interest because they don't understand it and they can't see where it will lead. A report by a schoolmaster about Barry Sheene, the champion motorcycle racer, read, 'Barry has got to learn that fiddling with motor cycles won't get him through life!' We may have been good at butterfly and insect collecting when our parents were mechanically minded. We may have loved the ballet and music, when our parents were only interested in the house and garden. My mother found it odd that I liked to walk on my own through the fields where we lived, dreaming. For a while I felt ashamed for my 'oddness' and tried hard not to be a dreamer. I can see now that this was the time I naturally reflected alone and collected dreams and thoughts. This is now an important nourishment for writing and therapy.

Go back to the time of your early growing-up period – age four to twelve – and think about what your own interests were then. Write them down. Include the ones you might be tempted to dismiss.

List the things you were drawn towards then that are still part of your life today.

If they have been driven underground how can you resurrect them?

Was the opposite true in your family – that talent was overemphasised and looked for even when it wasn't there? Did you feel you had to oblige and come up with something to please and gratify your parents' desire?

Sometimes parents who have a particularly strong talent hope it will come out in their children. Parents hope that their children will do the things they were unable to do, living out their own unfulfilled life through them. I know a young man who is naturally quite introverted and shy, and whose mother is the same. She dislikes her shyness but has never done anything about changing it, and she projects the extrovert person she would like to be onto her poor son. As a result, he is bullied into joining things that do not suit him and wearing clothes that are loud and fashionable. She tells false stories of his daring deeds, which make him curl up with embarrassment. He tries to oblige her by having a go at the more extrovert tasks, overcoming quite a lot of fear on the way and aligning himself with friends who expect him to be always full of bravado and loud jokes. It is killing his spirit.

Did you feel that you had to work hard to be what you are, not in order to please your parents' fantasy of what they wanted from a son or daughter?

Are you still having to live up to that today?

Does it suit you?

Do you want to change it?

Sexuality and gender
Have a look at how your sexuality was formed against the background of your family.

What was physical touching like in your family? Was it:

☐ encouraged
☐ not allowed
☐ allowed too much so you weren't sure of the boundaries between what was acceptable and what was not

---

Were you helped to feel good about your body or were you ashamed of it?

At what age did you first become sexually aware?

Could you talk freely about sex in your family? Did you want to? If not, what did you feel?

Were you told about sex:

☐ at school
☐ at home
☐ via a brother or sister
☐ other relative

What did you make of it when you heard about it?

In the family's attitude, did sex mean one thing if you were female and another if you were male?

Write down some of the myths you received about sex as you were growing up.

Was homosexuality talked about and, if so, in what way? What feelings did you have about it for yourself; for others?

If you discovered you were more attracted to people of your own sex, when did you become aware of this and how?

Were you able to talk about it and find a partner or has it remained hidden still?

A lot of people say, 'I feel very screwed up about sex.' Can you identify with this? If so, make a list of things that bother you about yourself and sexuality:

☐ always ends in an emotional row
☐ makes me feel great/other person feel great/both feel great, feel closer
☐ embarrassing
☐ humiliating
☐ gets in the way
☐ causes anger and disappointment
☐ it makes me scared

Spend some time looking at the mixed messages you have received about your body, your gender and your sexuality.

If you were sexually abused as a child, how does this affect you now:

☐ by feeling guilty and contaminated
☐ by being unable to feel safe enough to get close
☐ by self-abusive behaviour such as promiscuity, drinking
☐ by allowing others to abuse you by taking you for granted, hurting or depriving you

There are now many special agencies to help survivors of incest and sexual abuse. You may wish to contact one of these. You may prefer to find a counsellor or therapist who will help you with your journey of healing this most difficult and painful of wounds, a person who will treat your story with care, confidence and compassion. A guide to choosing a therapist appears in Part Seven.

Illness

Did illness or ill health affect your family much? Was one family member, yourself perhaps, ill more than the others?

Make a list of all the ill health within your family, with dates and the length of the illnesses and any periods of hospitalisation.

Make a list of all your own periods of ill health, with dates and kinds of experience.

How was illness referred to: was it with fear and reverence for operations, pills and doctors; or with a more cavalier approach, where it was left to nannies, grandparents or neighbours to look in or visit?

If you were ill, who looked after you? How was your illness handled, how much did you know about what was happening to you?

When small children are admitted to hospital they sometimes 'forget' who their real parents are and attach themselves to nurses or other staff members as a way of protecting themselves from the pain of grief. Look carefully at the number of separations caused by illness, and try to get in touch with the feelings of this time.

Who, if anyone, did you play with during those separations?

What fantasies did you have about your parents?

Sometimes parents do not believe us when we say we have a pain or problem, and this can be very hurtful.

In many one-parent families where the parent is the sole breadwinner, and going to work means the difference between eating or not, the onset of a child's illness can be a frightening prospect, and may be treated with fear and denial, before time and energy sees the situation accommodated.

Were you believed about your illness?

Were you treated crossly as if your illness was a nuisance, an inconvenience that upset the routine?

Parent's illness

Children often come to fear 'Dad's heart' or 'Mum's wheezes', and can be made to feel that they will make the problem worse by their behaviour. They mustn't laugh too loud, be rowdy, indulge in rough and tumble, play tricks, roll about in bed with parents first thing in the morning, in case they cause deterioration, or worse, death.

What did you know of any illnessess your parents had? Or were they mysterious, not referred to, hushed up?

Did their illnesses become barriers to your being with your parents and having fun with them?

So often what we retain of childhood impressions – smells, bandages, potions, creams, prostheses, coughs, wheezes, noises, dark clothing – remains like a pastiche. Myths about health and sickness spring from these times when things were not explained properly.

What was the nature of parents' or grandparents' or other family members' illnesses?

How much has your experience of other people's illness affected your own attitude to health, sickness, to control or feeling out of control, to life and death?

Accidents

Accidents often stand out in the memory during childhood. Accidents such as burning, scalding, falling, bumping heads or knees, grazes, stings, swallowing foreign bodies, being bitten, often stand out in memory for us and can influence the way in which we subsequently take care of ourselves. We may become overcautious or, in defiance, reckless. Childhood accidents are often accompanied by parental anger and blame – 'I told you not to take your bike on that road/play with the neighbour's dog' – and the association of fear, danger, pain and panic with blame, disapproval or rejection can actually convince us that we are bad or foolish and that we mustn't try anything unusual or difficult or exciting, or we may put acceptance at risk.

Some children are punished for getting dirty or tearing their clothes, long before they are mature enough to look after themselves and take responsibility for such adult ways. One girl I knew, who had had a number of hospital admissions for various illnesses and accidents, subsequently became very depressed and was unable to communicate properly. After some months we did come across the memory of her experience of being twice scalded badly enough to go into hospital for several weeks when she was under ten years old. The most powerful memory for her in her revisitation of the image of these events was her mother's fear and worry, and her overwhelming sense of being burdened by a large number of children and now a child suffering from burns. The daughter vowed inside herself that she would never complain about anything, that whatever happened to her would be her own fault, and she must not burden anyone with her feelings. When she did become unwell later in life she returned to these feelings, and was so overwhelmed by them that she turned inwards into depression.

exercise

Write down any accidents that occurred and the attitudes that accompanied them within your own family. Put them in date order. If necessary, ask about hospital admissions and treatments you received.

Death

Were there any deaths in your family during your childhood or adolescence, which made a big impact upon you? If the person who died was your mother or father, please go to pp. 158–9.

Write something about the person or people you lost, what you lost most at the time, what you most missed. Write something about what you learned from them about the world and about yourself. There might be negative things as well as positive.

How was the event of death handled in your family? Was it talked about?

How soon after the death did you know that the person had died?

Were you told how they died and where?

Were you allowed to go to the funeral, hold flowers, take part?

Could you talk about the death, did you feel free to express what you felt, ask questions, or were you told to be quiet or made to feel you had upset someone too much?

As you flick back the memory album, see yourself as a small person in whose family someone has just died. Imagine yourself, dressed and standing or sitting in a room in your house. Get as strong a picture as you can of that small person and then sit beside them in adult form. Can you feel into your child of that time? Did you:

- ☐ withdraw
- ☐ go silent
- ☐ go off your food
- ☐ throw things around
- ☐ scream and yell
- ☐ have nightmares
- ☐ find it difficult to sleep
- ☐ find yourself clinging to another adult or a soft toy
- ☐ find yourself being drawn to one particular place
- ☐ become ill in any way yourself
- ☐ have fantasies or dreams about the dead person, hear their voice, see them as if they'd come back to life

In the years following the death, how was the person spoken of:

___

☐ never again
☐ never without tears and upset
☐ you were told off for talking about them

Were anniversaries remembered, did you take part in them?

Today, how much do these deaths live on in your memory, or have they been blanked out?

___

Sometimes when a family death occurs early in our life, and we are not allowed to discuss it or mourn, it can produce 'magical guilt' which may unconsciously undermine our later life. It's as if, when very small, we take responsibility for the death (and also for things like the serious illness or miserable life of, for example, a parent or sibling). There are two ways in which this can work. We may have had some negative thoughts about the person who dies, and because we are small and our thinking is not sophisticated we presume that these negative thoughts had something to do with their death, that they contributed to it in some way. We may carry this magical guilt (magical because we couldn't possibly be guilty) unconsciously for years, until we reconsider it and decide to free ourselves from it.

We may also develop a sense of magical guilt because of our own survival: someone close to us died and we did not. Why should we survive and they not? Do we deserve it? Sometimes we think not. This undermining idea may also develop if there is a damaged or very ill parent or sibling in the family. We feel as if our health and wellbeing, or success and happiness, is at their expense, that if we grow up and claim our lives fully it will mean a rejection of the other's life, and that somehow instead we should be limited, damaged and as ill as they were. It's a very uncomfortable idea that our happiness has only been achieved at the expense of someone else's unhappy life. And so it lives on unconsciously inside us, coming out as self-jeopardy, self-sabotage, arranging things so that we do not fulfil our potential or really embrace fully what we can do. In the process of change we have to face those feelings of terror and guilt when we want to carry something through fully for ourselves, but the rewards in terms of self-acceptance and a wider sense of personal horizons are vast.

Sometimes, if a parent dies when we are very small (under eight), we feel guilty about it – especially if we have favoured the living parent and thus feel disturbed about 'gaining' anything from the death). We may then cover our 'magical guilt' by idealisation or hero worship of the dead parent. Sometimes loss of a parent can affect the way we relate to people of that parent's sex.

Loss of a father
Men who have lost a father early in life do sometimes have difficulty relating to other men, particularly older men, and this is more so if there were no other good male figures after the father's death. Sometimes men can grow

155

into adulthood feeling that their masculinity is 'on hold', not yet formed. One man said to me, 'It's as if I'm waiting to grow into a man ... still I feel like this and I'm forty-five.' Some men feel they have to overcompensate for not having had a father, by being more in charge, powerful, strong and successful to make up for the loss. This is often encouraged by the widowed mother, who may view her son as a replacement husband. This means inevitably that the sons grow up way before their time, trying to fit into dead men's shoes that they cannot possibly ever fill. Left behind is the 'fatherless boy' inside them. Unless he is claimed properly, later in life he will still be there – lonely, sad, cut off from a possible mentor, champion, friend, example and mate – possibly dominating the inner life of the man, and preventing him from fully claiming his manliness. Getting in touch with this fatherless boy is an important part of mourning for the loss, which may never have been accomplished. When the father is mourned for by the boy who has become a man outside, but wants to feel one more fully inside, something important happens to the growth process.

A girl who loses her father early in life may later on have difficulty relating to men freely, because of fear of losing them. Sometimes people who have died are made into heroes irrespective of what they were like in life. It may then be difficult for a woman to find a man who lives up to the hero her father has become. In her idealism, no man may match up to him. She may find herself searching for the 'perfect' man only to feel more and more disappointed, but without realising why.

A parent's death may also cut a child off from that side of the family, their values and lifestyle. I have known many people who knew nothing of their father or mother's family because they had died early on. The remaining spouse either could not bear to be reminded of their deceased partner in any form and did not keep up with the family, or remarried and they lost touch. Sometimes in rediscovering what a dead parent was really like, by using old photographs or writing to anyone who knew them, people reclaim the character and flavour of their lost parent and can also claim that part of themselves. The individuality of the dead parent may have been forgotten, or hidden, and the child left may be quite like their lost parent but not realise it and feel odd or different.

At forty-eight, ALICE discovered a host of relations in Russia whom she had never met because her mother had lost contact after her father's death. She found they shared her love of music and dancing, of colour and of melancholy verse, qualities her mother had criticised in her and which she had come to feel were undesirable, extrovert and pretentious. Finding that she did indeed carry some of the essence of her father was a real gift to her.

During therapy, ANNE brought many old photographs of herself as a child with her parents. Her father had killed himself when she was three, and the subject was never referred to. He was made out to be a 'bad lot', unstable and generally no good. She was convinced that not only was there a poor quality running in her blood, but that her father hadn't cared enough about her to stick around.

156

By writing to one of his friends, whom she had discovered quite by accident, she was able to piece together her father's last few days, when he was hospitalised and suffering from shell-shock during the war. He had believed he was responsible for killings in Germany and France which his conscience could not tolerate, and in a frenzy of self-hate and acute misery he had leaped out of an eighth-floor window. This friend went on to describe to Anne some of the horrors of war and the lack of help available to people, such as her father, who were sensitive and conscious of what they were being asked to do.

Anne was herself a pacifist, and this realisation changed her given view of her father's character. One day she brought to the session some old photographs (discovered in the drawer of her aunt's desk) of her father holding her as a small child. Her arm was firmly round his neck and she was smiling radiantly. He was the image of a proud Dad, holding her as if she were the most precious thing on earth. Suddenly tears welled up in her eyes: 'I feel as if I was loved by him,' she said, 'even though I didn't have very long with him!' This realisation made a profound difference to her, and although she had to work through her ever-present fears of rejection from men, and her habit of reading rejection into everything that happened, she had begun the process of building a more solid core to herself, upon which could be built other profound experiences.

Loss of a mother

When a small child loses their mother it is an extremely sad day. Mother, or whoever is mother for us, is the earth into which we were planted. We share her unconscious for the first two years, and she represents our link with care and nourishment in the nursery years. She is the person who makes our emotional and physical world safe. When we lose a mother our most basic world is shattered and we feel frightened, alone and very vulnerable. Although others may take her place and give us mothering, we have lost our link with someone who, whether liked or disliked, was the centre of our world. As she is often the actual centre, family life is seriously disrupted when a mother dies and children may be fostered or farmed out to other families while help is found.

The loss of a mother may live on throughout the following years like a yawning gap. Part of us may stay 'on hold' internally from the time of our mother's death. Our instinctual, emotional and intuitional life may remain undeveloped as we struggle to survive in what to us is an alien world. Later we may look for 'mothering' influences to allow us to complete the unfinished work of our development. We may seek quickly to become mothers ourselves, or conversely, avoid mothering, because we know the excruciating pain of loss.

A man who loses his mother early on may be deprived of a feminine influence, thus not developing the feminine side of himself and finding it awkward to make relationships with women. Whatever the way of compensation, the wound inside will be deep and the need for appropriate mourning and release of sadness is important, as well as looking at ways in which we have overcompensated for the loss in our personality.

Questionnaire: Loss of mother/loss of father

How old were you when your mother/father died?

Describe your world until that point if you can – where you lived, your own room, toys, playtime, school, atmosphere.

What is your most lasting memory of your mother/father? Paint this picture if you can, with all the details you can manage.

Do you feel you have properly mourned the death of your mother/father? Is the mourning process held up in some way:

☐ by the lack of knowledge of facts of the death – time, date, place of burial, nature of death
☐ by not talking enough about her/him, about how you felt for her/him, what you miss about her/him
☐ because part of you has not let her/him go, not accepted that she/he is dead

How does she/he live on in you? By the nature of:

☐ how you live
☐ your work
☐ family
☐ ideas
☐ religion
☐ ambition

Are you still carrying a candle for her/him in an appropriate way, having accepted her/his death and now remembering her/him lovingly; or inappropriately by trying to live as she/he would have, or wanted you to?

Does she/he have an unconscious presence in your life:

☐ through dreams
☐ through ideas of how to 'be'
☐ through 'magical guilt'
☐ as a force that drives you which is not your own

Do you feel you have to compensate for her/his death?

If you feel you have lost out on mothering/fathering, how does this manifest itself in your life?

If someone else took on the mothering/fathering, what is your relationship with that person or people now:

☐ grateful
☐ happy
☐ satisfied
☐ resentful
☐ angry

Take a fresh page in your notebook and write down the positive and negative aspects of the mothering/fathering you received after your parent's death.

How much have you been able to take on 'mothering'/'fathering' or looking after yourself? Are you:

☐ kind
☐ gentle
☐ encouraging to yourself
☐ harsh
☐ neglectful
☐ demanding

Can you change this if needs be?

Parents' relationship

Were your parents happy together? If not, do you know why?

What was the atmosphere like: when they were together; when father or mother came home and one of them was already there?

How long were they married before you were born?

How did they meet?

What were their fantasies about each other – Marilyn Monroe or Clark Gable …?

Did they agree how you should be brought up, or did you go to one parent for some things and the other for others?

Did they have a good physical relationship? Did they touch and hug each other? Did you reckon they were active sexually? Does this idea seem repellent; could you never imagine your parents making love?

Have you wanted to keep them as 'Mum and Dad' and not as ordinary human beings?

Did you prefer one to the other? How did this affect family life?

Did you feel your parents stayed together 'because of the children'?

Did you feel you had to intervene on behalf of one of them, to protect each from the other?

Many of these acts, although not conscious, may have been automatically taken on board. In defining ourselves alongside one parent we may be unconsciously rejecting what it is the other parent stands for. Many children of an alcoholic parent try to take on a role that will protect the non-alcoholic parent or the whole family from stigma, only to find later on in life that they partner an addictive-type person or become at risk themselves from addiction. Again, it is as if the psyche is trying to restore balance and to ask us to claim what it is we have rejected.

Divorce and separation

Children always suffer when there is a marriage or partnership failure. Parents are the small person's rock and security. To have this threatened is devastating. The after-effects can be softened by the way in which parents act afterwards, and how much they each help the children not to feel guilty, or to feel that they have taken sides. Although a parent may say, 'It's your mother I'm leaving, not you', the rejection is no less absolute.

For a girl whose father leaves the family in her early adolescence, there is the additional blow of feeling rejected as a growing woman at the beginning of her maturity. A son whose father leaves the family may feel pulled between mother and father – wanting to see his father, and aware of a new role as surrogate father with his mother. Younger children may feel pulled from one place to another as they have to adapt to new places and faces, and to weekend fathers or mothers. There may be no memory of the actual event, but what will be absorbed is the atmosphere and emotions of those undergoing the separation.

When a mother leaves a relationship, children experience the same feeling of rejection, or a sense that she left because they weren't good enough. If the mother has been the centre of family life it may feel as if the heart has gone out of it, that their world is a very cold, unforgiving place.

If your parents divorced or separated:

How old were you at the time?

Who told you what was going to happen?

How did you feel?

What were your first thoughts, fears? Did you voice them? Did you get heard?

How much did your life change at this point – at home, at school, with friends?

Did you carry on seeing both parents?

Was there a difficult atmosphere or competition between parents for your attention?

Did you feel you had to take sides? Did other family members approach you?

Did you miss the parent you saw least? What was it you missed most?

Did you feel angry inside? Perhaps you did not express it, but do you think now that it came out in some other form – angry outbursts, tantrums, breaking things, banging your head, shouting, spitting, etc.? Do you still feel angry now?

Do you feel it was anyone's fault?

Did you blame yourself?

Could you talk to anyone about it – brothers, sisters or family members?

If you grew up with only one parent, what were your fantasies about the absent parent? What kind of relationship, if any, did you have with them? How was the absent parent referred to:

☐ lovingly
☐ adoringly
☐ disparagingly
☐ with a curse
☐ critically
☐ as a hero/heroine

What effect has this had upon your attitude to, and relationship with, members of the opposite sex, and with members of the sex of the parent you grew up with?

What do you feel about being the child of a single parent:

☐ different
☐ deprived
☐ hostile
☐ ashamed
☐ embarrassed
☐ odd
☐ it was good fun
☐ it was an adventure
☐ it was special

Note what it was that your feelings were specifically attached to.

If either parent remarried, how did this affect you? Did it change your relationship with your parent? If so, how? What did you lose or gain? Were there new family members, step- or half-siblings? How did you feel your place in the family changed?

What effect has the experience of separation and divorce had on you? Has it made you nervous of relationships or a commitment? Has it not made any difference at all?

part five

making the change

10

Writing our life story

By now you have a notebook with lots of writing, some pictures and some ideas of how your life has been so far. You probably feel as if we have been opening a lot of boxes, some of which may have been tightly shut for a long time. You will have been noticing how your internal dialogue operates, both with other people and within yourself. You may be feeling a bit worried about the more painful life issues you were previously unaware of. Do not be alarmed if there seems to be a lot. Trust your own natural self-regulatory processes. Remember what it was that made you pick up this book now and look at your life more closely.

This next stage of the book shows ways in which we will use all that you have been through and put it together in a useful and, hopefully, creative way. You are going to be listening to the different dialogues within yourself and writing out how things have been for you and how you have coped in the only way you knew how. And in your writing you will be nourishing the healthy island within yourself.

Some people protest that they could never write anything about themselves, and are so daunted at the prospect that they don't even begin. It really is amazing how this fear (inbred, I believe, from school, where what we write is always judged) simply melts away when we allow ourselves to play with the images and understandings we already have inside of us and get involved in our own creative process. This next section is for no one but you. You need not show it to anyone. No one will be awarding gold stars or dunce's caps. Once you allow the ideas, images and metaphors to inform you, the sentences will form themselves.

How to start

Get one large sheet of paper or several small index cards. Take your notebooks and flick through, casting your eyes down the pages. Take the words, shapes, images, forms or phrases that leap out at you, or any particular words you seem to have used a great deal. Don't worry about being dramatic or self-conscious. The simpler the phrases you can find to describe something the clearer will be the picture of your life and development, and the more powerfully will the images stay in your mind as you begin the process of change. Some of the phrases that come up in the seven examples of life-story writing that follow are:

Sitting on a volcano – Death waiting at my shoulder – Wild Janet and Controlled Janet – Black hole – Ostrich attitude – Can of worms – Stolen child – Busy Lizzie – Child behind the chair – Anxiously skidding away – Puppy dog – 'What … little me?' – On the treadmill – Scared rigid – On automatic – 'Knew inside'.

Take your own examples and either brainstorm them onto the large sheet of paper, or write each one on a card. When you feel you have enough, begin elaborating upon each phrase or image. For example, 'I grew up in a family where …' or, 'All my life I have felt that …' or, 'Early on I remember feeling that I was …' or, 'I have few conscious memories of my early life, but having begun to question how things are in my life I can guess that I took on the position of … early on'. Give as much detail as you can. Facts, memories, realisations.

When you feel you have the important experiences and facts you would like, put on your 'observer' hat (or ask your co-counsellor), and analyse what effect your early environment and your attitude to this has had on your thinking about yourself, and on the way you act in the world. The process needs to go something like this: because of 'a' and 'b' I believed that I had to be 'x' and 'y'. This has led me to having an 'e' attitude to others and to behave as if 'j', 'h' and 'l'. Your story might then begin something like this:

Most of my life I've been afraid of other people thinking I was stupid. This seems to go back to the time when I was very small and the youngest of several brothers who were all very clever. They used to call me 'dolly dope' and 'slow coach' … I felt helpless and upset. I tried to keep up by running after them and pleading with them to let me come on their outings, but they only laughed and said they could never have girls around. Both my parents were out at work all day and were too tired to listen. They expected my brothers to take care of me when they weren't there. I feel these experiences have contributed to a pretty low self-esteem inside me, which I fight by being quite aggressive and macho. I give as good as I get. I play the toughie and tell crude jokes, but inside I am hurt and sad and I wish someone would notice. But things don't happen by magic and I have to learn a way of being with others, especially men, where I don't have to appear so tough. I would like to risk taking off my tough mask from time to time and just seeing what came out. It's a risk, but I've got to get something to change how things are or I will remain on my own, the butt of others' jokes. I drink far more than is good for me, and I know this is related.

Remember to write something about your healthy island, about the things that you feel good about, are drawn toward positively and about parts of your life you can see from observing that actually you have survived well enough.

The final process is to end your story by writing something about what changes you would like to make and how you might begin to achieve them. This will involve changes in self-perception, in 'faulty' thinking and in false beliefs. There may be a need to recognise and challenge traps such as avoidance or pleasing, isolation or thinking negatively. All involve facing fear. This might be the only change needed.

In dilemmas, we must change from living lopsidedly to being more balanced, finding a third position from our extremes. In snags and self-sabotage we need to learn to recognise times when we unconsciously arrange to spoil our happiness. Name the reciprocal roles that are most problematic for you and name those reciprocal roles you would like to develop. All change means embracing the things we have learned to fear, and reframing our experience by challenging the 'as ifs' that live on from the past.

You may wish to write your story in prose form, or you may prefer to illustrate it with sketches, drawings, cartoons or colour paintings. Alternatively, you may like to write poetry or in a stream of consciousness. Another way is to use a flow chart or tree, showing the passage of your life from roots to branches, with images or words to illustrate what has happened during growth.

Writing the story of our life is always a powerful experience. It can be very moving. When we write the stories and then read them out loud during a therapy session, something quite special happens. Usually it is the first time we have heard exactly how life has been for us, and how our early formed attitudes to ourselves and others have contributed to our present difficulties. And we begin to understand how, by changing these attitudes, we can move away from what we may have believed were indelible footprints or entrenched habits over which we had no control. It may be the first time we have a glimpse that we can be in control of our life. Writing our story also helps to sort out confusion, and to give us a clear vision of how things are and how they have been, rather than our muddling on any old how and hoping for the wind to blow in another direction.

Seven examples of story-writing

The following are seven different examples of life stories taken, with their permission, from people working in therapy. Names and professions have been changed to protect identities. You will see how varied they are and how completely individual. They may help you to get more ideas about how to write your own story.

SYLVIA

I grew up as the *wide-eyed eldest child*, taking everything in and not always sure that things were right for me. I felt special love from my father – when he was home – and from Grandma – when she was allowed to show it to me. But otherwise I don't remember there being a readily available lap or someone to pick me up when I fell. I felt like *the child behind the chair*. It seems my mother was not very enamoured about having children, and perhaps we were a hindrance.

Because now feeling things deeply is very painful for me, and because I didn't have a safe framework in which to express feelings, I have developed ways of keeping feelings at bay. I do this either by *showing off* intellectually, observing and commentating, often very astutely and with flair, but in the head, or by *controlling things rigidly*. This control also extends to relationships, when I sometimes feel anxious and threatened and prone to angry outbursts unless I am in control. I feel as if something is holding me back from claiming my life fully for myself. Perhaps the *child behind the chair*, who represents my deeper and more painful feelings, is wanting recognition, and I perhaps need to relinquish some of my tactics for keeping feelings at bay, even if experiencing feelings is painful. Then I can be more rounded and integrated as a person and move forwards to claim my life, without *anxiously skidding away* from real feelings.

JANET

I grew up in a lovely family where I was the youngest and felt *special*. We were very close and I feel upset when anything happens to break that closeness. When I broke out to 'do my own thing' it hurt my family and I feel really guilty about it. I feel God is punishing me for it by letting bad things happen to me.

I live now as if I have to keep my *feelings bottled up* and bend over backwards to please people and be a good mother, wife and daughter, so I don't hurt people. I feel that if I make trouble, they might stop talking to me, and that is terrifying for me. It reminds me of when I was seven years old in hospital after I had my tonsils out, and when my sisters weren't allowed to see me. I can remember how lonely and frightening that felt, and perhaps that is why the panic attacks I get now often feel as though something is stuck in my throat (like the pain after the tonsils were removed). Sometimes it is as though anger and strong feelings, which I'm frightened to express, get stuck in my throat too. But I daren't let them out because they would hurt people.

In the past two years a number of things have happened that have threatened the safety of my *special family*: my mum's illness, Mike's [husband] dad's death, and the dog biting Shân [daughter]. This has shaken my security and I feel 'anything could happen', as though I am *sitting on a volcano*, or as though *Death is waiting at my shoulder*. I'm very frightened that something bad might happen and that I might die. This probably causes me to have panic attacks (sometimes sparked off by outside events like the boy getting hurt in the playground). At times I have experienced a sort of *black hole*, feeling there's nothing there, as though the anxiety and fear are so great that it makes me cut off from the world around me.

Perhaps I also have this fear of death because I feel my life is passing by and that I'm missing out. Although I like being a good mum, etc., I don't really do anything for *me*. Perhaps deep down I feel if I do what I want it will hurt others, and that I don't deserve to put myself first. But I also believe that there are parts of Janet that want to come out and express themselves. I have tried to blot out *Wild Janet*, but perhaps I need to feel that it's OK to be my full self, and accept all of me, to like myself and express my feelings. And I need to realise that, by doing these things I won't be hurting people and the world won't come to an end.

STEPHANIE

I was born into a family where I somehow seemed to be carrying the pain of generations. My father was born twenty years after a 'black sheep', his father died when he was eight and his mother died in front of him when he was fourteen. My mother came from a family who avoided conflict. Like my father, she was the only graduate of the siblings, and her older brother and sister died young, so she may have had to make up for them in some way.

In our family, Barry, my brother, and Jennifer, my sister, had special places. Barry is the boy and the oldest and he is like the prodigal son who returned from the threshold of death. Jennifer is special because she is the youngest and there was a belief that everyone must be nice to her because she is fat.

I am in the middle, and it feels as though the bad fairy at my birth wished that, no matter what I did, I would never be good enough. Spilling the orange juice as a very little child is still an unexpiated crime for which I cannot gain forgiveness, no matter how hard I try. I was labelled clumsy when I was six and that label has stuck – as 'exotic', 'difficult', etc. Since then, I have always felt that I'm treading carefully, trying to negotiate a minefield laid by my father. I'm aware of this little bright face, eager to live, eager for approval, always being knocked down, bouncing back, but somehow being left behind. So it feels that I have never been able to flourish: I am the shrivelled bud of my poem, who has never been nurtured or allowed to grow properly.

As a result of this, I have become caught in a trap of 'trying to be perfect'. In order to be acceptable, I aim at perfection. I never feel good enough, but still try to please, and eventually feel let down and out of control, which reinforces my sense of worthlessness. So I try again, even harder.

Another way I have of coping is by taking all the knocks on the chin, trying to bounce back no matter how much I've been knocked down, keeping the face bright, even if bits of me are left behind. But in this cycle, I come – more and more – to expect to be hurt, and I have begun to believe that I don't deserve anything good.

In some ways, this is what happens in my relationships. With men, it seems that I recruit those who fulfil the '*prophecy*' of my never being good enough, of deserving nothing for myself and of expecting to get hurt and abused. Getting herpes is like a physical manifestation of this, an emblem of the transaction where I try to give everything that's good and joyful and get back an increasingly more threatening sexual disease. They leave me, and that's my legacy – so now I feel completely diseased. It's the same feeling as I exposed in the 'letter' to my father: 'I tried to think of an image to describe how it felt to be your daughter. What came to mind was that when I was small, over a period of time you slit me open, placed a box of maggots between my heart and my stomach and slowly and deliberately sewed the scar away. Your living legacy was that I could never again feel peace, goodness, satisfactions; just rottenness at the core ...'

In my relationships with women, it sometimes feels that, in the give-and-take equation, the only part available to me is the giving, and I have learned to interpret this as being as valuable as actually receiving. I have the image of me as a plant that grows legs and moves out of the range of any nurture that may be intended for me – so convinced am I that I don't deserve to receive. Perhaps therapy is an opportunity to change this pattern. With a few women, it feels that they are strong enough to force me to receive, although then I feel controlled and trapped as if medicine were being forced down my throat.

One of the family sayings is, 'Stephanie has only one problem and that's Stephanie.' And I have come to believe it in some way, as though I am eternally snagged in trying to be fully myself. I have the feeling that I have never been heard and that I therefore have never been really connected with someone. Deep down I am still the deprived, needy child craving recognition, warmth and acceptance for who I really am. But I daren't show this neediness, so I try to behave well and please and give, treading carefully and thinking before I speak, terrified that the neediness will seep out and make a dreadful mess and doom me to more verdicts that I am clumsy and impossible. I wanted to star in the play, but ended up being cast as the ugly, grunting troll.

I often intellectualise my feelings – carefully releasing words so that I don't overwhelm people. But I am entitled to experience my feelings fully, even if they are very painful. And I do have some profound self-knowledge, as, for example, expressed in my poetry. There are some good bits on which I can begin to build the full, real, lovely Stephanie: my closeness to Barry; the warm, creative and admirable part of my mother which doesn't seem to judge me and is also close and very special to me; and the newly acquired sense that I have an '*angelic overview*' of the minefield – as an allegorical picture of a Tuscan field, with my father laying mines as I fly above, unseen, blowing raspberries at him!

I need to believe in the shrivelled bud – that it is good and valuable at heart, that it will and can grow, that *I* am the one who can nurture it and allow it to flower, and that I don't need to find ways of being special other than as the 'fortunate victim'.

I need to start learning to take as well as to give, without feeling I need to spit out the goodness. I need to feel I can stand tall; the little, bright face can become the full, bright Stephanie.

ALISTAIR

I have very few memories of my early life, and it's possible that much of my feelings from that time have been buried under my need for control. I saw my father as a strict authoritarian, a hardworking research scientist who was rarely at home. My mother seemed to spend most of the time in bed depressed, and was always trying to leave. I followed my very clever brother to boarding school and felt the pressure of expectations to continue in his footsteps. Just before boarding school, at eight years old, I had a frightening experience of racing in the school playground with another boy – the fastest boy – and slipping and hitting my head so badly against a brick wall that I was hospitalised for two weeks and at home afterwards for several months. I have no memory of my parents visiting me, only an overwhelming sense of loneliness and fear of being made to go to school. The one positive element was my nanny, who waited to get married until I went away to boarding school so that she could look after me.

I think that probably the early part of my life was quite deprived emotionally, with the feelings of the child I was at the time unexpressed and unexplored. The natural response to *depriving/rejecting* in relation to *deprived/rejected* is feeling hurt, angry, abandoned, and also needy, jealous, vindictive and destructive. There was no place for expressing any of these feelings. I coped by learning to control everything connected with feelings. The only way I hoped to receive anything for myself was through my achievements. I constantly tried to win. Mother said, 'Let feelings out,' but I didn't believe it. Father said, 'Chin up, son.'

I felt in control and good about myself later on at school, because I could do things well and be in charge. Life at home was extremely difficult, because I was trying to keep my parents together during their increased threats to divorce. And again I felt alone and lonely, and took responsibility for the adults, missing out on getting help for myself over the choice of career.

All this has led me to have an *ostrich attitude* to my inner feelings and needs. I feel that I have to strive constantly to win, that if I stop I have failed. And even when I do win I don't feel satisfaction or pleasure, but the despair of feeling I have to go on winning. I have tied my life up in such a way that I have to stay *on the treadmill*. There is little room for self-reflection, for connecting with the imaginative artist in me, or the creative dreamer. This self-deprivation has resulted in my being terrified of illness, loss and death, as if this were a metaphor for my own creative, free life being snuffed out by the desperate need to control my own life and win. I feel that if I let go it will all go wrong, or be a dead end like the brick wall. I was recently intensely moved by a piece of music. I found out it was called 'The Stolen Child'.

I would like to be able slowly to get in touch with some of the pain of my early childhood feelings, allow them space and air, through therapy, talking or through drawing and painting. I would like to make this vulnerable area within me less anxious and afraid, less the *can of worms* I fear it to be. In doing so I realise I may have to face the fear and sadness and lose some of my more controlling side for a while, until a more appropriate balance is restored and I feel freer to make more comfortable choices for myself as a whole. I would like to be brave enough to open the can of worms, rather than spend my life trying to run away from it and putting myself at risk of exhaustion and ill health.

FREDA

I was the elder of two girls in a family who were very keen to get on in the world and achieve both social and material success. My father was an immigrant from South Africa and my mother had a northern background. Both had quite strong accents which made them self-conscious of how they spoke, and each struggled to overcome this. My sister and I were sent to elocution classes when we were six. We had to practise our vowels on every car journey and to practise reading aloud. We were harshly scolded if we got things wrong, and mealtimes are full of bitter memories of being corrected over the way we pronounced things.

In between my sister and me there had been a brother who lived only a few days. I think my mother never got over it and she was always depressed and looked sad.

My father often said, 'Oh don't go on about it. What will be, will be,' and she would shut up and tears would roll down her face. I think they both would have liked a boy, and my sister and I reacted to this in different ways. My way was to try to be as pleasing as I could, do what they wanted, be the person they wanted me to be. My sister was actually very clever, but never felt she got the encouragement she needed. She felt they were always expecting her to make up for not being a boy, and although she was clever she always spoiled it somehow. She would go in for the exams and mess them up, and she left college in the middle of her training and went into a job that didn't really satisfy her.

I don't remember Mum losing my brother directly, but I remember a lot of muttering and whispering, and that certain things were never referred to. She drummed it into us that having a baby was the worst pain of all, and always went into big emotional silences whenever someone was expecting. It seems as if, looking back on it, Mum did have the exclusive use of the emotional realm. Somehow I always felt that whatever I felt it could never be as bad as her – losing a baby and all that. So I grew up used to putting the lid on what I felt, and later on not being aware I felt anything really. I did somewhere inside me, but it was very deep.

When I was about seven my sister started her illnesses. She used to be ill most of the time, and no one ever knew what was the matter with her. She got labelled a hypochondriac. When she was fourteen she stopped eating and the school sent for my mum and dad, and we all had to go to see a psychiatrist. It was awful. Mum was crying and saying to Lyn, 'Why do you do this to me?' Dad was saying, 'After all we have done for you!' I think I tried very hard to make things better. I tried to keep the peace, to listen to everyone, and it was around this time I began to be expected to be the one who coped. Until then I had been quite clever too, and good at sports, and much was expected of me, that I would bring honour to the family, but I didn't. One of the reasons for this was that I started to put on a lot of weight because I couldn't stop eating. I was very ashamed and tried diets and running it off, but it just made me eat more. Now my parents had two children they were ashamed of and our holidays were pretty miserable. I tried to escape into books and reading, but was called selfish and ungrateful. My mother really wanted me to sit with her most of the day and entertain her; my father was quite pleased if I did this as I took her off his hands, and he was pleased if I tried to encourage my sister to eat. But other than that he had really given up on me, because I was nothing to be proud of.

What I have realised is that I have never really been a small child. I don't think I've had much freedom or fun. I've always had to be very grown up, and this has left me not really capable of letting go. I appear serious and I'm overconscientious. I take on much more than my share of tasks and become a general dogsbody. I'm beginning to see that I've used eating as a way to fill up the emptiness inside, which is related to feeling basically I'm nothing unless I'm serving or giving out to others. The eating has a tyrannical self-punishing role, because I fill myself up when I'm bothered – usually when I'm cross with my husband or I'm taken for granted by others – and then when I'm full up I feel so guilty and disgusted with myself I go for long runs and also take laxatives to try to get rid of the food.

I married a man who is a mixture of the negatives of both my parents – a depressed bully in other words – whom I try to please and serve and long for a few crumbs of affection. My *puppy dog* attitude brings out the bully in him. I take menial jobs because I haven't dared believe that I can do anything better, or that I'm entitled to, and I often catch myself thinking, '*What … little me?* in a *martyrish* way, when I really know inside that I could do something better for myself.

I envy others their success and long to be free, but it's as if something pulls me back. I would like to find out what there is inside me that was there before my little brother died, because it feels as if something of me died at the same time. I would like to give up believing I have to please others all the time in order to gain approval and love. I would like to feel the healthy island inside I sort of know about, instead of the groaning emptiness that gets stuffed with food and then punished for it. I would like to free myself from the guilt about not being a boy, about my mother's depression, about my sister's anorexia and at not being able to make these things better. Oh! And I would SO like to be angry sometimes, to actually know what this feels like and find a way of expressing it without being terrified. And I would like to have a good belly laugh.

MARTIN

It seems as if in my early years I was the centre of my mother's life. My parents married late and I was an only child. My father was away travelling for much of my childhood, and when he was around, took little interest in me. He's still a difficult and uncommunicative man. My mother felt he wasn't intellectual enough and often ridiculed what he said and did. It feels as if she looked to me to fulfil her ideals of what a man should be, in her eyes. I was forced to be centre stage, feeling unconsciously that I must conform and be hard-working and good, perhaps to make up for my mother's disappointment in her husband, perhaps to ensure that I was loved and accepted. As a result, I was often lonely and anxious. I couldn't let it show, but I was intensely bored and bit my nails ferociously, both of which made me feel very ashamed. Negative or angry feelings were a no-no, and I learned early on the habit of pushing away anything negative that might come into my head. I learned to be vigilant about all my actions, to judge myself constantly and to fear things that came into my mind that did not conform to the image I believed was mine to live up to and upon which my survival was placed.

It seems as if in some way I have remained on the *treadmill* developed out of my early life through my professional training, repeating the pattern of trying to live up to what I believed was my lot through excessive hard work. I have believed that I must be all things to all people in order to be a good, caring professional. It seems as if I have felt it necessary to provide what is expected of me from others or I will not be recognised and valued.

Since my mother died, the pattern of things in my life has begun to change. The feelings I have never allowed to the surface have made themselves known, and the natural resentment at having to live my life entirely for others in order to be recognised has made its point. I am frightened by my angry and negative feelings; they seem to rock and threaten my entire equilibrium. I find I cannot control my thoughts, which swing from one thing to another. I can understand that many of these feelings are ones which have been repressed since childhood – they are natural and ordinary feelings. But because they were not allowed earlier on, they still carry with them potency and fear. I find I desperately want to gain control of what is happening to me inside. Some days I want a 'magical cure', when I will wake up and it will all be over; other days I feel despairing and hopeless and am plagued with guilt about what is happening to me, and seek reassurance that all will be well.

Some days it is very difficult for me to acknowledge what is happening to me and that I can have an active part in the transition from survival self, which was very restricting, to being more real, saying what I really think both intellectually and emotionally. I need to believe more in my own capacity to make change, to use my own insight, to listen more directly to the voice inside which allows stillness. My religious faith says: 'Be still ... and know ...'. One of my biggest hurdles is to get over feeling bad and guilty when I am angry, envious, cross or impatient with anyone. I would like a more active relationship with everything that is happening to me, so that I may use some freedom of choice and get to know sides of myself previously in eclipse. The reciprocal role of *powerfully controlling* to *guiltily submissive* is the hardest for me to work with. I sometimes take refuge in helplessness and then my controlling rituals begin. I am working on trying to be noticing/accepting/supporting in relation to myself in order to feel accepted and supported for myself as a whole. Warts, feelings, problems and all. I do know that the strength I have is something of my own which is flexible and not dependent on others.

SUSANNAH

Susannah came into therapy because of issues in relationships where she felt merged and lost her own separate identity. This made her feel frustrated and used. She had recently separated from her partner of fifteen years and was feeling the loss of this closeness and the pull to return to the relationship for the wrong reasons – in order not to have to see her ex-partner suffer or because of her loneliness. She felt that her 'bid for freedom' to be herself was a breakthrough, but it meant she had to face many unresolved issues around close relationships with others and patterns from the past. The following are extracts from the reformulation letter we created together:

We have shared some insights into your experiences in relationships and understood a reciprocal role of striving in relation to a conditional 'other'. Also the dilemma of being either close but taken over and losing a sense of yourself; or, free but alone and cut off. You are particularly in touch with the feelings around this dilemma since your separation from Pete [your partner] last June.

Possible roots for these patterns would appear to be in your fairly strict childhood. You were a shy child kept on reins by an anxious mother. There was a sense of keeping your natural self-expression back in order to please her and keep her happy, as well as yourself safe from her withdrawal if you were not as she wanted you to be for her. This, and the controlling sense of order in the household, may have contributed to a fear of 'making your mark' and 'going over the mark' in your life generally.

The ending of your marriage to John was devastating and the deeply upsetting feelings of hurt and betrayal are still fresh for you, feelings that perhaps you bottle up for fear of mess. The ending of your marriage pressed your fear of 'not being up to the mark' and you seem to have taken more blame and responsibility than is your share. You felt guilty and ashamed at your children not having the secure background you wanted for them.

After your marriage ended you felt vulnerable to your next partner, Pete, and his need to merge and be close was at first comforting. It gave you the 'arms' you longed for and for many years the sense of safety and comfort was welcome and often creative and happy, but you were always aware of the more stifling aspects and your need to be and express yourself differently.

To balance the restricted feeling of needing to please is the need to break free of constraints. Sometimes you recognise 'if I must, then I won't', in relation to joining clubs and networks where conformity is overt. You can be anxious about being 'up to the mark' at work and can envy colleagues who get ahead. Breaking free also carries the fear of hurting others and being seen as mean by those you care about, and it also leaves you with a deep sense of loss and loneliness, and unresolved feelings about your own unmet need in close relationships.

I feel that our work together needs to concentrate upon helping you befriend the anxiety about your own self-expression, your own 'mark' either with others or at work, in order to have a more robust relationship with your own power, self-expression and skills. This will entail recognition of when you restrict or place conditions upon your own response or go along with others' conditions in order to keep the peace.

I feel that the conditional regard for yourself which has led to a restricted striving sense of self needs to be loosened to become unconditional. This may mean experimenting with new responses in order to revise their feeling and impact.

The dream you had early on in the sessions, of you and your manager measuring feet against each other and finding them to be equal, gives us a positive and hopeful image of the authority already present in you. Your description of the qualities of the manager – sharp, open and very nice – can be seen as a reflection of your own robust and lively self that needs permission and space in order to flourish and find her own mark.

At the end of Cognitive Analytic Therapy both therapist and patient exchange goodbye letters that reflect their work over the sixteen sessions. My goodbye letter to Susannah refers to the dream:

At the end of the reformulation is the image from the first dream in therapy, of you measuring your feet with the manager and finding them to be equal. We spoke of this dream as containing a positive and hopeful energy, symbolising the robust and lively authority already present in you, and that one of the goals of therapy was to give this authoritative self permission and space, and to experiment, to learn to make her mark and become integrated.

We have shared a lot of sadness connected with the ending of your relationship with Pete. You often connected with this in the few minutes' mindful space at the start of the sessions. There has also been the anxious questioning – 'have I done the right thing?', followed by connecting with your very strong need to 'break free'. There was the sadness at losing the intimacy of the 'arms' followed by the realisation that the arms could at times be 'conditional tentacles'. There was the fear of being seen as 'mean' and seeing Pete suffer, followed by realising you had merged asking for your own needs to be met with being mean or unreasonable.

So the work of therapy has been to recognise your relationship with 'other' and how you can lose a sense of yourself and the reality of your own feeling by disappearing into others' needs. We imagined that this was a pattern of relating learned from your relationship with your anxious mother, for whom you had to make things alright, whose arms were there only if conditions were met. It was hard for you to develop a safe sense of your own needs and voice, or to make your own mark without feeling guilty or selfish. In allowing an understanding of these patterns you have opened to the harshness of the 'stolen ease of being' and begun to allow a kindness to yourself. You could also see that the gap left by unmet need had been filled with an idealisation of how things 'should' be in terms of duty to others, in order to feel alright yourself. From this position you were able to articulate the wisdom that came from the recognition and acceptance of your own feelings. You said: 'Freedom comes from within myself, in accepting the reality of what I feel and seeing things as they are rather than how I feel they "should" be. Right now there is too much anxiety, sadness and longing in me to be comfortable. So I need to wait.'

At session eight you had the dream about the stolen bag. We shared a lot of sadness at the feeling of this dream, of having to plead to have back what was rightfully yours. In the dream you did get back fully what was yours. And this dream was followed by two others that seemed to reflect both your fear of danger and also, like the first dream, a balancing factor. In one, under pressure from others, you were climbing along a ledge over the sea and were frightened. Then after rounding a corner you drop down onto the sand and the feeling was of relief at being finished with danger.

The reciprocal roles of conditional/controlling/merging in relation to restricted with 'stolen sense of ease', and critical bully in relation to hurt victim, have softened and a new psychological position of playfully caring for yourself in relation to meeting your own need joyfully and growing your own 'arms' has been created.

So the post-Pete part of therapy has been about consolidating this new sense of self. We made a new diagram that included 'growing my own arms, supporting my needs separately from others; being mindfully free to make my own mark'. There is the image of your own kingdom, your own path and an ease of being. You are also aware of putting more energy into making your mark at work and making plans to travel next year and deciding what you would most like for yourself.

And last session there was the opportunity to re-explore the way you can experience a 'silenced emptiness' when you fear not knowing what to say and the 'other', me in this instance, is in the position of being judging and demanding. I was glad that we had the time to share this reciprocal role and the understanding that rather than being empty and not knowing what to say, it is when you get hooked into the reciprocal role of being emptied by 'other' that you lose your voice and a hold on your liveliness.

Susannah wrote the following in her 'goodbye' letter:

Two significant dreams brought me in touch with my own desperate longing, indeed, pleading, to reclaim my precious, lost, stolen, self. I liked 'ease of being'. I dreamed of escaping from danger, fear and demands, by 'breaking free' from the narrow ledge above the raging sea by jumping down and experiencing the safe, firm sand under my feet. I went on to see my own vast kingdom in front of me, green, irrigated and open for exploration into the far distance, with no set paths or restrictions. Depicting this marked the reawakening interest in painting.

If I had checked my lung capacity before therapy and again now there must be an increase in volume! I am learning to breathe in as well as out, and to channel the air, nourishing in itself. Getting to the end of therapy made me wonder if I would manage alone and last week heightened how vulnerable I am in relation to questions, demands or expectations of 'the other' and how I can feel anxious and depleted. I know, however, that what I have experienced in therapy cannot be taken away, that the kingdom is all around me and I am walking on ... The concept of Maitri has been important. I have never known the unconditional in my life, let alone the unconditional acceptance of myself – thoughts, emotions, reflexes and behaviour. Some of the time it eludes me, but when I can enter this freeing, caring place I am filled with tears of relief and gratitude. Thank you for this gift. I know it is mine forever and what better way to navigate a new journey – to navigate a change of path.

You will see that everyone's story is quite different, that the images, phrases and what each made of the different experiences was highly individual. **Your story is your own and you need to claim it as your own story and place on the journey so far.** It should contain enough of the essence of what you feel now and something of an understanding of how that has come to pass, even if you have to hypothesise because you cannot know all the facts. (Even when facts are known everyone will make something different even of the same life events.) Include in the story both how you feel things have come to be as they are in your life, and something about what you hope to be relieved of and what you would like in the future.

11

Targeting the procedures that create problems and deciding on aims for change

We have been seeing throughout this book how we can name early beliefs such as 'Only if I behave in a certain way (please others, avoid action) will I survive' and that these early beliefs keep us in a placation trap and possibly depressed. Whilst pleasing may have been an important survival mechanism, these old beliefs and procedures shape our everyday behaviour and restrict us.

This chapter is devoted to naming the restricting procedures that we take for granted and setting realistic goals for change. We will look at how Sylvia, Janet and Alistair made charts of their problem procedures and developed their aims for change. In Chapter 13 we will see how Alistair, Martin, Freda and Susannah also made use of diagrams to focus upon the way their procedures grew into the sequences that led to problems.

You may choose to make either a chart for rating procedures and aims for change, or a diagram of the problem sequences as you recognise them. Once they have been created, it is useful to carry these diagrams or charts around with you, so that you can turn to them when you feel stuck, or feel the old responses and problems coming on. Recognising where we are in our learned sequences is the beginning of change, however far down the sequence we have travelled. **It is never too late to stop, revise and reverse!** When you have read Chapters 11 and 12, choose the best way to set about focusing on the areas in your life that need revision and change.

It is important to remember that what we seek to change are the **learned procedures that maintain the traps, dilemmas, snags and unstable states that limit our life and cause problems. It is essential to focus upon the learned procedures rather than the problems the procedures create.** For example, our problem may be an eating disorder, but the procedure underlying it may be that we bottle up feelings for fear of making a mess, or we stuff down anger for fear of being rejected. It is the procedure we need to address and change. We must stay off the symptom hook!

It's important too to be realistic and to start small, to start with what we *can* do rather than go for trying to sort out something large. Once we begin to change even the simplest thing, other changes follow, like the ripple effect of a stone on water.

Sylvia's target problems and aims

Problem procedure: *Either* in touch with the child and feeling and being in pain; *or* using my telescope to avoid.

Aim: To feel safe enough to let the child come out from behind the chair and be part of adult Sylvia.

Problem procedure: The 'Telescope' a 'performance trap'.

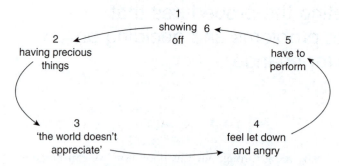

Aim: To value and love my whole self and listen to myself, first.

Problem procedure: *Either* controlling by being rigidly intolerant and tough on people; *or* being controlled and feeling I'm having my hair pulled.

Aim: To be aware of and trust my own strength, and not to take the wrong things too seriously ('tiger energy').

Figure 11.1   Sylvia's diagram of her problem procedures underlying her angry outbursts

Sylvia decided to look at her life when she began to have angry outbursts with people at work. She had also been aware for some time of feeling depressed and sad, and of a sense of meaninglessness in her life. As she worked with her reformulation (p. 167) she became aware of her inner creative spirit, her 'tiger'. Being in touch every day with her tiger has helped Sylvia to feel more 'whole', to become less depressed and to give up her 'performance' self. She has been much less frustrated and is less likely to burst out angrily (Figure 11.1).

Janet's chart (Figure 11.2) targets her problem procedures and aims. She monitored them over a period of a few weeks and they all changed dramatically. Janet had sought help from her GP because of her panic attacks, and was referred for short-term therapy. She identified with the 'doing what others want' trap and the 'I'm bound to do things badly' trap, also with the keeping things bottled up or making a mess dilemma. She also identified with intense, extreme and uncontrollable emotions and with swinging into emotional blankness.

After four months of working with her story and her target procedures and aims Janet was able to do without her valium! Her focused therapy helped to free her from the guilt which had led to her fear of death and panic attacks. In her final 'goodbye' letter to her therapist she wrote that she 'had a bad day now and again' but was always able to say what she felt and was enjoying the release and freedom after years of never having her say.

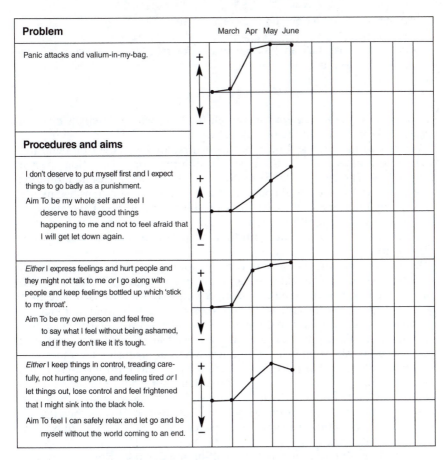

Figure 11.2   Janet's chart of her target problem procedures and aims

Alistair's target problems procedures and aims were as follows:

Problem 1:   High blood pressure and exhaustion.
Procedure: Overwork to stave off anxiety, fear, illness, death; no time for myself, anxiety leaks out, in the car, at weekends.
Aim: Make space for some anxiety and fragility to be accepted. Practise five minutes of relaxation.

Problem 2:   Eternal treadwheel and depression.
Procedure: Constantly striving in order to win, to cope with feelings of failure and inadequacy.
Aim: (a)   To recognise 'can of worms'. Recognise when activity is accelerated in order to cope with 'can of worms'.
         (b)   To find a container for these feelings (therapy).

Problem 3:   Can't let go and relax in any way.
Procedure:
Aim: Take half an hour every day for reflection, and writing in the
                journal.

Alistair also made a diagram for himself (p. 186), which describes his main traps. His story is recounted on page 170.

When you have worked out your own three or four target problem procedures and aims for over the next few months, copy the rating sheet in Appendix 4. The chart is divided into five sections which can be monitored weekly for twelve weeks as if you were in a CAT therapy. The chart begins after writing the life story. Each week, mark on the chart how you have managed, first in terms of **recognition**, then, secondly, in terms of **stopping and revising**, and lastly, the **aim. The symptoms or problems are not our primary aim at first**.

Remember, the aim may be simply to be more aware of the procedure itself, or it may be just to give yourself half an hour a day for self-reflection. Once your recognition of the issues is stronger you may find yourself able to be more specific about the aim, or to add to how the aim is brought about. For example, Susannah found that whilst her initial aim was to bear the anxiety of 'longing to merge' in relationships and her fear of hurting the other by being separate, she found that after a few weeks of practising awareness, she was able really to listen to what her own feelings and intuition were telling her. She said, 'I can just feel right now that I am not ready' and the value she could place on her own authentic feeling was vitally important. This is what happens when we start to recognise and challenge old habits: our healthy island starts expanding. The space and awareness we gain helps us in ways we could not anticipate.

Alistair is aiming to move from his half-hour a day reflection to allowing a space for the feelings he has never had time for. He has chosen to use music and poetry to help him with this and to keep writing about what happens. His next step will be to accept these feelings and find ways to integrate them and use them creatively in his everyday life, and ultimately to live more harmoniously with them.

12

Putting a diagram in your pocket

This chapter looks at how to make diagrams of the way you cope with inner conflicts. Having written about your life, you can find it very useful to create a working diagram of exactly how you have learned to cope with difficult feelings and core pain.

To make the diagram we need to find words to describe first the problematic reciprocal roles we have understood that we tend to bounce around. Then we need to put in the ways we have tried to cope with early care patterns, patterns such as striving or placating. And alongside this we need to remember what our core pain is and see how each of the traps, dilemmas, snags or unstable states often maintains our core pain and that we are caught in a management loop that does not release us from the deeper emotional pain.

Start your diagram by imagining trying to explain to me your findings from the psychotherapy file and Personal Sources Questionnaire. Together we will find the best words to describe your reciprocal roles and the procedures that maintain the pain caught up in them. Make a start by drawing out two or three boxes that look like the example in Figure 12.1. Choose two or three of what you feel are your main problematic reciprocal roles. Draw out one box for your 'healthy island' and healthy reciprocal roles, such as *listening* in relation to *listened to, giving kindness* in relation to *receiving kindness, caring* to *cared for.*

You might like to consider how you would describe the core emotional pain. Freda described her core pain of worthless/rejected as being maintained by the reciprocal role of *'deprived* in relation to *depriving'.* And *'feeding off* in relation to *fed off'.* She received no unconditional love from either parent and very early on took the position of the 'parental child', taking responsibility and magical guilt for her mother's loss and depression. She also recognised the *tyrannising/controlling* in relation to *tyrannised/controlled/restricted* role where her anger was turned against herself and the only way to express this was in her eating disorder. Here she was in a cycle of *rejecting* in relation to *rejected as worthless* and *controlling via placating* in relation to *controlled/kept guiltily caught.*

To find words for your core pain you need to feel into what, inside you, is your greatest fear and also your most overwhelming feeling of emotional pain. If you imagine being once again in the world of your childhood, you

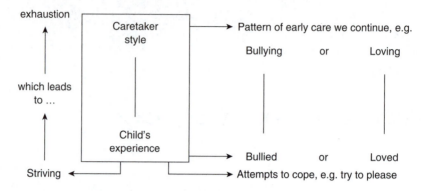

Figure 12.1   'Caretaker style and child response' example of learned reciprocal roles

might find the words to express your painful core feelings. These would describe the feelings you have worked hard to get away from through the learned procedures.

Some of the following examples might help find your own words:

afraid, terrified, lost, abandoned, forgotten, deprived, abused, left, rejected, lonely, in pain (physical, mental and emotional), angry, furious, in a rage, spitting, shrieking, yelling, crying, screaming, dropped, teased, tantalised, tyrannised, longing, waiting (to be held, loved again, picked up, nurtured, for Mum/Dad/ other), hungry, starving, empty, needy, intense

Spend time feeling into the words that best describe what you might be carrying inside. There will be other words you will wish to add to describe how you feel. If this does not come easily to you, ponder on this page and its ideas, and let your unconscious inform you of how to address your core pain. A sense of the reciprocal role procedures that maintain the pain may emerge naturally. An image, word or dream may come to you. Or you may just come across the word you need by keeping in touch with the feelings you have and by letting them indicate the right description.

Sometimes we are able to describe the nature of our core pain by first outlining the learned reciprocal roles that maintain it. For example, a demanding perfectionist role may be our way of coping with, but also maintaining, a harshly judged self, where core pain is experienced as humiliation and worthlessness.

The next stage in making your diagram is to describe the means of surviving the core pain which often lead to forming traps, dilemmas or snags, and to use arrows showing the sequence of what tends to happen. The self-survival procedures tend to loop back again to the core pain. You will see illustrated in Freda's diagram (Figure 12.2) that she coped with her inner pain of rejection and deprivation first by pleasing others, and later by overeating when placation no longer relieved her feelings and the core state feelings included depressed

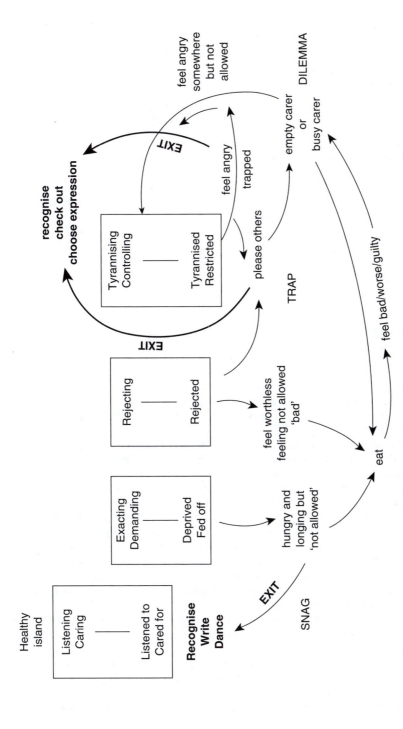

Figure 12.2 Freda's diagram

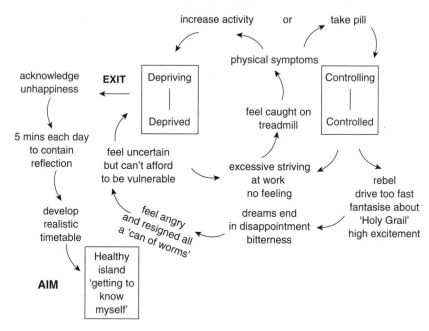

Figure 12.3   Alistair's diagram

and worthless. The diagram shows how each of her procedures, or coping tactics, while useful when she was small, in adult life trapped her in an actual circular trap, or were split into a dilemma. Each old coping pattern ultimately led her back to her inner pain.

Freda could see how the 'doing as others want' trap led to the perpetuation of her depression and restricted her own life. By using the diagram every day she could see exactly where she was at a time of difficulty or conflict. The eating to cope with the emptiness and feeling 'bad' made her guilty, for which she was self-punishing, and then felt alone. She 'snagged' her life in a way that deprived her of using her own creative skills. Her way out of the map, the exit point, was through recognising her ability to be able to cope, as she had done all her life. But instead of using it in a placatory way for others, she began looking at it as a natural skill that could be used to create a better framework for her attitude to herself and for her life practically.

Always try to keep your diagram simple. The most important thing is for it to work for you.

If you recognise that you avoid things, work out the feelings you are trying to avoid and plot the way you continue avoiding them in your life, as shown in Figure 12.4.

Alistair is currently working on his life story and diagram (see Figure 12.3). Because he has organised his life through excessive striving and control he has had no time for reflection, for letting his natural, spontaneous thoughts come to the surface, or for following his ideas. He had to suppress all of his

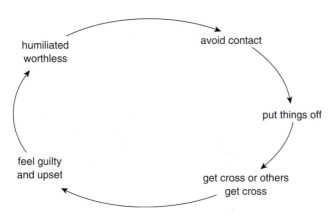

Figure 12.4   Martin's avoidance diagram

vulnerability early on in life, mainly because of a very tense family situation and because both his parents were largely absent. He had a very clever older brother, and he picked up early on that if he did not strive to win he would be left behind and regarded as a 'failure'. Thus, any feeling of which he was not in strict control has come to be seen as a failure. When we met he was so afraid of the out-of-control feelings that he had shut them off completely. They would 'leak' out, through 'odd' thoughts, dreams, irrational fears for his own health and a great flood of fear when two close friends died suddenly.

Alistair is now able to acknowledge how unhappy he has been and to look at what this means in terms of his life. This acknowledgement alone has allowed him to review the job he does (he works a fourteen-hour day every day, starting at 5 a.m.). Previously he had been 'on automatic', and his internal needs had reflected themselves in health problems such as a duodenal ulcer and abscesses. He could not allow himself proper time to take care of these matters, or to look holistically at the implications of his symptoms for his general stress level. Had he continued to deny his needs and difficulties, he may have developed an even more serious health crisis.

Martin had great difficulty with swings of mood and with obsessional thoughts, in particular his preoccupation with the word 'baptism'. He had been baptised a year before the onset of his depression, something he came to understand that was very important to him and an expression of his own need and devotional attitude. But he had always felt guilty about it because he believed it went against the wishes of both his wife and his mother. His chart shows how his survival-self mode was either to please others he considered 'perfect' and strong, or to work excessively hard to meet 'perfect' standards. Both survival modes restricted his healthy island and natural development and contributed to making him dangerously exhausted. He was caught between his desire to be himself truly and the guilt he felt when this conflicted with the two most important and powerful people in his life, his mother and his wife. The most intense period of his depression began after his mother died. Although free of her very tight hold, it was still inside him in his self *restricting*

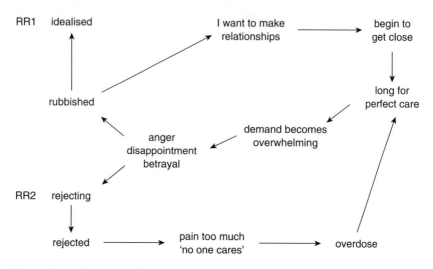

Figure 12.5 Karen's diagram: two reciprocal role patterns

in relation to *restricted* reciprocal role. This contributed to panic and guilt for wanting freedom to be himself. His guilt was unconscious and his map helped him see how much guilt he carried for every negative thought about anything or anyone. Every time he had the tiniest negative thought he would punish himself with feeling bad or by tormenting himself with the word 'baptism'.

One of the most wonderful experiences about the nature of suffering is that within the nature of the suffering is the key to the way out. Although the word 'baptism' could be used obsessively and as a punishment for not being 'good enough', Martin also needed to be 'reborn' into his real self and initiated into the adult freedom of choice about feelings in full range, without guilt.

Martin has managed to contain the extremes of his mood swings, and has been able to explore with his wife ways in which he restricts himself within their relationship and how she can be invited into the restricting role initially occupied by his mother. Restricting can make him feel contained and safe, and he panics when he is apart from his wife or with nothing to do; but restricting also makes him feel furious and trapped and he once again becomes the 'little boy'. Over time he has processed this change and now has a wider range of feelings without guilt. He does not have to be 'perfect' or centre stage in order for life to be meaningful.

Karen's diagram is shown in Figure 12.5. Karen was recommended for focused therapy after taking a number of overdoses. She had a pattern of making intense and immediate relationships with men that ended explosively after just a few weeks, when she would then make an attempt on her life. Karen was only eighteen, but had had five admissions to casualty over the previous two years. Her family background was unsettled. She had been fostered at age four, then adopted by a couple who split up when she was eight. She was 'parcelled round' to family and friends, but never settled anywhere. Two 'uncles' had sexually

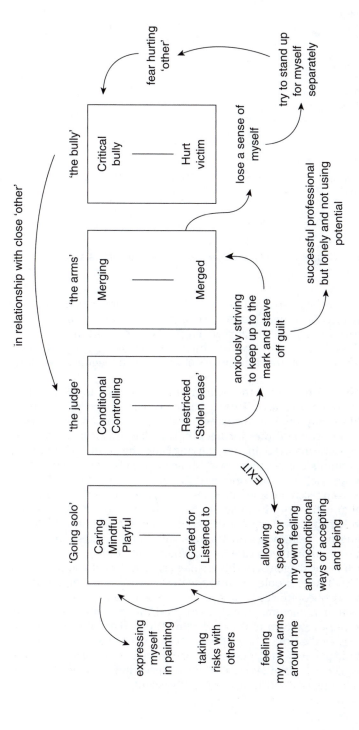

Figure 12.6 (a)   Susannah's first diagram

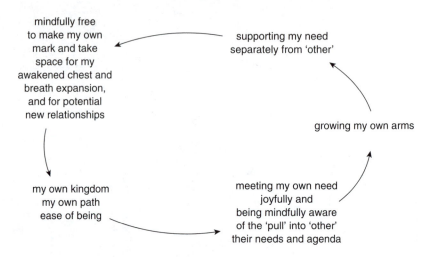

mindfully free
to make my own
mark and take
space for my
awakened chest and
breath expansion,
and for potential
new relationships

supporting my need
separately from 'other'

growing my own arms

my own kingdom
my own path
ease of being

meeting my own need
joyfully and
being mindfully aware
of the 'pull' into 'other'
their needs and agenda

Figure 12.6 (b)   Susannah's post-therapy diagram: the healthy island

abused her and she had also developed a pattern of bingeing and starving as a way of trying to control her confused feelings. As a result, by the time she began secondary school, and all her peer group were pairing off, she felt worthless, unlovable and that no one really wanted or loved her. All she could identify with were stories from romantic novels or an idealised longing for what we called 'perfect care'.

A diagram helped her to see the pattern of her responses to relationships which had led to her overdoses. This gave her a certain degree of stability, so that she could see why and how the patterns had emerged and begin the work of receiving 'good enough' care for herself. This diagram helped Karen see what patterns were involved in her starving/bingeing routines. What she began to work through in her therapy was how her idealisation had become a substitute for her grief at the loss and deprivation of her early life, and how it prevented her from receiving something that was 'good enough' for her needs.

We read Susannah's story in Chapter 10. In diagram (a) we see what she worked on in her therapy. Diagram (b) reflects how she was now exploring and nourishing her healthy island through mindful awareness, and using 'her own arms' symbolically to care for her emotional need.

Go over each of the diagrams in this chapter again and see if you can follow them clearly. Each stage should result in the next one by following the arrow. In a trap, the way of coping leads back to the core emotional pain, sometimes after quite a detour. A dilemma (the either/or, or if/then) results in a lopsidedness that also causes a return to the core pain. And a snag tends to keep the core pain as it is all the time. The exit point begins when we simply **stop** and recognise the old patterns. Revising the old patterns and trying something different follows. The exit point allows us time for space and self-reflection. This is also the beginning of nourishing our healthy island.

13

Techniques for working through the process of change

So far, we have described how to write the story of your life, how to make a chart of problems with aims for change, and how to make a diagram with exits for change. Also, we have talked about looking at these charts or diagrams each day and monitoring yourself in problem areas.

What we need to look at next is how we process the change we are looking for. How do we actually go about making change when some of our habits are lifelong and set? Please be encouraged by three things:

1. The human mind is capable of far more journeys, explorations and disciplines than is generally understood. Once you make a start on self-awareness and on the mindfulness practices designed to consolidate awareness you may travel further than you ever imagined.
2. The ripple effect – throw one small stone into a pond and the ripples are far reaching. Once you begin to change the smaller things – often the traps or dilemmas – other changes follow naturally.
3. Philosophical thinking such as ancient Taoism and modern psychology both share an understanding that nature – and humans are part of nature – abhor a vacuum and that the principle of homeostasis – meaning movement and balance – operates to prevent rigidity or lopsidedness. Life prods us to keep in balance. It gives us wake-up calls to keep aware. If we 'go with the flow' in respect of this principle we find ways to embrace dark and light, sun and shadow, the greys, blues and bright colour of different phases.

Perhaps you have had your jolt and this is why you are reading this book now; perhaps the book itself will act as a jolt. Perhaps it will work by confirming what you already knew somewhere but hadn't put into words. If you are seeking change and the change means making your healthy island more spacious, nourishing this space will help you. So often we get bewitched by the fear of change and allow ourselves to be limited by what others will think. Buddhist philosophy tells us that we already have all that we need, it's just that we don't see it. Clearing the mirror through which we look at ourselves is a good start to clearing space to get to know ourselves, freer of conditions.

There are many different ways of bringing about changes and shifts in consciousness, and there are many therapeutic styles which can assist in this. In this chapter we will look at a number of these, and you may be drawn more to one than another. **There is no one way of working, the best way is the one that works for you.**

I have divided this next section into **active** and **reflective** ways of processing change.

Reflective ways of processing change

Self-monitoring

We have mentioned the method of self-monitoring throughout these chapters as a way to help us develop awareness of our different patterns. It is best to choose something specific to monitor, like depressed or negative thinking, or the 'doing as others want' trap. Buy a small notebook that you can carry around and refer to easily. When you recognise the trap or dilemma write down the time of day, place, who if anyone you are with, what else is happening and **what you are thinking and feeling**. Keep this notebook for a week before looking at your entries. Sometimes we have to keep up the monitoring for three or four weeks before we can see any kind of pattern emerging.

The main purpose of self-monitoring is to increase your awareness of your own patterns and tendencies. With increased awareness you can become more astute about how one thing leads to another in terms of your own and others' reactions, and in time you can halt or change the process, once you have understood how it operates.

What do you monitor? Unwanted thoughts; strange sentences; odd feelings; obsessional words or acts; physical symptoms such as headaches, tinnitus, chest pain, feelings of nausea; forgetfulness; depersonalisation (feeling I am no one ... losing my sense of self); anxiety; fearfulness; not wanting to go out; ways of eating. These can all be monitored so that you can look at this aspect of yourself more clearly.

When you have your notebook with its entries, read through and select one or more words or phrases that you use frequently, and identify a repeated theme, person, time or place that links the monitorings. For example, through self-monitoring one man learned that his tinnitus grew worse whenever he was unable to be assertive. It became a reminder to express himself and not be passive or placatory.

Journal-keeping

Use a larger notebook or perhaps a special kind of notebook or hardback exercise book in which to write your thoughts, dreams and ideas. This is for the record of your inner life, what you are feeling and experiencing, what kind of thoughts you are having, what happens to you as you journey to know yourself more fully. You may like to keep your journal each day, or just for when you feel things strongly or have an idea about something.

At times of personal investigation or assessments, and particularly in times of crisis and despair, we often find that something in us tries to express itself in the form of symbol, metaphor or image. Some of us are drawn to write poems or pieces of prose; some write streams of consciousness with no particular process in mind, just letting what comes out flow; some like to doodle or draw, paint or colour what is happening to them. Whatever form it takes and however bizarre it may seem, don't be put off. Let whatever wants to, find form inside your journal. You may not understand it fully at first, but as time goes on, and certainly when you look back on it, it will give you a vital link with your inner world and to whatever meaning you might be seeking.

Mindfulness

Mindfulness, which was mentioned earlier in this book, is an ancient practice rooted in the Eastern spiritual disciplines. Its contribution in modern Western life is growing. The practice itself involves our concentration. We choose what is to be the object of our mindfulness and we focus on it, just as it is, without trying to change or control it. The object of mindfulness may be a sound, an image, a feeling, the body or breath. The purpose of mindfulness is to slow down the mental processes and hurry sickness that often dominate us. In mindfulness practice we allow thoughts to come and go, we just notice them, recognising them as 'just thoughts' and return to the object of our mindfulness. We do not follow thoughts, we release ourselves from being slaves to our thoughts. The results of mindfulness may not appear significant, but over a period of time we may find calm and clarity.

Vietnamese Zen Buddhist teacher Thich Nhat Hanh writes and speaks about the nourishment offered by mindfulness practice. He speaks of going back to the island within. In this practice we are nourishing our healthy island and we learn that in times of crisis we can maintain the practice rather than being swept away by our thoughts and feelings. This does not mean we are not affected by crises or that we do not feel. Mindfulness offers us a vehicle through which our experiences may be felt, processed and expressed. It can bring a quality of peace and relaxation into our lives, although this is not an aim in itself.

You will have read how Amanda and Susannah both used mindfulness as a way to help their more difficult feeling states.

In Appendix 3 there are mindfulness practices you might like to try: the Body and Chair Exercise; Mindfulness of Breathing; and the Unconditional Friendliness or Loving Kindness Meditation.

It's not possible to say more about learning mindfulness in this book, but some useful books are listed at the end of this book on p. 259.

Focusing

Another practice, close to mindfulness, is focusing. The technique of focusing can help us to be present with a direct experience of our emotions. This technique was developed by Eugene Gendlin (a student of Carl Rogers) and honed by John Welwood, who recognised its close connection to mindfulness. Here, the core pain (or soft spot) is connected to through becoming aware of a felt sense. In its simplest form focusing offers us a way of staying with a body sensation, a feeling or a word in a particular way that allows us to explore more of the initial presentation and without judging it or trying to change it in any way. In *Nothing to Lose* Nigel Wellings describes it in the following way:

> focusing can be done in a moment and brings our awareness close to our experience. Right now I am feeling a tightness in my throat which is best named with a sort of growling word. If I stay with it I find that it reveals a more hidden panicky emotion which then slowly fades away. Thus with only a minute spent on the technique I have gained two things: knowledge of what was really bothering me and an experience of allowing myself to experience it directly and witness it passing away. (Wellings and Wilde McCormick, 2005)

The following are steps that can be used for focusing, either on your own or in co-counselling:

1. **Clearing a space.** We ask: How are you/am I right now? This often evokes something of the 'story'. Concentrate upon what is underneath this by mentally scanning the body, particularly torso, chest, solar plexus, to see if a felt sense comes forward. If there is more than one, just stay with the one that demands more attention.
2. **Felt sense.** It's alright if the felt sense isn't clear. Just stay with it being diffuse and fuzzy. Go right up to it, but not so close as to become it.
3. **Handle.** Next we try to find the quality of this diffuse sense. Allow a word, phrase or image to emerge from the fuzzy felt sense. A word that describes the quality, such as sticky, tight, growling, shrinking, full. Stay with the felt sense as long as it takes for the word to emerge. (This is different from conceptually finding a word and labelling.)
4. **Resonating.** Then hold the word, phrase or image against the felt sense to check that they really resonate with each other. Changes may occur during this process. Continue carefully until there is a fit. An indication of this may be a small sigh or a feeling of 'yes'. Give it time, feeling it completely, the physical felt sense and its expression.
5. **Asking.** Sometimes the release of energy as we consciously connect with what is really going on in us gives us a deeper understanding of our situation. We can also try asking 'What does this felt sense need?' It is important that the answer comes from the felt sense itself and not the rational mind. Give lots of time. A real felt shift comes when the answer emerges from the felt sense and there is a sense of physical satisfaction and connection.
6. **Receiving.** Acknowledge the process that has just been experienced or shared, however large or small. Be still at this point so that true receiving has time to take place.
8. **Returning.** Give time to return to everyday consciousness. In co-counselling check that your colleague is ready to do so.

Imaging, visualisation, active imagination and body drama

There is no situation to which the creative use of your imagination cannot be applied usefully and safely. We all have this capacity, even though so many people say 'I've got no imagination'. To test yourself, close your eyes for a few minutes and lean back in your chair. Imagine yourself picking up a lemon from your fruit bowl. Place the lemon on a board and take a sharp knife out of your drawer. With the knife cut the lemon in half. Pick up one of the halves and put it in your mouth. Notice what is happening. Is your mouth watering, are your eyes tightening or squinting, is your tongue curling? If it is, then you have just imagined yourself eating a lemon with a full body reaction. There is no lemon in sight, so where did that reaction come from? Imagination!

Negative thoughts and damaging internal views are perpetuated by the combination of our thoughts and the power of the imagination to make them more concrete or more dramatic. In phobic disturbance and anxiety the most infectious negative thought is that 'It will happen again'. Many people who are fearful and seek to avoid their fears have images of what might happen to them 'if'. They will tell you, 'Oh I can't do that ... I'll be sick ... I'll fall off ... someone will come after me'. The range of our imaginings can be from imagining the worst questions as a schoolgirl in an exam to the pathologically jealous wife or husband who sees the imprint of the non-existent lover wherever there is a space.

Imagination, except in the world of the arts and music, is often dismissed or trivialised as in: 'It's only imagination ...'. Others consider it dangerous and, because it's non-scientific, it has had only a shadowy place in medicine or psychology. The power of the imagination is often feared. In the past ten years we have seen a debate in psychology and psychotherapy about 'false memory'. This centred on whether images and experiences raised in therapy represented literal 'truth' or were the product of an imaginative process misinterpreted by therapists. Memory is always selective, and it has a mercurial quality. Images and sensations, as we have seen from the section on focusing, have an individual world of their own meaning. We need ways to use its gifts to release us. We need to make sure we do not over-identify with the products of our imagination and harden down or take literally those images and sensations that emerge. These are just stepping stones to information.

> **If you discover through the exercises in this book that you have difficult painful memories or flashbacks, particularly of violence and abuse, please go very slowly and find someone safe, respectful of your needs and well qualified to work with you.**

Imagination has the power to bring forward hidden images from years ago that return when something triggers them. We have seen how imagining a lemon can make us salivate, we have seen that imagination can recapture the original fear of agoraphobia or the terror of a panic attack. If imagination can do all these things it can also be used as a resource and work for us positively.

Take your notebook and look at the number of images and descriptive words you have used, the number of times you have written, 'I feel like a ...' or 'It's like a ...'. You have created images and are already in the world of the imagination. When you are out walking, let yourself look at the shapes of the landscape rather than seeking to name trees and plants or count the number of bird species. When people are talking to you, whether on the television or in your life, see if you can find an image for them – something they remind you of, or a shape or colour. When you listen to music, lie on the floor and let the music conjure up images. When you are reading, read fiction, romance, poetry, fairy tales, children's stories, texts that are fun and full of simple wonder, that make you laugh. Getting into the realm of the imagination means getting out of the rational, logical, overfocused way of thinking. When you go to sleep at night, ask yourself for a dream.

Using the powers of the imagination positively and safely

Reframing problems through visualisation

You will already have used your imagination to create your life story and your diagrams. Choose now one or more of the difficulties you have. If you have identified with the 'doing as others want' trap, imagine yourself in a situation with someone you have always felt you had to please, and imagine yourself saying 'no' to them. Set the scene for yourself – a room, a place – and decorate it in your mind, giving it colour and shape. Choose where and how you will stand or sit, what you will wear. Watch what you do with your hands and feet. Place the other person where you can see their eyes. Make sure that your eye level is either equal or that yours is slightly above. (If we've found earlier that we tend to be always looking up at others, it might be that we always place others above us and ourselves in an inferior position.) Have an easy conversation with this person, speak to them as if you were in charge: say the things you would really like to say, rather than waiting to respond to their needs or questions. Then visualise that they ask you to do something you do not want to do. Smile at them and say, 'I'd love to be able to help out but I really can't at the moment.' Practise it out loud. Say it several times. There will doubtless be many other versions of things you would like to say which you can bring in here. Watch the other person's face. Notice what kind of look or gesture would normally trigger off your placatory response. Say 'no' to this gesture and look. Say it again. Practise it with a real person.

If you identify with the 'I'd rather be on my own' trap, imagine the most fearful situation you can create. Be the observer in this image and take note of all the ingredients. Who is in the image, where is it, what is the nature of the frightening quality, what is going on? Add to it as much as you want. Draw it in your mind with full colour and horror. Remember you are a fly on the wall. When you feel you have understood the full reality of the image from your observer position, prepare yourself to enter the frightening space. Choose a friend or special object, a 'talisman', to accompany you if you wish. Dress yourself for such a fearful journey (some people choose armour, skins, fancy dress, the dress of heroes) or find images for the qualities you would like to have – courage perhaps, or attractiveness, relaxation, humour. Imagine yourself dressed or armed with these attributes, and visualise how you would look. When ready, go forth in the changed image. Remember you are dressed appropriately for the encounter. Let yourself into the part. Do what you have to do. Experience what would be the most useful aspect you could bring back from this image to use in everyday life. Just one thing will help you to begin the change from having to be on your own because of fear.

Using images

The 'either/or' dilemma gives us two quite specific images to work with. Take the dilemmas you have identified in your life and ponder on them using your imaginal level. See if you can find images, shapes or colours for how you feel at each end of your dilemma.

TRACEY identified 'bottling-up feeling or making a mess' with 'having to give into others', and with 'having to do what others want', and found that her main dilemma in terms of relating to other people was that she felt she was either a *battering ram* or *modelling clay*. She felt that she had been modelling clay all her life, giving in to others, doing what they wanted. But if she expressed some of her feelings or was assertive in any way, she felt as if she were a battering ram. One week she spontaneously reached a middle position which married the positive value of each pole of her dilemma. Her image and her new position and aim was to be 'like springy steel'.

Once we have realised the images, we need to explore them. There are several ways to do this.

Imaging
Stay with the image in your mind's eye, either sitting or lying down with your eyes closed. Just let the image be there before you and ponder on its shape, colour, size, what it is made of, what, if anything, is around it, the age, sex, function, feeling, description and every possible detail of the image. Even if you just get a red blob you can still explore it: what kind of red; what shape is the blob; is it moving or still; is there anything else around it; does it have a name; does it remind you of anything? Each answer might lead to something else. In each case **let the image tell you**. Give it time. Do not force it to do anything.

If you are co-counselling someone, just let them stay as long as they can with the image by quietly encouraging them: repeat the name or sense of the image in the same voice they used to describe it to you; ask simple questions that will help amplify the image and expand its meaning.

With imaging techniques we may stay just with one image at a time, or we may see where the image wants to take us. We may put two or more images together, either imagining them side by side, or feeling first into the language of one and then moving on to the other, seeing how they may change or what they may need from each other.

Painting and drawing
Images may be anchored by painting or drawing. Keep these as spontaneous and natural as possible. Do not judge your spontaneous drawings as if you were in an art class and looking for an exact replica. Many people are upset

that their drawings do not represent the richness or vividness of the images they carry inside them, but what we are looking for by anchoring the drawings is a reminder of the nature of our images and their details. Make the paintings or drawings as soon as possible after the encounter with an image whilst it is still fresh with all its detail. Interpretation or meaning can come later. Sometimes we don't understand the exact nature of an image until later, when something happens and the impact of the image becomes clear. Once we become accustomed to using our images creatively, as part of our lives, we are rewarded by other images and other insights into the potential use and meaning of our images, and we realise that we have inside us a rich resource for future assistance with struggles and difficulties.

Drawing and painting are best done on the floor, as if we were playing, using colours freely without constraints. As well as painting or drawing we may like to model something in clay or Plasticine, Play-doh, papier mâché or whatever is handy. One woman made masks for the different parts of her and used them to help her be aware of their impact.

We may also use magazine or newspaper pictures to conjure up the images or feelings of what we experience inside. They may not be images we have created ourselves, but sometimes seeing a photograph or picture can trigger or inform us of memories and feelings, and we may prefer to use this method. You might like to cut out pictures and stick them onto paper as a collage, or as a wheel with different segments to portray the nature of your dilemma or trap.

When you have arrived at the image that suits you, keep it somewhere where you can look at it every day – in your wallet, diary, over the cooker, by the bathroom mirror, etc. Be proud of what you produce. Do not judge it or take notice of anyone else's judgement.

Exploring traps or dilemmas through the body

Images or feelings may also be enacted by finding a body posture to capture those feelings or images. Stand, sit, lie or get your body into a position that describes your image or your feeling. Stay with the posture and let your body tell you something of the nature of this posture as you hold it.

One woman wanted to use this technique to get in touch with the tremendous tension she felt. In letting her body tell her about it by forming itself into the position that would encapsulate the feeling best, she found herself literally trying to climb the wall. She was shocked to find how extreme this was and how evocatively her body behaved when asked to express itself.

Another person who described their dilemma as 'either I'm a doormat or one of the Furies' manoeuvred her body into the position of a doormat and experienced the sensation of everyone walking over her. When asked to describe the nature of the doormat, its colour and shape, she said, 'It's soft and brown and it's got WELCOME written on it'. In contrast, her body position for the Furies involved spinning, spitting, scratching, kicking, hissing and twirling. Her 'Furies' had never really been explored but remained hidden and repressed, and this had frightened her, thus aiding and abetting her doormat side. In this exercise she moved between the two positions, spending a few minutes in each. Gradually a third position appeared, as her body spontaneously placed itself straight upright, looking ahead, arms swinging to and fro freely, shoulders back, knees supple. 'I'm ready for action,' she said. 'I can move fast or be still as I wish.' In this third position she felt in control, and in charge of her choices. In the other two positions she had felt trapped, caught, unable to respond in any other way than the limited and extreme nature of the dilemma demanded.

Sometimes we are able to explore how we feel by actually being aware of what our body is doing in different situations. Becoming aware of how we sit or stand when talking to difficult people tells us a lot about our unexpressed feeling. Being aware of how we use our body, either when we are on our own or with others, can help us to examine the feelings that are being expressed unconsciously through the body. Sometimes we tell two stories: out of our mouth may come 'I'm fine thank you' whilst our eyes are looking dead and sad and our body is as tight as a drum or heavy with pain, telling a different story.

From this section we have established there are two main ways of using our observation of body language: (1) by a general awareness of what we do with our bodies and what others do; and (2) the direct use of body postures to act out the drama of an image or feeling, to allow us to take on board the full extent of our feelings, and to bring about change. Sometimes the smallest body change, from arms tightly folded when talking about the narrowness of our life, for example, to those same arms opening out widely to embrace something new, can begin an actual change, as what is depicted by the body change is taken into life experience. The woman who got into the position of the doormat never did it again in quite the same welcoming way, nor was she hurled about inside by the Furies. Something memorable always happens when we work directly with the body.

Exploring traps, dilemmas and other problems through objects

Make a box of small objects of a mixed kind, containing some you like, some you don't like, some to which you feel indifferent – shells, stones, toys, sticks, glass, ornaments, eggs, bits and pieces you have in your room or around your house. Clear a space on the floor for the objects you have chosen and place a rug or cloth in the space. This will be the boundary for your 'drama' enactment. Now get down on the floor, either on your own or with your co-counsellor. (This exercise can be fun to do, either alone or helping someone else.)

Decide which trap, dilemma, decision, family scene or relationship struggle you wish to depict. Choose first an object for yourself, to represent you. Don't think too hard, just go for something you really like that will stand for you as you are now (or perhaps as you were in the past, if you are depicting a past situation). Hold your own object for a while and get the feel of it; get to know it well. When you are ready, place it in the centre of your space on the floor. Next take an object to represent one of the people in your current drama.

That could be father, mother, uncle, aunt, sister, brother, friend, colleague, lover, neighbour, animal – anyone you wish. After you have chosen the object, look at it and see why you have chosen it for this person, what qualities they have. If this is not immediately clear, the reason may emerge as you go on with the drama.

Go on choosing objects until you have one for everyone you intend to include. Place each one on the floor as you imagine them to be currently in your life, or as they were in the scene you are recapturing. Notice the spaces between each one and ponder on what they might mean. If some are close, how close are they? Notice if some block others in their closeness. If others seem far apart, ponder on this and the nature of the apartness. If you are depicting a scene from your past, for when you and your siblings were together, you might like to get the feel of what happened when the scene changed, as when someone left home or went into hospital, or when someone new entered. When you do this allow the objects to show you the whole scene, let the objects themselves take on the drama and give you the impact of what happens rather than concentrating upon which object is which person.

It is quite fantastic what strong feelings this exercise can evoke when the objects are allowed to unfold their story. For example: objects may be all of similar size or material and then suddenly something quite different is introduced; everything about the *gestalt* then changes. There may be distinct groups of very different substances; you may notice that, in order to communicate with certain members/objects, you have to make huge leaps across the floor.

Everything that happens in terms of the objects is useful in portraying family structures: pairs and triangles; sizes and shapes; who is easy to approach and who isn't; what is needed in terms of change or movement; what needs to happen for one object to reach another; how it feels for the rock that is your father to approach the tiny shell that is your sister or the piece of string that is wrapped around your uncle.

You might like to focus on a particular event and then ask the question: 'How should it have been different?' And let the objects show you.

Spend no more than half an hour with the objects. This is a powerful exercise. Let it inform you, and give you an idea of how you would like the patterns of things to be in your own life now.

Writing letters you never send

This is useful when there are many things left unsaid to people who are perhaps dead or unapproachable. Start the letter, 'Dear Mum . . .' or whoever you wish to write to. Then begin with something of what you feel. For example, 'I am writing to you because I could never find the words to say what you meant to me', or 'All my life I feel you have put me down'. Go on into the letter and let out all the feelings you have never dared embrace. Write as if your heart would burst, that your aches, longing, griefs are so full they would spill over. Write as if this were your last chance fully to express what that person has meant to you or brought out in your life. Do not flinch from any word or image that you use. Do not let guilt get in the way, or any moralising about blame or fairness or pride. You will never send this letter, but you need to write as if you were having a vibrant conversation with a living person. It may be gratitude and love you want to express, that you regret not passing on in the person's lifetime; or, it may be more painful and negative feelings, as in the following unsent letter, written by Stephanie from Chapter 10. Here is the letter she wrote to her father:

Dear Dad,

I tried to feel what life would have been without you; it was unimaginable except for the feeling of an immense weight lifting from me. Life without that burden. When I tried to imagine life without my mum, I could imagine some other good woman looking after me well enough.

I tried to think of an image to describe how it felt to be your daughter. What came to mind was that when I was small, over a period of time you slit me open, placed a box of maggots between my heart and my stomach and slowly and deliberately sewed the scar away. Your living legacy was that I could never again feel peace, goodness, satisfactions – just rottenness at the core. That shocks me. It is like hating and blaming my own limb to hate and criticise you. You seem old and often very pathetic, and nothing at all to do with the person who came and planted the maggots. I feel very sorry for you, but it becomes confused with feeling sorry for myself.

I do feel like I have been tortured enough, and I would like you to let me go now please. You and Mum tut-tut about the relationships with men that I form, but each is modelled on the way things were with you. I had to learn to trust and love somebody who hated parts of me, loathed others, merely criticised most and demanded that I thrive and flourish and serve their every need.

I was at Uncle Jack's house lately. He thinks you have been a pretty dreadful father to me. I was there for an evening and he wanted to do something nice for me. He offered me a drink and brought me a cup of coffee – no strings. It made him feel good because he had done a nice thing. It made me cry, because in twenty-seven years my own father has never done such a simple act of kindness for me.

Guilt and mixed feelings apart, I think that I have to tell you that you have been a complete bastard. It fills me with an anger which I transfer to many people, and in particular all of the men I meet. Every skill you gave me you used against me; you tutored my brain, then devoted yourself to undermining my intelligence. I have many an amusing story to tell on these subjects; if someone is treating me badly I can't call you in to protect me because you would agree with them, etc. But the humour is a thin veneer on top of hate and anger.

Such a small and pathetic man, not content with losing his own chance of happiness and satisfaction, you had to have mine too. I would like to destroy you. I would like to spit all that hatred back at you. Strange that I should think you smaller and more pathetic than your own child. Strange that I should believe that even a fraction of the hatred you gave to me could destroy you. And you had my mum completely devoted to salving your every need from the moment you met aged fifteen. She has become quite a contortionist to be able to constantly feed your every need and still remember to keep herself alive.

Life with you has been like living in a minefield. Allan picked his way through first, but you set a different pattern for me and threw in a few booby traps for good measure. Jane made notes and tiptoed round the edge. They have got to the other side now, but I find I am still searching for mine years after the fight is supposed to be over.

I wish I had had a different father. I hope I can trust enough to allow the manly half of the human race to make some positive contribution to me and my life.

Monitoring your progress with problems and aims

Make yourself a chart containing your problems and aims like the one in Appendix 4. Use this rating chart every day. Keep it in your diary or pocket-book so that each day you can at least glance at it to remind yourself particularly of the aims. Once a week have a concentrated look at the chart, and mark on it how much the aims have altered, if at all. There are lines for 'no change', 'better' and 'worse', and you will need to mark where you feel you are in terms of your aim according to these markings. As the weeks progress your marks will form a graph. Some weeks will be better and others worse. In a week when you mark the rating down be sure to understand why that is, what happened to put you off your aim and perhaps led to your being caught up in an old pattern. Don't be discouraged, but use the information to help you understand your need for change, and let yourself have some compassion for the struggle this part of you may well be having. Sometimes our progress with one aim drops as others are achieved, because we are testing out traps and snags. We may well feel 'snagged' by getting more assertive or stronger in some aspect. Marking this on your chart will help to highlight these problem areas and to focus upon them.

Do not judge how you are doing or be tempted to mark all the ratings as high as possible. Just stay with a realistic view of how things are. Make sure that the aims you have given yourself *are* realistic. If you begin with the more straightforward aims, such as getting out of the traps and becoming more assertive, you will be encouraged to challenge some of the more difficult problems, like fear of dependency, sudden mood swings and more embedded difficulties with anxiety or physical symptoms.

Change is best consolidated if achieved slowly and thoroughly. Take your time, quietly focusing upon your task. A major change may already be happening, that of self-reflection and self-observation. This change will already be bearing fruit. Once you have begun to accomplish small changes you might like to make a new chart, including other problems or a more detailed version of your existing problems and difficulties.

Dreams

Dreams are the language of the unconscious, a rich symphony of yet undis-
covered material which reaches the daylight of consciousness through
imagery, motif, story and feeling. We all dream every night, but not all
dreams are remembered. When an important dream occurs we wake up and
we know that something has happened. The feeling evoked by a dream can
stay with us throughout the day and beyond. Dreams can contain insights
that are useful. They offer a balancing influence upon consciousness by making us aware of our unconscious longings, symbols and unfinished business.

How to work with our dreams

Keep a dream notebook to record your dreams. Write them down as soon as
you wake, even if it is in the middle of the night. If a dream wakes you it is
important. If you go back to sleep thinking you will record it in the morning,
it will slip back into the unconscious. If the dream message is important it will
come again. Learning to listen to the language of dreams can help us release
what is blocked and help to restore balance as well as offer us exits and third
positions for traps and dilemmas.

When you have written your dream down, ponder on its general shape, on
its images and motifs. Note the feeling of the dream. Notice the time and
place in the dream – current time or past time, your age if you are represented
in the dream. Note the time of day and consider its meaning. Morning or
afternoon, evening or night.

The most important question when pondering on your dream is: **what
does this mean to me?** If you appear as age seventeen in your dream and you
are in fact thirty-five, what aspect of your seventeen-year-old self is being represented in the dream? What was this time about for you? What does it
remind you of? Does the figure seventeen hold any other significance? What
does the memory or meaning of being seventeen mean for your life as it is
now? Why are you now having to think back to when you were seventeen?

It is helpful in the amplification of your dream if this approach is followed
for all other aspects, symbols or images. If there is a house in your dream, what
kind of house is it – colour, shape, size? Is it familiar? What country or place
does it remind you of? Where are you, the dreamer, in relation to the house?

FREDA dreamed a great deal and was interested in her dreams, and so she
began reading about them, and about myths and fairy tales. A number of
animal motifs appeared in her dreams, and she became especially fond of a
fawn and a frog. She saw that these creatures had been banished to the
darkness of her unconscious because they represented aspects of herself that
she presumed were negative. She used the words: 'jelly-like, slobs, pathetic,
losers'. Because the dream had drawn her attention to them she looked at
them afresh. She realised she liked their simplicity, their instinctive nature: they

knew how to live naturally. As she got to know and welcome the energy and life in these dream animals she started to move her own body differently. We went to dancing class and started writing in her journals. The urge to binge because of emptiness lessened. She started feeling more content and started enjoying the countryside.

Another important aspect of amplifying your dream is to consider the order of events in the dream. There seems to be no ordinary linear time in dreaming, and death in dreams does not necessarily mean mortal death. Death in a dream is a symbolic death and may be interpreted on many different levels – as an ending, a transformation, a dying off, a falling away, as the death of a particular aspect of your life.

Look closely at the order of the events in your dream and see if you can understand some of the links between sequences, events or images. For example: 'In the dream an old lady rides a bicycle down a steep hill. At the bottom of the hill she is stopped abruptly by a small girl bearing a bunch of flowers. She wants to keep going, to use her downward speed to help her gain impetus to ride up the hill, but has to accept the flowers from the child first. She then begins her difficult ascent up the hill, but as she is going more slowly she sees the view of the fields more closely.' The order of the dream indicates that the old woman (an aspect of the dreamer) has to curb her irritation to stay with the child, and in doing so the dream shows how she gets another view of the fields as she travels on her way. The event of the child and the flowers precedes the climb and has to be encountered before the nature of the climb can be revealed.

Sometimes dreams come in series, and the series may occur all in one night. In these cases the series forms one whole dream which is trying to communicate a theme, a development and an idea over a number of dreams. This is one way in which the psyche alerts us to an unconscious process that is ready to be made conscious.

Dreams may produce images which are frightening, startling or powerful and which bear no resemblance to anything we know rationally. When this occurs, what is hidden in the image that is of importance to us wants very much to be noticed and understood before incorporation into our everyday living. Draw, paint or act out the nature of your dream figure, and share it with another person if you feel the dream content to be too disturbing or worrying. Although the figure in the dream may represent something you don't like, once explored and made conscious the figure and what it represents is never so frightening or overwhelming.

AMANDA (see p. 46) had two significant dreams during her depression that drew attention to her suicidal impulses. In one dream she is swallowing pills with people around her encouraging her to continue. There is a feeling of ease in the dreams of just continuing taking the pills and quietly fading away into oblivion. The dream had such a powerful feeling that on waking Amanda felt terrified that it would be easy to go along with the dream. She remembers speaking to her therapist on the telephone who indicated she was in fact in control of whether she took her own life or not and the important thing was that she could be in charge of the choice. She was not being told what she should or should not do, although she writes that she remembers the therapist suggesting that she took all the pills she had stored in her cupboard into a pharmacy for disposal!

The other dream was of someone trying to smother her and was recurrent. She explored it through role-play in her therapeutic session with the therapist approaching her with a pillow and Amanda working at stimulating the muscles of her arm to push the pillow away. She was being encouraged to develop her own assertive resources and to say 'no' to destructive forces. For a while the dreams left her. Then about a year later the dream returned; she still could not resist or shout out except in her head and she realised that she was not frightened but very very angry. She also knew that she was stronger, that the dream in itself couldn't harm her. Amanda had been able, through her therapy and its work with her dreams, to acknowledge her angry feelings that were so deeply buried. In doing so she gained a sense of freedom from the destructive anger that was turned against herself, that could have led to her killing herself.

If you become interested in your dreams and in knowing more about how to work with them in your life, you may be helped by reading any of the selected books listed in the Further Reading section.

Assertion and aggression

Changing always ignites all our traps, dilemmas and snags as well as our more unstable states! Be alert to this! See it as a chance to keep in there, to keep noticing, revising and trying something new. We may need to be more assertive about our ideas, thoughts, needs, wants and desires. It's easy to confuse assertion with aggression and thus hold back from expressing ourselves, and this confusion can get in our way. You may find, having got this far, that it is difficult for you to be assertive, and express your needs directly. You may have noticed your 'fear of hurting others trap', believing that saying just what you feel, simply, will be hurtful; or you may fear being seen as aggressive, as too 'pushy'. Keep on noticing the old beliefs. Keep trying to refine the way you express yourself with others so that you *are* clear and straightforward in what you ask for or how you express feeling. If we avoid being assertive out of unrevised beliefs, others may well ignore or take us for granted, because *they* actually do not know what we think or feel.

For all of us, being assertive is perfectly acceptable. People who do not respect us as human beings must either be stood up to or left out of our life.

Learning the art of assertion may be an important part of your change. Once you realise this is a skill you lack and which you need to learn, there are many places where this can be achieved and practised. Joining a group or class to practise the art of assertion can really help to consolidate the changes you may wish to make. Having a living person or group to whom one practises saying 'no', or saying what one thinks, or with whom one tests out the new-found ideas or strengths, is a potent and lasting way of keeping hold of change.

Part six

changing within a relationship

One of the secrets of equable marriage is to accept one's partner for the person he or she is. Each can have only what the other has to offer. Expecting more leads to frustration and disappointment.

Susan Needham, Chairman,
London Marriage Guidance Council 1990–1995

14

Love is not enough

Relationships *always* bring our individual procedures to a head. Whether they are relationships with people at work, in groups, within our families or with friends. And intimate relationships are most likely to press us on the core pain we carry: on our fears associated with getting close, feeling dependent or needy, our fear of rejection or abandonment, of feeling jealous and envious. It's possible, through revision of our individual procedures and the way these interact with those of our partners, to elicit changes that free us to enjoy relating.

It seems too that collectively we need to make relationships with others in a clearer way. Duty, religious belief, social tradition or just love are not enough to sustain relationships through the current times in which we live, and the basis upon which people live together must meet a new challenge. The increasing divorce rate and the number of children born outside marriage, together with a sense that the family has failed, points to a human struggle about relating. While this book will not debate political or sociological issues, Cognitive Analytic Therapy can contribute ideas about how we might establish more flexible relationships with ourselves and with others. By understanding the interplay of reciprocal roles, we change how we become entangled or enmeshed with other's roles.

Idealisation and reality in relationships

In his book *Love is Never Enough*, Aaron Beck (1988) writes about how marriage or intimate relationships differ from other relationships. He describes how the intensity of living with someone fuels dormant longings for unconditional love, loyalty and support, and sets up expectations and desires. These are often based on an idealised image of love and acceptance. Idealisation is present in every hope and is useful for initiation, but it can set up impossible and unrealistic standards that cannot be met by another person. People with a history of early losses or poor bonding sometimes develop an over-idealised image of how relationships should be in order to compensate. While dreaming about this imaginative, 'happy ever after' world helps us to cope with a miserable home life, it cannot serve as a basis for relationships with others. When there is an over-idealised idea of how relationships 'should' be, whatever a partner does or does not do tends to be judged against a variety of these expectations or desires. Relationships can then become stuck, as each individual blames the other for their disappointment and sense of failure. And relationships can become blocked when each person carries one end of the reciprocal role and there is no room for flexibility. The relationship then remains at this superficial level and the deeper layers of potential within the couple cannot be reached. Relationships can only be truly satisfying when we learn to live with the other flesh and blood person we are not trying to reform.

Falling in love and sexual attraction are only the initial (but important!) triggers that draw two people together. *How* two people live together and sustain differences and difficulties is a test of maturity, generosity, endurance and humour. If we remain individually limited in our thinking and movement, we lack the flexibility required to dance in time with another, perhaps very different, person. Revising individual beliefs when they are redundant or damaging can be the beginning of allowing a relationship to flourish.

We have seen in Chapter 4 how the internal core pain from our childhood is carried by the internalised child self and maintained by both the learned procedures based on old beliefs and by the internalised adult or other. Thus it's easy to understand how, until revised, we may choose partners from our internalised child self who confirm the old beliefs of that child self and maintain the core pain. Someone with a crushed child self who expects a conditional other will tend to be drawn to someone whose attitude will confirm this; or, they will tend to see only the conditional response in the other, and react to this in the old way. Even when there is goodness between two people it can be undermined by these old, now outdated procedures. Someone with an over-idealised view of relationships who was neglected as a child will long for fusion and closeness, and yet at the same time fear being abandoned. They may set up impossible demands which force their partner to flee, so confirming their belief that it is not worth getting close because everyone always neglects or leaves you in the end. What needs revision is the procedure for dealing with deprivation. Instead of longing for fusion or perfect care, the internalised child self needs to be recognised and cared for first, so that we do not expect this hunger to be met totally by another. The core procedures that dominate relationships and maintain pain need to be revised together.

We have seen many other patterns of relating throughout this book. We have seen someone who, when close to another person, becomes 'mother' or 'father', taking care and control of the other and denying their own needs, only to feel used and lonely. We have seen how the fear of loss of control can lead someone to seek to take charge of every interaction, creating a suffocating atmosphere where sooner or later one person will either explode or hit out, so establishing the very chaos the control pattern was designed to avoid.

Suggestions for couples

This section is for couples who are concerned about their interaction with each other and wish to make changes. Work individually first to establish your own individual pattern of procedure.

Read through Chapter 4, 'Problems and dilemmas within relationships'. Then make your own individual diagram for reciprocal roles, as guided in Chapter 13. It might help to notice how you feel with your partner at certain times when things seem to go wrong. Are you feeling like a crushed child or a furious parent? A critical carer who can only be martyred or a rebellious infant who wants to stamp its feet and run away?

Keep a journal individually (without reference to the other), for one week, of the times in which you have been pressed on a core pain place, or pushed into that bottom-line 'as if' core pain statement. Try not to make assumptions or judgements, but simply keep a record.

Having read through the chapters on traps, dilemmas and snags, write down which of these apply to you, and which procedures for coping with core pain are most dominant in your life.

Complete your examination of traps, dilemmas and snags by predicting which your partner would identify. Then look together at how each of you sees the other, and how this differs from your individual identification of traps, dilemmas and snags.

As part of gathering information, you might also like to go back in time and make a note of the qualities that attracted you to your partner in the first place. Qualities such as spontaneity, warmth, fun, humour, caring, depth, perception, strength, intelligence. What were you hoping for from these qualities? Having made this note, make another column to record how you feel about these qualities now. If they seem to have changed, ponder on this. Sometimes when we are drawn to certain qualities in a person it is both because we like and respond to those qualities, and also because we want to develop them in ourselves.

Drawn to opposites: FRANCES and MIKE

Frances, an only child, grew up in a very serious household. When she met Mike, who came from a large, noisy, fun-loving family, she was immediately attracted to what she had not experienced. For Frances, living with Mike was both a rebellion against her serious parents, who thought Mike a renegade and drop-out, and a challenge to her own learned seriousness. She hoped that Mike would help to heal her loneliness and allow her to expand her spontaneity. While this was ultimately a healthy option for her, in their first years she found herself being snagged by feelings of guilt for choosing such a different life from her aloof parents, as if her fun was at their expense. She had visions of their lonely existence in front of the one-ring gas fire while she was dancing the night away. This made her anxious, but she dared not confide in Mike because she did not want to spoil their enjoyment. She began to have panic attacks and to fear going out, returning instead to lying alone in bed and to the idea that she was not, after all, meant to go out and enjoy herself. A revision of her 'magical guilt', and speaking to Mike and her parents about the reality of their lives, helped her to begin to claim the life that she had chosen.

211

Drawn to similarities: BILL and EMILY

Bill chose Emily because she was just like his mother. Bill hated change, which he saw as rocking the boat. He wanted someone to be there for him when he came home from work, who would look after him and serve his needs. For Emily, who came from a rather cold background where she had had to placate in order to feel a sense of worth, it was heaven to be so wanted. But over time, because the glue that bound them together was based on earlier needs, they began to come unstuck. Bill found Emily boring and demanding – just like his mother in the *bad* sense. And Emily found his need of her oppressive and began to have angry outbursts and tantrums. She felt that he never listened to her but was always demanding, and she started to dream of being alone, of leaving, or of having an affair with someone she was attracted to at work.

If each set of individual procedures is locked together unhelpfully, without revision, the relationship can reach crisis point where the only solution seems to be to get out. This does not have to be so.

Hidden complementarities: FRANK and MAGGIE

Frank and Maggie find it difficult to live together without continual angry rows, when things get said which are regretted, only to be used as fuel for the next argument. They have separated several times, but found it equally difficult to live apart. Figure 14.1 is a diagram of how their relationship moved from initial closeness to anger, separation and then loneliness and reconciliation.

Frank and Maggie had actually separated when they first came to see me, and saw our meeting as a last-ditch attempt to save the relationship, although both were pessimistic, and both were deeply entrenched in their survival modes. Maggie was frightened, shaking and withdrawn; Frank aloof, controlled, calm, but his face white and muscles tense. By the time we had worked on their individual stories they had got together again and were both moved when each read out their story to the other.

In the early days they worked by doing simple self-monitorings. Frank was to monitor each occasion when he thought, 'I've had enough, this is terrible, I'm getting out'; similarly, Maggie was to monitor the times she thought, 'I want more, this isn't enough, this isn't how it *should* be'. It appeared as if these thoughts developed into a compulsion to act which, when followed through, served to keep the trap going. Both found self-monitoring very difficult. But as they gradually came to understand more of the other's history and to allow for each other's fragility, they were able to hold on to the space long enough to listen, and later to have a discussion. To this end, they used their tape recorder to record conversations, later setting aside time together to listen to what had transpired between them. They were frequently shocked and moved by what they heard.

This is what I wrote and then read aloud to Frank and Maggie in therapy:

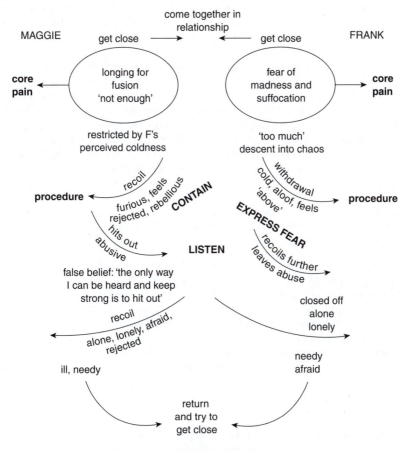

Figure 14.1   Frank and Maggie's relationship trap

The three of us agreed to look afresh at the situation within your marriage, which operated to make it difficult to live together or apart. You had been in different therapies, both individually and together, in a quest to find answers to the dilemmas you both face as a couple. A great deal of perseverance, time and effort has gone into this quest, perhaps indicating a desire to find a way to be together more harmoniously, and perhaps out of a yet not understood love for each other. The individual reformulations (life stories) gained over three sessions, reveal similarities. You are both intelligent people with damaged siblings. There is considerable self-negation and disappointment in all four parents' lives. 'Magical guilt' is strong in both of your lives. You both learned not to appear too well or happy. Magical guilt presupposes that we have received something good at another's expense, and that if we have what we want later on in life someone else will be damaged.

In Maggie's case, her unconscious involvement with self-sabotage revealed itself immediately in terms of the appointments we made, and that it took us five arranged appointments to result in three actual sessions. It was 'as if' something operated in Maggie's life to prevent her from getting help, fulfil obligations or grow and become happier and more fulfilled. Maggie has recognised how she follows patterns of depriving and punishing herself in order to feel good about herself, and talked about the fact that she doesn't dress as well as she might because she feels she doesn't deserve it. All good things, because they make her feel 'bad' and guilty, have to be either denied or demolished in order to fulfil the unconscious pull of self-sabotage. Maggie's self-sabotage feels at its heaviest when it links in with the part of Frank she sees as 'Superman': superior, clever, successful, controlled and better than herself. Because her antennae are tuned to expect personal demolishment and criticism, it gets set up unconsciously, again confirming the myth of magical guilt. And when this happens, and she feels criticised or punished, she falls back on survival tactics, becoming either rebellious and aggressive or passive, ill and in need of care.

Self-sabotage in Frank's life seems to operate in the way he does not feel free to express himself emotionally or with any vulnerability, and in the fact that he feels compelled to 'walk on eggshells' for fear of triggering Maggie's wrath or abuse. Early in his life, control, success and intellect were very important, and emotion and feeling were associated with chaos and madness. His professional life is successful and free of chaos. But in personal relationships there is another challenge. He was possibly drawn to Maggie because it would enable him to become more in touch and comfortable with a whole range of feelings. At difficult times he experiences emotional inertia and feels stuck, putting up with unpleasantness and appearing cold and unresponsive, or, more recently, allowing anger to surface.

Magical guilt carries with it the fury and rage at the restrictions it imposes. Each of you offers the other a vehicle for this magical guilt. Freeing yourselves individually from this would mean that it would not have to be played out in the drama of marriage.

The other area that links you together negatively at present is the struggle around closeness and intimacy. It seems as if you have opposite ideas, and idealised ideas, of what being close means. For Frank, closeness is self-contained and intellectual, and anything else feels suffocating and frightening, out of control. For Maggie, closeness is fusion, being constantly together, contained and safe, perhaps reflecting an inner longing to be held in a complete, symbiotic way. If you keep holding on to these polarised ideas your relationship will be a constant battle. Perhaps if you question the validity of these ideals and work towards making them less absolute, you could find a reasonable place from which to be close to each other. Freeing yourselves from magical guilt would mean that you could allow for, and maintain, good feelings and closeness, without having to sabotage it by all the 'as ifs' we have mentioned.

This is what Frank and Maggie wrote in return:

What we've taken home

We are learning that each of us carries substantial burdens from the past, which result in 'snags'. For example, for different reasons, each of us has difficulty with intimacy. Rage and frustration always get in the way of our being close. We are each well advised to make the effort to accept the reality and validity of these snags in the other, even though we may not always like the resulting behaviour. To deny and reject these personal characteristics in the other is futile. It also devalues the other person and therefore causes unhappiness.

So, we need ways to cope. We must learn to use them effectively. First, we can understand them and empathise. We can also gracefully fall back and use and cede space. Apartness need not be rejection, and sometimes can be constructive.

On top of this, we realise that each of us has difficulty delivering on some of the other's primary needs. These were detailed by Liz in one of her reformulation documents. Just sensitising ourselves to this reality is a step forward. We must also think constructively and take more initiatives.

Finally, it should be said that our continuing resolve and application shows that we love and need one another. But it's a rocky, non-placid road that we are gradually learning to travel. The good times are worth it.

Frank and Maggie are still struggling to listen to and contain the feelings produced by their very different responses to getting close. Although their relationship is not easy, they are still together, and there are some good times which make the effort feel worthwhile.

SEAN and MARY

Sean and Mary sought help as a couple because of the painful rows which threatened their relationship. Their dreadful quarrels seemed to develop a life of their own and escalate out of control. They each began to look at their individual traps, dilemmas and snags, and kept a record of exactly what happened, what they were thinking, what was said and when they had a row.

Sean's early experience was of a critical father, before whom he felt inadequate. Mary felt that Sean constantly criticised the way she did things. Her own pattern was to take the blame for any disagreements. After one of their rows, each drew up their own diagram (see Figures 14.2a and b).

Changing within a relationship

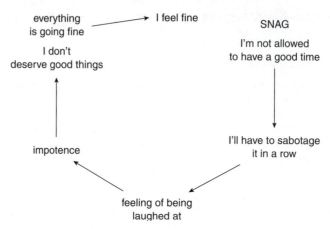

Figure 14.2 (a)   Sean's diagram

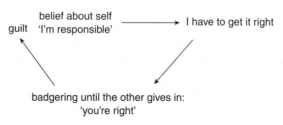

Figure 14.2 (b)   Mary's diagram

> One row occurred when they were laughing and joking, and about to make love. Mary said something which she thought was very funny but which had a dramatic effect: Sean turned away, seemed to lose all interest and became very angry. Mary became upset, and very soon they were deep into a conflict from which they could not extricate themselves. When Mary had made her jokey remark Sean had experienced her as the critical and contemptuous castrating father. For Mary, Sean's withdrawal was devastating. She needed desperately to please in order not to be rejected. She took the blame for the row and badgered Sean to tell her what she had done. This only increased Sean's feeling that he was being harried and put down, and that he must give in to Mary even though he did not agree with her. Following the row, and Mary's appropriation of the high moral ground, Sean withdrew, which left Mary feeling frightened and abandoned, just as she had experienced as a child.
>
> Sean and Mary quickly saw how their responses to each other had been affected by earlier maladaptive ways of communicating, which were now preventing

them from seeing each other clearly. For Sean, Mary had become the castrating, rejecting father; and for Mary, Sean represented the rejecting father for whom she could never do anything right. It was a shock for Mary to discover that Sean's perceptions were entirely different from her own. One of the values of working together in this way is the opportunity it gives to each person to hear the other's side and to witness their learned patterns of response.

The following is an account of the focused therapy Sean and Mary had with two cognitive analytic therapists.

The previous hypotheses of Sean and Mary's traps and dilemmas were given added confirmation during the following session. Once again they had had a row which had lingered on in a desultory fashion. It was as though Mary had to keep picking at Sean in an attempt to put things right, trying at the same time to do and be what she thought he wanted of her, and in the process ignoring what she wanted. Sean, unaware of Mary's needs and feeling only a sense of being smothered and of her underlying withholding of approval, retreated behind his newspaper resigned to the fact that the situation could not be resolved. Later they decided to go out to the park and then on to an AA meeting. This, however, only intensified the tension between them, because Sean had to wait for Mary to get ready, all the time becoming more and more irritated at the delay. From this we were able to tease out the trap and dilemma that Mary was in (see Figure 14.3a).

What seemed to be happening for Sean was that he felt, once again, he could not win. This brought back two important memories of his father. In the first, he and his father were staying with a much-loved jovial uncle in the country. The two men had arranged to go somewhere. Sean's father, up and ready early, stood in the middle of the room, jingling his keys and almost bursting with irritation at his brother, who was taking his time putting on his boots, completely unconcerned by the other's impatience. Clearly, in the incident with Mary it was Sean who had become the irritated, impatient father, while Mary had assumed the role of the laid-back, disorganised uncle.

The second memory involved Sean's desire to become a car mechanic. His father, however, had wanted him to have a more respectable, higher status career in management. Unable to go against his father and choose what he wanted to do, but equally reluctant to go along with his father, Sean fell between two stools and ended up in a series of jobs where he did just enough to get by. It was as though if he were to succeed, particularly at something his father disapproved of, he would incur not only his father's envy but also his anger. On the other hand, if he failed he risked his father's contempt. It seemed as though the only course was simply to get by. This was seen not only in his work but in his behaviour at home. He would start something – putting up shelves, decorating etc. – have piles of wood all over the flat, and then leave

Changing within a relationship

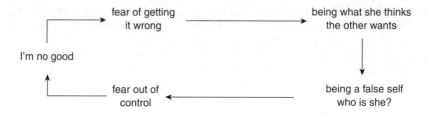

or to put it in terms of her dilemma:

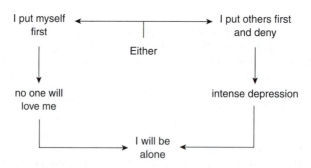

Figure 14.3 (a)   Mary's trap and dilemma diagrams

the jobs half-done, a source of irritation to Mary and incomprehension to them both. We were able to see here how the memory of his father once again seemed to be intruding (see Figure 14.3a).

In the fourth session we linked their responses to the relationship between them to possible past modes of behaviour. For example, in response to the first trap, avoidance, Mary felt responsible for Sean and for the possibility that they might split up, so she had to prevent this by trying to do what he wanted. This had parallels with her earlier life, when she had needed to be both in control of her siblings and responsible for their welfare, particularly after her mother died.

With Sean, his fear of standing up to his father leads to a self-fulfilling prophecy that he was no good, followed by inevitable depression. What became very clear was that his fear of succeeding in his relationship with Mary stemmed from his conviction that he must pay for success, and so he has to sabotage it.

Both Sean and Mary were very afraid of something within them that seemed out of their control. Sean's other procedures were his avoidance of his feelings about partings and loss, and his destruction of his creativity, which he longed to enjoy. For Mary we highlighted her need always to take responsibility for others' feelings, and her pattern of being unable to value, and thereby destroying, her creativity.

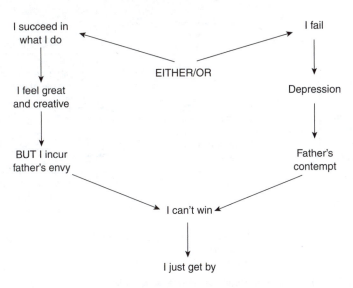

Love is not enough

I succeed in
what I do

I fail

EITHER/OR

I feel great
and creative

Depression

BUT I incur
father's envy

Father's
contempt

I can't win

I just get by

Figure 14.3 (b)   Sean's trap diagram

The nub of the work over sessions 6–15 focused on analysing together any rows they had had during the week, and seeing where their individual false beliefs got tangled up with the other's in these quarrels. Sean and Mary became very good at this, which gave them a sense of control that they had never experienced before. The weekly sessions became both a safe place to defuse explosive feelings held about the other, and a place to learn techniques to take with them for the future. Both Sean and Mary liked the idea of seeing their often repeated procedures caught on paper for them to refer to, and would regularly point out where they saw themselves as being on their diagrams. Sean put it this way, 'It's like opening a book and seeing all the stuff in my head laid out plain on the page. I can see how all my life I have got into the same patterns.'

In the early and middle weeks of our work the reported rows were fierce and felt catastrophic, but it was exciting to see how quickly Sean and Mary began to recognise patterns from childhood in their behaviour. Both came to see how their fathers' voices chimed in on them so often and stopped them from being themselves and expressing their spontaneity. In session 8, Mary talked about her struggle to confront her daughter's unjust and hurtful behaviour in saying things about her to a third party that were untrue. We saw her caught in the now familiar dilemma (see Figure 14.3c).

She was able to see that the exit here was to hold on to the right to her own feelings, and to express them. Sean witnessed her struggle with this problem and was able to be protective and supportive in a helpful way. At the end of session 8 we suggested each of them compose a description of themselves, as if written

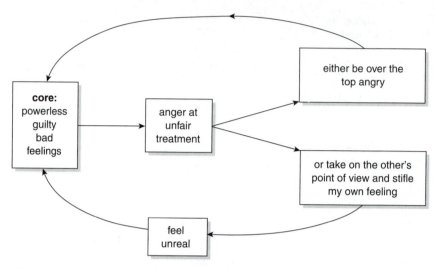

Figure 14.3 (c)   Mary's diagram of Sean's false belief

by a loving friend. Mary, we found, was able to really enter into this fully and present herself as the warm, ebullient person she is, but Sean found it hard to see himself in a favourable light and could only come up with a description of how he would like to be. This brought home to Sean how hard it was for him to be appreciative of himself. His father's critical voice was pervasive.

In the middle of our work, in session 9, there was a big row that seemed to be connected with their feelings about the therapy coming to an end. Apparently they felt they were not getting enough from us, and were taking out their anger about this on each other. Mary said she had left the last session without feeling the closeness to Sean that she usually experienced at the end of a session. She felt let down, and this was transferred onto Sean. She said Sean seemed depressed, and in swung her need to jolly him out of it: if he were down, it must be her fault (as with her parents when she was a child). She then felt guilty and that Sean was critical of her (when in actual fact he did not feel that at all at the time). It was clear to see how plugged in to each other's moods Mary and Sean had become. They could see this and were able to identify the points at which they had each pinned their own feelings on the other.

A key issue for Sean came up at this time. Mary was bringing to the sessions her painful feelings at the death of a close friend, which in turn resonated a whole untouched area of feelings about the death of her father. She was able to express her rage and hurt forcefully, and explore some key issues about the rejection by her sister and mother. This was so hard for Sean to witness, as his pattern had always been to swallow feelings about loss and endings. He was surly and irritated at Mary's outpouring of feelings of grief at the death, and by the fear, anger and hurt she displayed at the thought of losing us. Sean was able to say it frightened him. We noticed at this point that his false belief charts showed that no progress had been made on changing his usual pattern of avoiding grief, so this became an area of focus. We realised we had been colluding with him on this. As the weeks went on he was able to make two significant steps in dealing with this problem: (1) actually to tell his son, when he was leaving to return to Ireland, how hard it was to say goodbye to him and how much he loved him, and (2) to tell us how much he would miss the sessions and was afraid he might not manage without us.

Another area that Sean confronted in the middle sessions was the child part of him that needed constant reassurance from Mary that he was allowed to do something (e.g. watch football on television). This pattern worked quite well between Sean and Mary for much of the time, as Mary would be the reassuring mother to Sean's reassured child.

At this point the therapists sketched the diagrams shown in Figure 14.4.

At times, however, his need would exceed Mary's ability to keep giving, and we traced the rows that ensued. Yet another pattern for Sean was his jealous and rivalrous feelings when Mary paid attention to others. (She was a sponsor for other AA members.) They would often phone, and she would spend considerable time talking to them, sometimes adopting what Sean called a flirtatious manner. He would then become sullen and withdrawn, which would in turn evoke Mary's need to take responsibility for his feelings and her sense of guilt – his moodiness was her fault. Both were able to recognise this pattern, as well as the way in which Mary's attention to others evoked the insecure jealous child who was afraid of rejection in Sean. These feelings also came out in a dream Sean brought to the session at this time. He dreamed he was on a coach sitting beside Mary who was making love with the man next to her. In the dream Sean went off and sat by himself away from Mary.

A breakthrough came in another session over the escalation issue. There had been a small row over a football match. Sean and Mary had both been watching the game on television. Mary left the room to do something during a break for advertisements, but Sean failed to call her when the match started again. The reason for jubilation was that Mary, rather than nursing her anger and allowing it to swell inside with a kind of masochistic pleasure, was able to let go and the row did not escalate. We all four felt triumphant at this (see Figure 14.5).

Another issue that surfaced at this time was that of differences. We all noticed and discussed how different were Sean's and Mary's patterns of response to situations. Mary tended to feel anxious and insecure if Sean saw things differently from her – for example, if he took an opposing view to her at an AA meeting – and could see how this was linked to the hurt she had felt as a child whenever differences arose between her parents. She and Sean were able to say, 'We are different, and it is acceptable to be different, to be ourselves.'

In sessions 12 and 13 the focus turned particularly to Sean's sense of despondency at never finishing anything creative he planned. He said he felt things would be better between himself and Mary if he could have something purposeful to do. We laughed and joked over all the unfinished DIY jobs, the half-completed bed. He was able to hear his father's voice clearly telling him

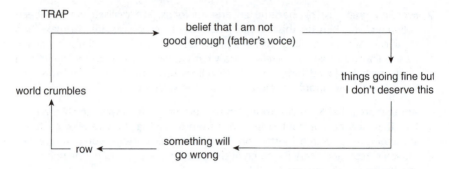

Figure 14.4 (a)   Therapists' diagram of Sean's false beliefs

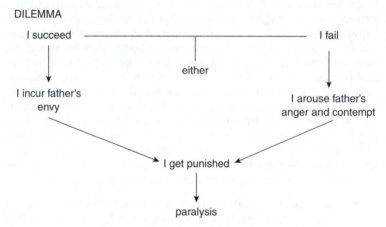

Figure 14.4 (b)   Therapists' diagram of Sean's dilemma

nothing was good enough. The exit from this snag was 'to have a go', he said.

The last four sessions were full of feelings about the ending and reported activities. Sean and Mary expressed their great disappointment that their respective son and daughter had let them down at the last moment by cancelling plans to visit them. This deprived Mary of her fantasy of creating a warm, happy, safe family, and she saw how her hurt over this could have been directed at Sean. This session revealed the pathological part of each of them, how the terrible, enraged, hurt, afraid child could burst in and destroy good things, especially their relationship. It was a sobering session. Mary had told Sean to leave and not come back when, or so it seemed to her, he had put his daughter ahead of her. Sean had replied, 'If I do it might be fatal', and Mary was then able to tell Sean that she hadn't meant it and they managed to de-escalate the row. We reminded them that it is alright to get angry and have rows.

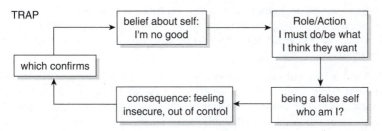

Figure 14.5 (a)   Therapists' diagram of Mary's trap

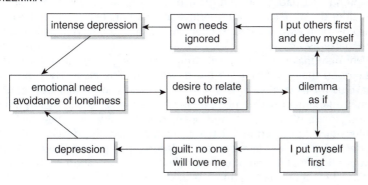

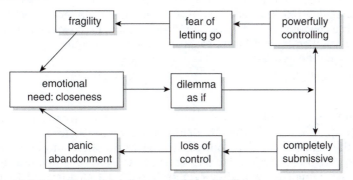

Figure 14.5 (b)   Therapists' diagrams of Mary's dilemmas

> The next session focused on how hard it was to bring our sessions to an end and on their sense of not having had enough. Even Sean was able to name this. There was some anxiety that there hadn't been a row. On one occasion Sean had felt resentful of Mary's laughter over the phone to someone else and he had been able to express this and be understood by Mary. Sean said in this session, 'Nothing in my life has made a bigger impression than this work.'

In the next session Mary reported that on three occasions she had succeeded in taking care of her own interests rather than putting the other person first. She was triumphant at her refusal to be domineered, and was encouraged in this by Sean.

During our last but one meeting the issue of ending came up very forcefully. Mary strongly vented all her fears and rage at losing us. Sean was more hopeful, saying he wished he had more time but that he felt they had the tools to go on by themselves. We confirmed that we would meet for a follow-up session in three months' time.

In our last session Sean arrived with a package which turned out to be a painting that had given him great pleasure to do. This was a great delight to all of us. We exchanged goodbye letters, ours being a joint letter to the two of them with separate sections for each of them. We spelled out again the patterns we saw that tripped them up, the enormous progress we had seen them make in finding exits from these snags, traps and dilemmas, and the good things we had got out of working with them. They in turn each gave us their goodbye letters. Each in their very individual way let us know what a landmark experience therapy had been for them. Sean's letter was much longer than Mary's, and once again we saw how they each felt the other must have performed better, as Mary convinced herself that Sean's letter must have been far more thorough than her own. Again we emphasised that it is alright to be different from one another. Both Sean and Mary felt they had gained a great deal of good experience and understanding to enable them to defuse their quarrels themselves, and both could see that using their creativity brought good feelings and was helpful in the relationship. They each expressed their thanks and sadness. We talked of all the changes we had witnessed, their courage, hard work and tenacity, and gave them more forms to enable them to continue the work of monitoring themselves.

Sean and Mary were able to use Cognitive Analytic Therapy to change their relationship. They were able to defuse their quarrels, to laugh at the tangles they got into and to confront things in the 'here and now' rather than carrying them around like a time bomb. Overall they had less devastating rows, which is what they originally set out to achieve in therapy. This change came about because they were each able to see how a lot of the anger and disruption really belonged to childhood experiences. For each, the procedure of trying to placate a powerful father loomed large and got in their way.

Sean recognised how the presence of his father's critical voice inside him created a trap, preventing him from enjoying his creative abilities and reducing his efforts, as well as ensuring that he withdrew from Mary whenever he heard his father's voice in her. He decided to 'have a go' and to enjoy himself, as well as reassuring his inner child and encouraging him to express himself.

Mary came to understand her fear of putting her own needs first for fear of others' rejection. Her difficulty with expressing her own needs remained hidden under her urge to punish when feeling rejected by being critical or withdrawing. When she began to express what she was feeling, particularly her fear at losing someone, this had a powerful effect on Sean, who was able to share and respect her feelings.

Sean and Mary write that now, five years on, they are still using the diagrams made in their therapy, and are communicating well.

---

exercise

Write your individual life stories, separately, using the third person – for example, let 'I' become 'he' or 'she'. It helps to step back and reflect. Pick a time when you can be alone together and each read your own life story aloud to the other. Put your observer hat on and just listen respectfully to the storyteller and the drama behind the story. Be as objective as possible and really listen.

Try not to *judge, criticise, object to, take personally, overrule or rationalise* the other's story. To do so would be to fall into a negative, internalised parent trap. If you do find yourself doing any of the above, just make a note of it so that you can refer to it later. Do not act upon it. Listen for the tone of the person who is trying to emerge, and communicate through the drama of the story. Note the way in which your partner has observed their own procedures and how they have survived their early life.

Give some time to the effect of reading the stories together and for each other's response.

Write something together about how your individual core pain and your procedures for coping affect the other.

Make a diagram for yourselves about the ways in which you repeat the ritual of your procedures during a row or difficulty. Note:

(a) the assumption or 'false belief' that leads to the behaviour ('I believe that ...')
(b) how this is received by the other which triggers their assumption ('so I do this ...')
(c) how this assumption results in behaviour ('he/she sees that I believe that ... so this makes me do ...').

Each keep a copy, so you can check where you are if you get into difficulties.

(Continued)

Spend the first week just observing and noting with each other what is happening. Don't yet try to change anything, but use your recognition not to get into the trap or dilemma to which your relationship usually falls prey. See what happens to the space, see what emerges or wants to emerge.

If you find yourselves having strong feelings, write them down, and see where or to whom they belong. How are the feelings connected to your core pain, and how can you best begin to relieve it?

When the energy in a relationship is not taken up with fighting old procedures there is time for other things. Experiment with *how* you like being together, and give feedback to each other on what works and what doesn't.

Storytime

Begin together to look at some of the powerful myths which you can see operating in your own histories, families, environment and culture. One reason for doing this is to evaluate where some ideas about relationships, and particularly marriage, originate. Another is to check how much influence these myths still have over you and your relationships, and whether they too need revision.

As you read, see which of the myths could be still influencing you in your life now.

Role myths
In my family:
    Men always came first.
    Women served men.
    Men never worked.
    Mum and Dad stuck together through everything.
    Women never worked.
    Dad was always there for me.
    Mum was always there for me.
    What happened within the family was confidential/secret.

Development myths
In my family:
    We had to better ourselves.
    No one read books.
    We always knew our place.
    There were no divorces.
    Marriage was for ever.
    All the men/women were labourers, white-collar workers, professionals, etc.
    To be ambitious was to be selfish.
    Any change was bad.

Sexual myths
In my family:
    We never talked about sex.
    Men were always unfaithful.
    Women were always unfaithful.
    Sex was OK for men but not for women.
    Sex was dirty.
    Mum and Dad never had sex.
    Men have got to have it, but women can wait.
    Sex always led to trouble.
    Sex was very difficult.

Sexual attraction myths
    Men only like 'good girls'.
    You have to play a game to get a man.
    Only if you are a size – will you get a man.
    Never trust a man until he's put a ring on your finger.
    You have to look – to be sexy.
    Sex appeal: you've either got it or you haven't.
    Independent women are not sexy/are very sexy.
    Men can do and look as they wish and still be sexy.
    A man doesn't have to be sexy to get a woman.
    Girls will be as sexy as they can until they've got you hooked, and then they turn into their mothers.

Myths about feelings
In my family:
    No one was close.
    We believed, 'Never wash your dirty linen in public'.
    Anger was a dirty word.
    Feelings were bottled up.
    Mum/Dad/Gran/sister/brother, etc. had the monopoly on feelings.
    Women could have feelings, men couldn't.

Myths about caring and love
    Caring means looking after/being looked after.
    Love means being strict/harsh/hurting.
    Love is only for special people.
    Love and caring means never being cross.
    Love and caring means giving into others.
    Love and caring means sacrifice: others are more important.
    If you love a person of your own sex you are homosexual.

Moral and religious myths
    Only God knows.
    Marriages are made in heaven.

God can see everywhere and he knows you are bad.
To break a commandment means being punished for ever.
God gave you to us so we can mould you for Him.
To be good and loving is to serve God in forgiveness, even those who have
    hurt you.
Mother and Father always know best.

Family relationship myths
Should be happy ever after.
You make your bed and lie on it.
Should always be hard work or they're not worth anything.
Should come naturally or they're not true.
Should be as good as Mum and Dad's, Gran and Grandpa's.
Being in a relationship is better than being on your own.
Relationships make you whole (joining a 'better half').

Myths about behaviour
You can never do anything right.
You always make me unhappy.
If you really cared or loved me you would ...
You will only be happy when you've ...
You must win to survive, life is a contest of winners and losers.
Be seen but not heard.
If you get what you want you will be unhappy.
Only if you get what you think you want will you be happy.
Waiting for the 'perfect man/woman'.

---

exercise

Predict which myths rule your partner's actual thoughts and beliefs, as well
as their *hoped*-for myths.

Name the myths which *together* you feel dominate your relationship.

Write the myths as you would like them to be!

---

part seven

holding on to change

Equanimity combines an understanding mind together with a compassionate heart.

Jack Kornfield *A Path with Heart* (1993: 331)

15

How to hold on to change

In this book we have been challenging old beliefs, having seen the way they can influence what we think and believe about ourselves and other people. Self-monitoring and writing about it help to move hidden ideas from the obscurity of our minds into the daylight and allow us to look at them afresh. Some of us might be amazed at the influence of an apparently simple but mistaken belief. This awakening may be sufficient to bring about change. Many problems, however, result from strongly built-up defences against early woundings, and the difficulty in changing these defences appropriately comes about because the fear involved is very great. We said at the beginning that change takes courage. It takes courage to risk feeling into our fears rather than avoiding them. It takes courage to go with anxiety rather than letting it limit us. But in finding ways to be more present with the reality of difficult feelings, and trying out new responses, we are bringing ourselves into conscious life, often for the first time.

Staying with, and feeling into, are not the same as giving into or being passive. We tend to give up on new ways or revised ideas because we lose heart at keeping them going. Anything freshly learned needs time and practice to become established. If we think that the old patterns of thinking have been around for most of our lifetime, it is not too much to ask that we give a proportion of time to practising the revised patterns. The most important learning I have received is that if I fall back into old habits or patterns, I need to recognise this and get back on the new road again. **If you fall down the most important thing is to get up again, not to lament the falling down.** The quality of Maitri, of unconditional friendliness, will be your companion to help develop the new reciprocal roles of *kindly accepting unconditionally* in relation to *supported/encouraged*, assisting you during the process of change.

There is usually relief, but there can also be loss, when we change how we think and what we presume. If we have built relationships largely upon our 'survival' self then these patterns of relationships will be challenged. Someone who has been used to us pleasing them, giving in to them, caring for them, may be disgruntled at first when they see us operating differently, and they may even be actively discouraging or threatening. Change does challenge all levels of our life and in particular those we are closest to. Living with what may feel like the opposition of our partner or closest friend or colleague is hard, but it is important that this opposition does not put us off. If it does we are colluding with the original fear that kept our old beliefs unrevised, and things will go back to being just as they were, with our healthy island still compromised.

What I have found is that when friends and colleagues realise the importance of change to the person trying to change, and how much relief there is when old redundant patterns are eradicated, they too are pleased. Only when relationships have become fixed and one-sided do things tend to get more heated. Then each of us has to make a choice. And the choice is frequently 'him (or her) or me?' If we risk losing others because they want us to stay the same we must ask whether we really want or need those others in our lives. Sometimes we have to step into an open space and believe that we will make new friends and acquaintances.

The first priority for holding on to change is therefore courage and the determination to stick with it. What follows is a checklist of ideas for holding on to change. Not all will need to be considered. Pick out four or five which are helpful and write them out for yourself. Look at this checklist everyday to encourage yourself to stay with the changes you have chosen.

- Keep up your courage and strength to carry out the changes you have decided upon, even when others seem to discourage you or disapprove. Internal changes that need to be made to release more of the healthy island will not harm other people; rather they will tend to enhance your exchanges with others.
- Believe in what you are doing and allow others to see your quiet conviction.
- Recognise yourself for what you are. Stop trying to be like other people or as other people demand you to be.
- Know that there will be times when you will need to go through a 'pain barrier'. Changing is not easy, and many fears are being challenged. Know that sometimes it will be hard and that you must just keep going and stick with your newly made story and aims.
- Develop tolerance for yourself instead of feeling you have to give in to the demand for instant gratification, which could lead to slipping into the old habits you are trying to change.
- Celebrate your feelings and your needs. Don't let them isolate you.
- Know your fears and take them with you into situations and bring your mindfulness practice to be alongside them.
- Know you are anxious and take your anxiety with you by the hand.
- Don't judge yourself with thinking: 'I shouldn't be like this, I'm silly.'
- Learn the art of listening to yourself and to others. Listen to yourself speak and note the tone you use. Listen to what your body is telling you, notice your body language.
- Be aware of the destructive power of negative thinking and don't let it get you. Be firm when you have a negative thought and tell it to go away.
- Be aware of the power of positive thinking and the healing that can be achieved from letting good vibes in.

- C.S. Lewis (1961) believed that only a real risk can test the reality of a belief. Take risks and check out your own beliefs.
- Make sure that you laugh every day. Be with people who make you laugh or with whom you have fun. Read or watch things that are amusing.
- Use your images in your everyday life. 'It is like ...', 'I feel like ...'. Let the symbols or images that have emerged during your reading be useful to you, so that you can say, 'Ah yes, this is how I'm being ... this is where I am right now ...'.
- If you get stuck at times or feel faint-hearted, say to yourself, 'It doesn't have to be like this', or 'This isn't all there is'.
- Every day give yourself permission to change and to hold on to change.
- Give space for your healthy island and the experience of yourself you have in this space. It might be raw and new at first. Let it have a proper life: give it the soil, light, air, water and careful nurturing that you would give to the ground in which a precious seedling is entrusted to your care.

Finding a therapist

Having read this book you may feel that you would like to consult a therapist, and the material raised by this book may be pressing you to do so. The subject of 'what is a good therapist' is still hotly debated in both professional and lay circles. You may find someone with excellent qualifications with whom you have no rapport; you may be seduced by someone's kindness and friendliness, only to find they have no stamina when the going gets tough. Finding a therapist with recognised qualifications is important, because it means that they have had to meet both personal (all good therapists have to have their own therapy or analysis for a required period of time) and professional standards and commitments.

If you are attracted by the ideas in this book, which come from Cognitive Analytic Therapy (CAT), you may want to consult the Association for Cognitive Analytic Therapy at www.ACAT.me.uk. Or write to: ACAT, P.O. Box 6793, Dorchester, DT1 9DL. The telephone number is: 0844 800 9496 (calls from landlines cost 5p per minute). Emails should be sent to: admin@acat.me.uk. Office hours are 9 a.m. – 5 p.m. Monday to Thursday. Through the website or by email to the office you may find a CAT-trained therapist in your area. There are CAT-trained therapists in England, Scotland, Ireland, Finland, Spain, Australia and South America.

There are now a growing number of CAT-trained therapists working within different settings – doctors, psychiatrists, psychiatric social workers, community nurses and psychiatric nurses, occupational therapists, social workers, GPs, counsellors and psychotherapists – who are working in short-term therapy within their speciality using the methods outlined in this book.

You may also consult the websites suggested in the resources section. Accredited therapists have to meet a wide range of standards and requirements and be in regular supervision.

There is no therapy which is 'perfect', and the 'perfect' therapist should not be sought. A 'good enough' therapy will allow you to explore most things safely and within manageable boundaries, at the same time as encouraging you to develop the healthy island already present within yourself.

What is a 'good enough' therapist?

A good therapist should have completed a recognised training, be in regular supervision and should receive you as a client or patient with equality, acceptance and an open mind. Every therapist will have his or her own individual style, just as you will do. The chemistry in the working therapeutic partnership is crucial. Having read this book you may know more about your reciprocal roles and be aware of how they might be activated with another person. In the close working alliance of a therapy many reciprocal roles will be enacted and this is good because it gives you an opportunity to see them in action in an almost laboratory setting. You can scrutinise them, express the unexpressed feeling in a safe place and also begin to develop new, more helpful reciprocal roles.

Do not feel duty-bound to put up with a therapist who:

- doesn't speak to you properly, or at all, for the first month
- abuses their position by trying to be overpowerful, over-interpretative, or who does not adhere appropriately to boundaries (for example, the therapeutic hour is yours: a therapist who is continually late, takes phone calls, leaves early or who is frequently distracted is not adhering to the boundaries of the therapy, for which you may well be paying fees)
- who is judgemental or disparaging about your feelings and your life
- seems overly interested in some aspect of you for his or her own personal purposes.

It is not helpful if a therapist talks too much about themselves or their own life. Whereas there may be times when personal disclosure is timely, appropriate and a real gift to you as client or patient, too much too soon destroys the freedom and sanctity of the professional hour. The same can be said for physical contact. Some body-orientated therapies use touch as this is the basis for the professional clinical work. Therapies which are unclear about touching and physical contact can create confusion, and as a client or patient we can feel invaded. A therapist who hugs you when you arrive and when you leave, or who touches you in some way during the session when this does not seem appropriate, may feel cosy and accepting at first, but this situation can create difficulties, confusion and misinterpretation of motives, as well as lack of freedom later on. Again, there may be times when one hug or hold is exactly right for the moment, and is mutually anticipated, but these genuine moments are rare, and a lot of woolly mistakes in the name of 'warmth' occur when physical boundaries are not adhered to with integrity and honesty.

Transference

There may be times during a therapy when you have very negative feelings for your therapist: anger, fury, fear, hate, despising, contempt. These feelings are usually part of what is generally known as 'transference' (i.e. they are 'transferred' from some other person who has affected you, and who may have originally produced such feelings, or from part of yourself). They form a useful part of the therapy, because these feelings can be discussed, interpreted and understood, and although painful, can be liberating.

CAT is a particularly useful therapeutic model for anticipating and naming the sort of transference that might well be invited in the therapeutic relationship because of the description of reciprocal roles. Together you can look at where you and the therapist might be on the diagram and what sequential loops you might be encountering.

If you have any negative or difficult feelings, like being attracted to your therapist, talk about it and allow it to be part of the work. If your therapist does not allow such feelings to be part of the work, but takes them personally or judges you for them too harshly, you may need to be challenging and confrontational, and to leave the therapy if the issue does not reach a satisfactory conclusion.

Practicalities

Most therapeutic 'hours' are fifty, fifty-five or sixty minutes. Reliable time-keeping is important. Many areas within the NHS now offer psychotherapy or counselling. In the private sector there are many more therapists and a wide range of training. Fees vary from between £35 and £75 per session. The higher range of fees tend to be charged by therapists who also have a medical background. Most good therapists work on a sliding scale of fees if they possibly can. The value of a short-term therapy is that the cost is known in advance and limited. If you feel that your therapy is not going well, or if you have any reservations about your therapy after reading the above, talk about it to your therapist. If you are not satisfied with the response you are perfectly free to go elsewhere. Everyone who enters therapy needs to feel that they are receiving something useful before too long, no matter how obscure the nature of the usefulness, which will be personal and individual to all people who become clients or patients. As a 'consumer' looking for a therapist you are allowed, indeed entitled, to feel valued, respected and to be given help by the therapist.

Having decided upon your choice of therapist, take along your notebook of findings, drawings or personal recollections and realisations that you have gleaned from this book, and share them, at whatever pace you choose, as part of your process in therapy.

Mindfulness practice

If you are attracted to learn more about mindfulness look for opportunities in your area to join a mindfulness meditation group or course and try it out. Look for a teacher who suits you. This may take time. Once we are open to looking for an appropriate teacher one often does appear, often unexpectedly. The important thing is just to start practising exactly where you are, right now, in the present moment. Choose from some of the titles in the suggested Further Reading and start from there.

appendices

Appendix 1

The Psychotherapy File: an aid to understanding ourselves better

In our life what has happened to us, and the sense we made of this, colours the way we see ourselves and others. How we see things is for us how things are, and how we go about our lives seems 'obvious and right'. Sometimes, however, our familiar ways of understanding and acting can be the source of our problems. In order to solve our difficulties we may need to learn to recognise how what we do makes things worse. We can then work out new ways of thinking and acting to change things for the better.

These pages are intended to suggest ways of thinking about what you do; recognising your particular patterns is the first step in learning to gain more control and happiness in your life. You should discuss this questionnaire with your counsellor or therapist.

Keeping a diary of moods and behaviour

Symptoms, bad moods, unwanted thoughts or behaviours that come and go can be better understood and controlled if you learn to notice when they happen and what starts them off.

If you have a particular symptom or problem of this sort, start keeping a diary. The diary should be focused on a particular mood, symptom or behaviour, and should be kept every day if possible. Try to record this sequence:

1. How you were feeling about yourself and others and the world before the problem came on.
2. Any external event, or any thought or image in your mind that was going on when the trouble started, or what seemed to start it off.
3. The thoughts, images or feelings you experienced once the trouble started.

By noticing and writing down in this way what you do and think at these times, you will learn to recognise and eventually have more control over how you act and think at the time. It is often the case that bad feelings like resentment, depression or physical symptoms are the result of ways of thinking and acting that are unhelpful. Diary-keeping in this way gives you the chance to learn better ways of dealing with things.

It is helpful to keep a daily record for 1–2 weeks, then to discuss what you have recorded with your therapist or counsellor.

Starting to change

You may get quite depressed when you begin to realise how often you stop your life being happier and more fulfilled. It is important to remember that it's not being stupid or bad, but rather that:

1. We do these things because this is the way we learned to manage best when we were younger.
2. We don't have to keep on doing them now we are learning to recognise them.
3. By changing our behaviour, we can learn to control not only our own behaviour, but we also change the way other people behave to us.
4. Although it may seem that others resist the changes we want for ourselves (for example, our parents or our partners), we often under-estimate them; if we are firm about our right to change, those who care for us will usually accept the change.

Working with the Psychotherapy File

There are certain patterns of thinking and acting that do not achieve what we want, but which are hard to change. Look through the descriptions of traps, dilemmas, snags and difficult states on the following pages and mark how far you think they apply to the way you feel. Some will be familiar, others will not. If a description feels familiar but is not quite right cross out the words that do not apply and write in how things are for you in your life. Remember there is no way of doing this badly or of getting it wrong. Discuss what you have discovered with your therapist. You and he/she can work together to work out what your unhelpful patterns are and get the descriptions as accurate as possible as the first step towards making helpful changes.

TRAPS

Traps are things we cannot escape from. Certain kinds of thinking and acting result in a 'vicious circle' when, however hard we try, things seem to get worse instead of better. Trying to deal with feeling bad about ourselves, we think and act in ways that tend to confirm our badness.

Applies strongly ++   Applies +   Does not apply 0

1. Fear of hurting other people's feelings trap

Feeling that it is wrong to be angry or aggressive we can be afraid of hurting other people's feelings so we don't express our feelings or needs with the result that we are ignored or abused which makes us feel angry; this confirms feeling that it is wrong to be angry.

Applies:

2. Negative thinking trap

Feeling that we will mess up tasks, relationships or social situations we can believe that if we try we will do it badly so when we do try we are ineffective and things go wrong; we often feel that things went disastrously which confirms the feeling that we will always mess things up.

Applies:

3. Anxious thinking trap

Anxious that we won't be able to cope with tasks, relationships or social situations we worry that we will mess things up and we anxiously worry about getting things right, resulting in panicking, stress and exhaustion; this makes us feel more anxious about things.

Applies:

4. Trying to please trap

Feeling uncertain about ourselves and wanting to be liked we try to please others by doing what they seem to want with the result that they take advantage of us; we can feel angry and used but also as if we have failed to please which confirms our uncertainty about ourselves.

Applies:

5. Can't say 'no' trap

Feeling that it is impossible to say 'no' to others leads to feeling out of control in relationships so to feel more in control we avoid others by hiding away or letting them down with the result that they get angry and can reject us; we then feel guilty which confirms that we shouldn't say 'no' to others.

Applies:

6. Avoiding upset trap

Feeling anxious and believing that we mustn't upset or displease others we avoid upset by doing what they seem to want, anxiously trying to please them; as a result others don't get upset, we feel relieved but trapped in not upsetting others.

Applies:

(Continued)

7. Social isolation trap

Feeling that others may find us stupid or boring we lack confidence in social situations and feel anxious, so we don't approach others or respond when others approach us; as a result others may see us as unfriendly and go away which confirms our feeling that we are stupid or boring.

Applies:

8. Worthlessness trap

Feeling that we can't ever get what we want or have what we need, it can feel that if we try to get needs met we will be punished, rejected or abandoned; sometimes it feels as if we have been born cursed. We give up trying and feel hopeless and helpless and can even feel suicidal as if everything is impossible.

Applies:

9. Self-punishment trap

Feeling bad, weak or guilty, we can feel agitated or upset and feel as if we must punish ourselves. We can hurt or harm ourselves in different ways which can make the feelings of badness or guilt go away briefly but only confirms that we are bad and should be punished.

Applies:

DILEMMAS (False choices and narrow options)

We often act as we do, even when we are not completely happy with it, because the only other ways we can imagine seem as bad or even worse. Sometimes we assume connections that are not necessarily the case – as in 'If I do x then y will follow'. These false choices can be described as either/or or if/then dilemmas. We often don't realise that we see things like this, but we act as if these were the only possible choices. Do you act as if any of the following false choices rule your life? Recognising them is the first step to changing them.

Applies strongly   ++   Applies   +   Does not apply   0

1. Upset feelings dilemma

When I feel upset *either* I bottle up my feelings, others don't notice that I'm upset and so ignore me or take advantage of me or abuse me *or* I express my feelings, sometimes explosively, and others feel hurt, attacked, overwhelmed or threatened and respond by attacking me or rejecting me.

Applies:

2. Deprivation dilemma

When I feel needy *either* I spoil myself, take what I want or get what I need and then feel guilty or greedy as if depriving others and then feel cross with myself, bad and frustrated *or* I deny myself things and don't ask for what I want or need and feel modest and self-righteous, as if giving to others and then feel as if I am punishing myself.

Applies:

3. Perfectionism dilemma

Feeling inadequate or not good enough *either* I try to be perfect, which is impossible and very stressful and leaves me feeling an exhausted angry failure, *or* I just let things slide and feel guilty for not trying and feel like an angry and dissatisfied failure.

Applies:

4. Dealing with demands and criticism dilemma

Feeling bullied or criticised *either* I gloomily submit to demands and feel trapped and crushed, miserable and hopeless *or* I passively resist demands, put things off, drag my feet and feel anxious but still get criticised and bullied.

Applies:

5. Sabotage or rebellion dilemma

Feeling bullied or criticised *either* I secretly resist demands and sabotage what is demanded of me but end up attacked and bullied *or* I actively rebel against demands and attack others and destroy things and feel hopeless and end up feeling trapped and punished, a hollow victory.

Applies:

6. Responsibility dilemma

Feeling over-responsible *either* I look after others, take charge, meet their expectations of help and feel needed but also taken advantage of and can feel angry and trapped (even though I'm in control) *or* I don't look after others, don't take charge, others don't expect me to do things for them and I feel unwanted, rejected or without a role and can feel lonely, anxious and out of control.

Applies:

7. Self-sufficiency dilemma

Feeling that I should be self-sufficient or that I shouldn't want or need anything, if I reach out for what I want and get it I feel childish, guilty and

(Continued)

undeserving as if I shouldn't want things, that I should contain myself; *on the other hand*, if I don't reach out or don't get what I want I can feel angry and deprived (as well as saintly) and that I should have the things that I want or need and that I should be more assertive.

Applies:

8. Anxious control dilemma

Feeling anxious about what may happen I try to keep things, feelings, plans in perfect order, pay obsessive attention to details in order to keep in control but feel exhausted and overwhelmed by the endless tasks and so feel like letting go and giving up; *on the other hand*, if I let things go and get into a mess by avoiding or ignoring things then the brief relief is followed by feeling anxious and panicky about the mess and I feel an urgent need to get back into control.

Applies:

9. Not knowing how to react in relationships dilemma

Feeling unsure how to act towards others *either* I stick up for myself too much, don't join in or take my turn and find that others reject me or don't like me which leaves me feeling confused and unhappy *or* I give in and do too much to try to please others and get taken advantage of and end up feeling angry or hurt.

Applies:

10. Approval vs feelings dilemma

I want to express my feelings but also need approval from others so mostly I feel I have to bottle up my feelings in order to be approved of or accepted so I don't cry or be angry or tender or playful with the result that I am accepted or approved of but feel frustrated and cut off; *on the other hand*, when I express my feelings, be myself or do what I want or need, I can feel childish or rebellious and angry with the result that I am often rejected or disapproved of and feel my feelings and needs are unrecognised.

Applies:

11. Approval vs independence dilemma

I want to be independent but also need approval from others so mostly I feel I have to do what they want to be approved of or accepted, I have to submit and can't be myself or do what I want, I feel accepted but at the same time frustrated and miserable; *on the other hand*, when I do what I want and be myself I can feel rebellious and angry and am often rejected or unrecognised, disapproved of and unacceptable to others.

Applies:

12. If involved then smothered dilemma

It is as if when I get involved with or too close to others I can feel smothered, engulfed or taken over by them and then feel suffocated, trapped and desperate; so I keep distant and feel safe with breathing space and room to move but can also feel lonely and miserable.

Applies:

13. If involved then abused dilemma

I fear that if I get involved with others I will be abused so when I get involved I can easily feel taken advantage of or used and feel angry or miserable *or* I don't get involved and feel safe but also feel lonely and miserable.

Applies:

14. If involved then admiring dilemma

I feel that I need a lot of attention and seek others whom I can admire or who will admire me which feels good; *on the other hand*, often this does not last and then I don't admire them in fact I often feel contempt towards them; or find that they are contemptuous and rejecting of me which can leave me feeling bad or worthless so I seek a new relationship.

Applies:

SNAGS

Snags are what is happening when we say 'I want to have a better life, or I want to change my behaviour but ...'. Sometimes this comes from how we or our families thought about us when we were young; such as 'she was always the good child', or 'in our family we never ...'. Sometimes the snags come from the important people in our lives not wanting us to change, or not able to cope with what our changing means to them. Often the resistance is more indirect, as when a parent, husband or wife becomes ill or depressed when we begin to get better.

In other cases we seem to 'arrange' to avoid pleasure or success, or if they come, we have to pay in some way, by depression, or by spoiling things. Often this is because, as children, we came to feel guilty if things went well for us, or felt that we were envied for good luck or success. Sometimes we have come to feel responsible, unreasonably, for things that went wrong in the family, although we may not be aware that this is so. It is helpful to learn to recognise how this sort of pattern is stopping you getting on with your life, for only then can you learn to accept your right to a better life and begin to claim it.

(Continued)

Indicate by ringing the number if: you recognise that you feel limited in your life:

1. By fear of the response of others: for example, I must sabotage success
    (a) as if it deprives others
    (b) as if others may envy me or
    (c) as if there are not enough good things to go around.

2. By something inside yourself: for example, I must sabotage good things as if I don't deserve them.

DIFFICULT AND UNSTABLE STATES OF MIND

Some people find it difficult to keep control over their behaviour and experience because things feel very difficult and different at times. Indicate by ringing the number which, if any, of the following apply to you:

1. How I feel about myself and others can be unstable; I can switch from one state of mind to a completely different one.

2. Some states may be accompanied by intense, extreme and uncontrollable emotions.

3. Some states may be accompanied by emotional blankness, feeling unreal or feeling muddled.

4. Some states may be accompanied by feeling intensely guilty or angry with myself, wanting to hurt myself.

5. Some states may be accompanied by feeling that others can't be trusted, are going to let me down, or hurt me.

6. Some states may be accompanied by being unreasonably angry or hurtful to others.

7. Sometimes the only way to cope with some confusing feelings is to blank them off and feel emotionally distant from others.

DIFFERENT STATES

Everybody experiences changes in how they feel about themselves and the world. But for some people these changes are extreme, sometimes sudden and confusing. In such cases there are often a number of states which recur, and learning to recognise them and shifts between them can be very helpful. On the next page are a number of descriptions of such states. Identify those which you experience by ringing them. <u>*You can delete or add words to the descriptions,*</u> *and there is space to add any not listed. If one state you have ringed leads on to another, join them with a line.*

DIFFERENT STATES. Everybody experiences changes in how they feel about themselves and the world. But for some people these changes are extreme, sometimes sudden and confusing. In such cases there are often a number of states which recur, and learning to recognise them and shifts between them can be very helpful. Below are a number of descriptions of such states. Identify those which you experience by circling them. You can delete or add words to the descriptions and there is space to add any not listed. If one state you have circled leads on to another join them with a line.

zombie – cut off from feelings or from others, disconnected	feeling bad but soldiering on, coping	raging and out of control	extra special – looking down on others, unrecognised genius	control freak – in control of self, of life, of other people	cheated by life, by others, untrusting	hiding secret shame
provoking, teasing, seducing, winding-up others	clinging, frantic, fearing abandonment	frenetically active, too busy to think or feel	agitated, confused, anxious, panicking, desperate	feeling perfectly cared for, blissfully close to another	misunderstood, rejected, abandoned, desolate	hurt, humiliated, defeated, always in the wrong
contemptuously dismissive of myself, worthless	vulnerable, needy, passively helpless, waiting for rescue	envious, wanting to harm others, put them down, knock them down	protective, respecting myself, respecting others	hurting myself, hurting others, causing harm or damage	resentfully submitting to demands, a slave, under the thumb	frightened of angry others
secure in myself, able to be close to others	intensely critical of myself, and of others	cheating others, cheating the system, lying, hiding the truth	feeling hopeless, no one can help, life is pointless, suicidal	spaced out – distanced from others, as if acting a part, double-glazed	flying away, running away, escaping	overwhelmed by grief and loss
seeking revenge, stalking, harassing, murderous	knight in shining armour, rescuing others, righting wrongs	as if poisoned or contaminated	like an unexploded bomb	watchful, suspicious, jealous, paranoid		

Appendix 2

Personal Sources Questionnaire (PSQ)

The aim of this questionnaire is to obtain an account of certain aspects of your personality. People vary greatly in all sorts of ways: the aim of this form is to find out how far you feel yourself to be constant and 'all of a piece', or variable and made up of a number of distinct 'sub-personalities', or liable to experience yourself as shifting between two or more quite distinct and sharply differentiated states of mind.

Most of us experience ourselves as somewhere between these contrasted ways. A state of mind is recognised by a typical mood, a particular sense of oneself and of others and by how far one is in touch with, and in control of, feelings. Such states are definite, recognisable ways of being; one is either clearly in a given state or one is not. They often affect one quite suddenly; they may be of brief duration or they last for days. Sometimes, but not always, changes of state happen because of change in circumstances or an event of some kind.

Indicate which description applies to you most closely by shading the appropriate circle

Complete ALL questions

Shade one circle per question only

**ALL INFORMATION SHOULD BE TREATED AS
PRIVATE AND CONFIDENTIAL**

NB. Shade ONE circle per question only

	1 Very true	2 True	3 May or may not be true	4 True	5 Very true	
1.	O	O	O	O	O	My sense of self is always the same / How I act or feel is constantly changing
2.	O	O	O	O	O	The various people in my life see me in much the same way / The various people in my life have different views of me as if I were not the same person
3.	O	O	O	O	O	I have a stable and unchanging sense of myself / I am so different at different times that I wonder who I really am
4.	O	O	O	O	O	I have no sense of opposed sides to my nature / I feel I am split between two (or more) ways of being, sharply differentiated from each other
5.	O	O	O	O	O	My mood and sense of self seldom change suddenly / My mood can change abruptly in ways which make me feel unreal or out of control
6.	O	O	O	O	O	My mood changes are always understandable / I am often confused by my mood changes which seem either unprovoked or quite out of scale with what provoked them
7.	O	O	O	O	O	I never lose control / I get into states in which I lose control and do harm to myself and/or others
8.	O	O	O	O	O	I never regret what I have said or done / I get into states in which I do and say things which I later deeply regret

The PSQ was developed by M. Broadbent, S. Clarke and A. Ryle at the Academic Department of Psychiatry, St Thomas's Hospital, London.

Appendix 3

Mindfulness exercises and meditations

Grounding Exercise

This exercise was first introduced to me at The Centre for Transpersonal Psychology by Barbara Somers and Ian Gordon Brown in 1974. I have given this exercise on many occasions and I also practice it myself. It helps us to connect with the natural energies around us when we find ourselves stressed, preoccupied and out of touch with the ground. It takes only a few minutes and can be done anytime, anywhere!

Remove your shoes.

Stand with your bare feet firmly on the ground, legs slightly apart and allow your feet to really feel the support of the earth underneath you.

Take a few moments to find a relaxed posture – you may find that gently swaying around your hips helps you to settle into a relaxed upright posture.

Make sure that your head is resting in a relaxed way upon your shoulders, just move the head around the shoulders slowly to find a relaxed position. Allow your back to relax. Allow your in-breath and out-breath to fill your chest and abdominal area.

Rest your gaze at about 45 degrees or just ahead.

Now place your attention firstly on your feet, and then on the earth beneath your feet. Just feel the earth.

Imagine that your feet have invisible roots pushing down into the earth. Push these roots as far as you can go.

Imagine now that your roots are contacting the fresh green energy of the earth. Allow this fresh energy to rise up through the roots into your feet.

Now allow the earth energy up through your feet into your legs, up into your pelvis, belly and abdomen.

And then allow the earth energy to course through your chest, heart and neck and shoulder area.

Cup your hands together at the area of your heart and allow it to be refreshed.

You may wish to leave this exercise there. If you wish to continue, one option is to remain standing with your hands cupping your heart area and to focus your attention at the top of your head. Now imagine the energy from above entering through the top of your head into your face, neck and shoulders, then flowing down into your chest and meeting up with the earth energy at the place of the heart.

Just spend a few minutes being aware of the connection between the energies of above and below.

Body and Chair Exercise

This exercise was given as part of a Continuing Professional Development Training day in CAT in Norwich, led by Integrative Psychotherapist and Trainer, Margaret Landale, in October 2007.

Take your seat on a chair. With eyes closed or just half-closed, allow your attention to rest on your experience of your body in the chair.

Notice the areas of contact between your body and the chair. Notice the support the chair is offering to you right now. Become aware that the chair is supporting your body right now by carrying most of your physical weight. Allow this to happen, allow a comfortable sense of heaviness to spread through your body, supported and carried by the chair.

Notice the rise and fall of the breath. Notice any tension you are holding within your body, the neck, shoulders, down the arms, the weight of the head. Notice any tension in your back down the spine, into your buttocks, legs, ankles and feet. Notice any tension in your belly or chest. Each time you notice any tightness or difficulty in these different parts of your body allow it to drain into your chair, be absorbed by your chair.

Just rest in this experience of being supported by the chair for a few minutes.

Whenever you are feeling anxious, unsupported or lonely, return to this practice which helps to build a nourishing reciprocal role such as caring or supporting in relation to being cared for or supported.

Mindfulness of Breathing

Firstly find your seat.

Find a comfortable sitting position with on a chair or on a meditation stool or cushion. You may like to feel your feet on the floor or sit with legs crossed.

Eyes may be closed or half-closed, just gazing at an invisible spot in front of you. The latter is good if you are feeling sleepy!

It's important that your back is straight and your neck and head well-supported by your sitting position and your back. The back should be in alignment and relaxed, not ramrod straight.

Take a few moments to feel into your body and allow any tension to be released.

Now place your attention on your breathing.

Notice how the in-breath begins. You might want to choose a place where you imagine the breath entering your body – the chest, just below the nose, the throat, the belly or from the earth. Once you have chosen the imagined point of entry keep this for the rest of your sitting practice.

Notice how at the end of the in-breath the breath naturally starts to descend and follow the breath down with your attention until it reaches the depths of your belly.

There is a moment here when, it appears that there is no breath. A point of stillness and space.

Then, of its own accord, without our having to do anything, the breath rises once again on the in-breath and the cycle begins once again.

When you are practising mindfulness of breathing you may just say as you are breathing in 'I know I am breathing in' or 'I know I am breathing out'. You may then notice 'I am breathing a long breath' or a slow breath, a smooth or a harsh breath. The main point of your practice is that your concentration is focused upon the process of breathing itself.

And distractions from our mind do arise, many, many times. What we do in this case is that we simply notice we have become distracted, either by a body sensation or a thought and we simply say to ourselves 'thinking' and then return to the breath.

This form of mindfulness practice is basic to all meditations. From this we gradually learn that thoughts are just thoughts – it is often our attachment to them and the emotion that arises from thoughts that produces our distress. Much emotional distress occurs when we get lost in ruminative thinking, going over and over the bad things that have happened to us, thus escalating our fears and our disregulation.

Befriending Fear Exercise

This next exercise uses the above exercise, the mindfulness of breathing, and incorporates promises on the in-breaths and out-breaths. When we are aware that what we are feeling is fear, we say to our fear:

'Breathing in, I know you are there my fear.'

'Breathing out, I will take care of you.'

We simply practice this over and over. We may also practice with our anger, or loneliness.

Unconditional Friendliness or Loving Kindness Meditation

Find a place to sit comfortably with your body and shoulders relaxed.

Take a few minutes to connect with the rhythm of in-breath and out-breath, allowing this rhythm to help relaxation in the body.

Then, allow some memories or images of being given kindness, however small, to arise. Notice where these memories touch you in your body.

Notice the sensations in your body – tingling, opening, softening.

Let the in-breath touch these sensations and the out-breath open the sensations further. Allow these sensations to expand until they fill your whole being.

Allow yourself to be cradled by these sensations and feelings connected to kindness. Become aware that you are being filled with loving kindness.

Let yourself bask in this energy of loving kindness, breathing it in, breathing it out, as if it were a lifeline, offering the nourishment you were longing for.

Invite feelings of peacefulness and acceptance to be present in you.

Some people find it valuable to say to themselves: 'May I be free from ignorance', 'May I be free from greed and hatred', 'May I be free of suffering', 'May I be happy'.

Once you have established yourself a centre of loving kindness you can take refuge here, drinking at this renewing and nourishing well.

You can then take the practice further. Having established the well of loving kindness within your own being you can let loving kindness radiate out and direct it wherever you like.

You might like to direct it first to members of your family or friends, visualising them and sending them loving kindness.

You can direct loving kindness toward anyone – those you know and those you do not.

You can also direct loving kindness to those you are having difficulty with.

And finally, you can direct loving kindness energy to all sentient beings, animals, plants and the universe itself.

Breath Poems

Practised by the monastic and lay practitioners of the Buddhist teacher Ven Thich Nhat Hanh.

This is practised using the first line on the in-breath and the second line on the out-breath and allowing the words to aid concentration at just being in the present moment. This breath poem, or 'gatha', contains the elements of helping us to remain in the present moment, to be solid like the mountain and also to recognise that we can be free, just where we are and that we are all inter-connected as living beings in the realm of all things.

I have arrived
I am home
In the here
In the now
I am solid
I am free
In the ultimate I dwell

The second breath poem is really helpful for allowing spaciousness within current close relationships or with those who have died with whom we wish to remain in loving connection.

No coming
No going
No after
No before
I hold you close to me
I release you to be free
Because I am in you
And you are in me
Because I am in you
And you are in me

Appendix 4

Personal rating chart

Symptom or problem

Target Problem Procedure

	Name:
	Start date:

A

RECOGNITION

Rate how skilled and quick you are at seeing the pattern

better

no change

worse

B

STOPPING AND REVISING

Rate how far you are able to stop the pattern

better

no change

worse

1	2	3	4	5	6	7	8	9	10	11	12

AIM

Alternatives or exits:

Further reading

If you have found the self-help approach useful, you may like to consider some of these titles for your own further reading. The list has been compiled with help from colleagues, friends and patients.

General

Bruno Bettelheim   *The Uses of Enchantment* (1976, Knopf)
  An analysis of fairy tales. We frequently identify with a figure from folklore or fairy tale, and this can help us in our understanding of ourselves and our patterns.
John Bradshaw   *Healing the Shame that Binds You* (1988, Health Communications)
  Helps us to look at how shame can be the core problem to many of our difficulties and behind many presenting problems. Includes exercises for releasing shame.
John Fox   *Finding What You Didn't Lose* (1995, Tarcher Putnam)
  A practical book aimed to help readers discover their inner poet and writer.
Eugene T. Gendlin   *Focusing* (1981, Bantam)
  Focusing is a well-researched technique to help us get underneath the presenting issue to the 'felt sense' underneath.
Allan and Barbara Pease   *Why Men Don't Listen and Women Can't Read Maps* (2005, Orion)
  A good and easy read about the struggle between masculine and feminine!
Dorothy Rowe   *Depression and the Way Out of Your Prison* (1986, Routledge)
  A practical and sensible approach to self-help and depression.
William Styron   *Darkness Visible* (1992, Picador)
Jon Kabat Zinn   *Full Catastrophe Living* (1990, Delta)
  Helps us to understand our stress response both physiologically and emotionally and its effect on our body and mind. It offers practices for awareness of stress and release from the effects of stress.

Bereavement and separation

Elisabeth Kubler Ross   *To Live Until We Say Goodbye* (1990, Routledge)
  A very moving book about the dying process of close friends and family.
C.S. Lewis   *A Grief Observed* (1961, Faber & Faber)

Judy Tatelbaum   *The Courage to Grieve* (1981, Heinemann)
   A sensitive and creative book for those suffering from loss, taking readers through the processes of grief and mourning, with stories and suggestions for how to complete the mourning process.
J. William Warden   *Grief Counselling and Grief Therapy* (1993, Tavistock)
   A helpful guide to the different stages of grief and mourning.
Alison Wertheimer   *A Special Scar* (1991, Routledge)
   An extremely sensitive and well-researched book about the painful experiences of people bereaved by suicide.

Cognitive Analytic Therapy

Anthony Ryle   *Cognitive Analytic Therapy and Borderline Personality* (1997, Wiley)
   The CAT approach to borderline personality diagnosis.
Anthony Ryle and Ian Kerr   *Introducing Cognitive Analytic Therapy* (2002, Wiley)
   The classic textbook of this effective short-term focused therapy now used widely within health service settings.

Relationships

Aaron Beck   *Love is Never Enough* (1988, Harper & Row)
   A practical, sensible approach for couples to understand the way their distorted thinking undermines communication problems.
Sue Gerhardt   *Why Love Matters: How Affection Shapes a Baby's Brain* (2004, Brunner Routledge)
John Sandford   *The Invisible Partners* (1980, Paulist Press)
   A Jungian approach to looking at the inner male and female components of men and women. Useful for readers wishing to explore their inner lives more thoroughly.
Maggie Scarf   *Intimate Partners: Patterns in Love and Marriage* (1988, Ballantine Books)
   A well-researched book offering insight into how inherited emotional and family history affects our pattern of relating.
R. Skynner and John Cleese   *Families and How to Survive Them* (1993, Ebury Press)
   A classic book. Psychology is made accessible, helping us to understand how our current patterns grow from our background.

Eating disorders

Julia Buckroyd   *Eating Your Heart Out* (1996, Vermillion)
   This book links the misuse of food with emotional hunger and gives practical advice for change.

A hopeful book about addiction with examples from artists and writers and the author's own experience with alcoholism.

Isaac Marks   *Living with Fear* (2001, McGraw-Hill)

Written by a well-known expert, this book looks at anxiety and obsessive compulsive difficulties.

Dreams

Ann Faraday   *Dream Power* (1973, Berkley)

Popular book about recognising and using the power of dreams.

Carl Jung   *Man and His Symbols* (1964, Aldus Books)

A look at the use of images and symbols in our everyday life. Many illustrations.

John Sandford   *Dreams: God's Forgotten Language* (1989, HarperCollins)

A lovely contribution from a Jungian to ways of looking at dreams.

Mindfulness

David Burns   *Feeling Good* (1999, Avon Books) and *The Feeling Good Handbook* (1999, Plume)

Two extremely popular and positive books based on cognitive therapy and self-help.

Pema Chodron   *Start Where You Are* (1994, Shambhala) and *When Things Fall Apart* (1997, Shambhala)

Buddhist nun Pema Chodron shares her own deep wisdom and personal experience of Western life.

Sue Gerhardt   *Why Love Matters: How Affection Shapes a Baby's Brain* (2004, Brunner Routledge)

An easy-to-read comprehensive book about the chemistry of early attachment and how this influences relationships.

Christopher K. Germer, Ronald D. Siegel and Paul R. Fulton   *Mindfulness and Psychotherapy* (2005, Guilford)

A very well researched book by American psychologists who have their own well-developed mindfulness practice, on the place and effect of mindfulness in psychotherapy. Very helpful for professionals.

Carl Jung   *Memories, Dreams, Reflections* (1989, Vintage)

Classic autobiography of the famous Swiss psychologist.

R. Kingerlee   *The Therapy Experience: How Human Kindness Heals* (2006, PCCS Books)

J. Kornfield   *A Path with Heart: A Guide through the Perils and Promises of Spiritual Life* (1994, Shambhala)

An excellent introduction to living a spiritually-based life. Gives meditations and visualisations for everyday life.

J. Kornfield   *After the Ecstasy, The Laundry* (2000, Rider)

A very grounded book about bringing mindfulness practice into everyday life and the pitfalls that can occur.

Thich Nhat Hanh   *The Miracle of Mindfulness* (2002, Beacon Press)
   The first of this Vietnamese Zen Buddhist teacher's many books about mindfulness in everyday life.
Thich Nhat Hanh   *Anger: Wisdom for Cooling the Flames* (2001, Riverhead)
   Zen Buddhist Thich Nhat Hanh focuses on his understanding of anger and its expression and offers mindfulness practices for being with angry feelings.
S. Saltzberg   *Loving Kindness* (1995, Shambhala)
   A warm, practical book with many practical exercises about working with loving kindness.
S. Saltzberg   *A Heart as Wide as the World* (1999, Shambhala)
   This book offers a collection of Zen Buddhist stories that are encouraging and heart-warming.
Charles Tart   *Living the Mindful Life* (1994, Shambhala)
   A practical book about practising meditation and mindfulness.

Resource addresses

Association of Cognitive Analytic Therapists

P.O. Box 6793
Dorchester
DT1 9DL

Tel: 0844 800 9496
Email: admin@acat.me.uk
www.acat.me.uk

Write for information about the availability of this therapy in your area. Cognitive Analytic Therapy is also available in Greece, Finland, Spain and Australia.

British Association for Counselling and Psychotherapy

BACP HOUSE
15 St John's Business Park
Lutterworth
LE17 4HB

Tel: 0870 443 5252
www.bacp.co.uk

Offers information about counselling and training in Great Britain.

beat (formerly Eating Disorders Association)

103 Prince of Wales Road
Norwich
Norfolk
NR1 1DW

Tel: 0870 770 3256
Helpline: 0845 634 1414
Youthline: 0845 634 7650
Email: info@b-eat.co.uk
www.b-eat.co.uk

Offers information about groups in different parts of Britain, and topical magazine *Signpost.*

MIND

See your local telephone directory for the address and phone number for your nearest branch.

The national association for mental health in Britain. Offers help and guide-lines for people searching for appropriate resources in their own locality.

Order of Inter-Being

www.plumvillage.org

The monastic community of Thich Nhat Hanh in France, the USA and Vietnam with sangha communities throughout the UK.

Samaritans

Tel: 0845 7909090

Samaritans offers confidential telephone or one-to-one conversation and be-friending, particularly for those feeling desperate or suicidal.

United Kingdom Council for Psychotherapy

2nd Floor
Edward House
2 Wakley Street
London
ECI 7LT

Tel: 020 7014 9955
Email: ukcp@psychotherapy.org.uk
www.psychotherapy.org.uk

Index